Simulation and Gaming for Mathematical Education:

Epistemology and Teaching Strategies

Angela Piu
University of L'Aquila, Italy

Cesare Fregola
Roma Tre University, Italy

A volume in the Advances in
Game–Based Learning (AGBL)
Book Series

Information Science
REFERENCE
An Imprint of IGI Global

Director of Editorial Content:	Kristin Klinger
Director of Book Publications:	Julia Mosemann
Acquisitions Editor:	Lindsay Johnston
Development Editor:	Julia Mosemann
Publishing Assistant:	Casey Conapitski
Typesetter:	Casey Conapitski
Production Editor:	Jamie Snavely
Cover Design:	Lisa Tosheff

Published in the United States of America by
Information Science Reference (an imprint of IGI Global)
701 E. Chocolate Avenue
Hershey PA 17033
Tel: 717-533-8845
Fax: 717-533-8661
E-mail: cust@igi-global.com
Web site: http://www.igi-global.com

Library of Congress Cataloging-in-Publication Data

Simulation and gaming for mathematical education : epistemology and teaching strategies / Angela Piu and Cesare Fregola, editors.
      p. cm.
   Summary: "This book proposes simulation games supported by the most recent discoveries and advances in theories of learning research, and gears operational decisions toward the development of an integrated system for the teaching of mathematics in primary schools"--Provided by publisher.
   Includes bibliographical references and index.
   ISBN 978-1-60566-930-4 (hardcover) -- ISBN 978-1-60566-931-1 (ebook) 1. Mathematics--Study and teaching (Primary)--Simulation games. 2. Simulation games in education. I. Piu, Angela, 1971- II. Fregola, Cesare.
   QA135.6.S564 2010
   372.7--dc22
                                        2009022720

This book is published in the IGI Global book series Advances in Game-Based Learning (AGBL) (ISSN: 2327-1825; eISSN: 2327-1833)

British Cataloguing in Publication Data
A Cataloguing in Publication record for this book is available from the British Library.

Advances in Game–Based Learning (AGBL) Book Series

ISSN: 2327-1825
EISSN: 2327-1833

MISSION

The **Advances in Game-Based Learning (AGBL) Book Series** aims to cover all aspects of serious games applied to any area of education. The definition and concept of education has begun to morph significantly in the past decades and game-based learning has become a popular way to encourage more active learning in a creative and alternative manner for students in K-12 classrooms, higher education, and adult education. AGBL presents titles that address many applications, theories, and principles surrounding this growing area of educational theory and practice.

COVERAGE

- Curriculum Development Using Educational Games
- Digital Game-Based Learning
- Edutainment
- Electronic Educational Games
- Game Design & Development of Educational Games
- MMOs in Education

IGI Global is currently accepting manuscripts for publication within this series. To submit a proposal for a volume in this series, please contact our Acquisition Editors at Acquisitions@igi-global.com or visit: http://www.igi-global.com/publish/.

Titles in this Series

For a list of additional titles in this series, please visit: www.igi-global.com

Student Usability in Educational Software and Games Improving Experiences
Carina Gonzalez (University of La Laguna, Spain)
Information Science Reference • copyright 2013 • 439pp • H/C (ISBN: 9781466619876)
• US $175.00 (our price)

Interactivity in E-Learning Case Studies and Frameworks
Haomin Wang (Dakota State University, USA)
Information Science Reference • copyright 2012 • 408pp • H/C (ISBN: 9781613504413)
• US $175.00 (our price)

Handbook of Research on Improving Learning and Motivation through Educational Games Multidisciplinary Approaches
Patrick Felicia (Waterford Institute of Technology, Ireland)
Information Science Reference • copyright 2011 • 1462pp • H/C (ISBN: 9781609604950)
• US $475.00 (our price)

Simulation and Gaming for Mathematical Education Epistemology and Teaching Strategies
Angela Piu (University of L'Aquila, Italy) and Cesare Fregola (Roma Tre University, Italy)
Information Science Reference • copyright 2011 • 256pp • H/C (ISBN: 9781605669304)
• US $180.00 (our price)

Gaming for Classroom-Based Learning Digital Role Playing as a Motivator of Study
Young Kyun Baek (Korea National University of Education, Korea)
Information Science Reference • copyright 2010 • 358pp • H/C (ISBN: 9781615207138)
• US $180.00 (our price)

Ethics and Game Design Teaching Values through Play
Karen Schrier (Columbia University, USA) and David Gibson (University of Vermont, USA)
Information Science Reference • copyright 2010 • 396pp • H/C (ISBN: 9781615208456)
• US $180.00 (our price)

www.igi-global.com

701 E. Chocolate Ave., Hershey, PA 17033
Order online at www.igi-global.com or call 717-533-8845 x100
To place a standing order for titles released in this series,
contact: cust@igi-global.com
Mon-Fri 8:00 am - 5:00 pm (est) or fax 24 hours a day 717-533-8661

Table of Contents

Section 2:
Theoretical and Methodological Aspects of
Simulation Games for Learning Math

Section 3:
Design and Conduct of the Games

Chapter 9
Description of Games **131**

Angela Piu, University of L'Aquila, Italy
Cesare Fregola, Roma Tre University, Italy
Anna Santoro, Istituto Comprensivo Statale San Giuliano Milanese, Italy

Chapter 10
The Conduct of a Simulation Game **158**

Roberta Masci, University of Calabria, Italy

Section 4:
Experimental Research Project

Chapter 11
A Review of Previous Studies **168**

Angela Piu, University of L'Aquila, Italy

Chapter 12
Research Outline **181**

Angela Piu, University of L'Aquila, Italy

Chapter 13
Angela Piu, University of L'Aquila, Italy
Cesare Fregola, Roma Tre University, Italy
Claudia Abundo, Roma Tre University , Italy
Salvatore Fregola, IanusLab Catanzaro, Italy

Eledia Mangia, Roma Tre University, Italy

Preface

The use of simulation games is a well-established practice in many countries in schools and training although the research into its educational benefits is uneven and fragmentary and little work has been done on the didactic justifications of its use in the educational field; indeed, what there is tends to be more geared towards commercial rather than educational ends with little attention devoted to the underlying structures and concepts or the knowledge or processes one would like to stimulate.

There is a considerable body of work on the design, realization and evaluation of simulation games in education but the variety of different criteria used indicates that there is no common theoretical framework regarding the learning epistemology in simulation games. Moreover, the work on methodological issues in the educational context is not explicitly orientated towards best didactic pratices.

Reseach of validity and effectiveness of approaches, applicable to educational contexts, opens important pedagogical prospects in the education to complexity, to the extent that they can relate to widespread systems of competences able to integrate the instruments and means application in learning-teahing processes, guided by theoretical models able to orientate decisions and behaviors of the teaching professionality.

The aim of this book is to draw attention on the epistemological and methodological aspects of learning through simulation games starting from a repertoire of meanings that can guide research in the educational field.

Simulation games in schools can, indeed, represent an important practical and methodological innovation in the teaching of various subjects and the use of new forms of educational technologies that offer a scaffolding for the construction of knowledge and the development of channels of didactic communication.

The subject area we have focused on in our work is mathematics, where there is a clear need to link different aspects involved in the learning process- cognitive, emotive social, motor and so on. The interaction in the games can activate connections that bring the aforementioned aspects together and contribute to the sharing of new meanings.

This work describes an educational research project based on the main characteristics and functions of simulation games, and aims to encourage the design and realisation of learning environments for the process of learning mathematics and discovering its relationship with reality with reference, in particular, to the acquisition and mastery of a mathematical language by children in primary schools.

Drawing on a vast theoretical background this work relates the ontology of simulation games and recent advances in educational psychology to the construction of a system for the teaching of mathematics within the context of an educational discourse from an ecological perspective.

Indeed, the spread of technologies, and consequently virtual worlds, have led to the development of environments which form reproductions reality; moreover, these advances in technology allow us to organise and design educational environments where it is possible to carry out simulations, thereby enabling us to highlight different facets and configurations of situations that otherwise it would be difficult realise in one place and time.

In this work simulation games are viewed from the perspective of the design of environments in which classroom interaction and the learning and teaching processes are informed by the most recent advances in research into theories of learning and inspired by systematic observation of certain typical types of behavior of children who have immerged themselves in video games rather than in the portals of cyberspace.

In this sense simulation games in schools can be reconsidered as meeting places between ways of learning about reality and ways of learning about virtual reality.

To sum up, the research focuses on the design, realisation and experimentation of simulation games applied to the learning-teaching process of mathematics with three priorities:

- Experiment with certain aspects of the evolution of educational science, that have made new learning models and teaching schemes available; these could act as a guide to launch a motivational process than achieves and sustains over time the learning of mathematical contents;
- Investigate certain structural characteristics and the dynamics of simulation games when applied to the learning process and the construction of a mathematical language based on abstraction and formalisation;
- Promote a meta-cognitive control within the game environment to develop self-efficacy in the learning of mathematics.

With regard to the research objectives, the goals are:

- Contributing to the formation of an accessible culture for the construction of learning environments for the teaching of mathematics, through the review and re-definition of traditionally familiar learning environments, influenced by the outcomes of innovation and research;

- Encouraging those involved in mathematics teaching to identify criteria for producing simulation games, by supplying concrete examples for the design of simulation games for mathematics that emerged from our research effort, and provide practical hints on their conduct and academic effectiveness.

The work is structured in four sections. The first section presents the introduction on the two central themes of the work: math learning and simulation games. As regards the first, the theoretical, epistemological and methodological guidelines for math learning are considered in the light of the changing realities and learning needs with a view to adapting math teaching to the new situation. Regarding the second, on the other hand, a study is made of different types of simulation games employed in social, recreational and educational fields. Our particular interest is the need to develop an ontology that can overcome semantic divisions and provide a basis for scientific progress.

The second section focuses attention on the theoretical and methodological aspects of simulation games for mathematics learning. In the light of the changes in society and the advances in educational psychology, the educational purposes of our work are outlined. Reference is made to transcoding and the processes of math learning in which not only cognitive elements play a part, but social and cultural ones as well.

The third section presents the theoretical framework and the methodological decisions taken for the design and conduct of the games, supplemented by various guidelines on how to operate the activity. This section also contains a description of the games designed for the research project along with teaching material and final progress tests.

The fourth section describes the Simulandia research project, complete with a review of the literature on simulation games and a description of the previous experiences of different members of the research group that have had a relevant influence on the research direction. In this section the research framework is presented on which the assumptions and procedures of the work were based, as well as an analysis of the initial results.

Along with the text there is a bibliography with n° 12 descriptions of the work of various authors concerning both the theme of simulation games and the question of the learning of mathematics.

Angela Piu
University of L'Aquila, Italy

Cesare Fregola
Roma Tre University, Italy

Section 1
The Teaching and Learning of Mathematics and the Ontology of Simulation Games

Chapter 1
Epistemological Framework and Mathematical Learning

Cesare Fregola
Roma Tre University, Italy

ABSTRACT

The aim of this chapter is to provide some indications on the background of our research regarding the use of simulation games for learning geometry and arithmetic. We reinterpret certain educational goals from the perspective of the anthropology of the virtual. Within this context, a number of important international commissions on math teaching are analyzed with particular reference to the difficulties involved in finding the right balance between the need for a formal mathematical language and teaching solutions to guide learning.

"Determine a reality that is within the child's grasp, describe the relations that the mind builds, the structure and the underlying models, and reconstruct linguistic codes for mathematics that form a communicative link between reality, thought, emotions, behaviour and the joy of discovery."

INTRODUCTION

Learning math is a difficult business and its acquisition entails many intrinsic problems that stem from the difficulties children find in mastering processes of ab-

DOI: 10.4018/978-1-60566-930-4.ch001

straction and the formal codes that characterize the language, that often undermine their motivation to learn. Moreover, it is complex process relating the mechanical aspects- internalizing and automatically accessing procedural knowledge- with the far more challenging task of learning the underlying structures, that leads to an awareness of the value mathematical concepts can have when applied to reality, to art, science and in intellectual and personal growth.

Today any serious consideration of math teaching must be based on the premise that the technological progress of recent years has led to a redefinition of forms of social communication causing friction between conservative and evolutionary forces in the educational field. In other words, the new forms of reality require a revision of how math teaching is approached in schools because the pupils are now part of a complex community that is used to interacting in real and virtual worlds and this can be of profound importance for the field of educational psychology.

LEARNING NEEDS REVIEWED FROM THE PERSPECTIVE OF VIRTUAL ANTHROPOLOGY

Up until the advent of the virtual world in every day reality every child arrived in class with learning needs clearly defined by organizational and social contexts. At school the children found a learning environment organized to respond, in a fairly predictable predetermined way, to their learning requirements; the roles (teachers, heads, admin staff, the organization itself) were clearly defined as were the tools and methods employed to teach certain facts and encourage certain behavior in the right way, often, vis-à-vis the knowledge to be communicated and the attitudes to be encouraged.

Up until the advent of the virtual world in every day reality every teacher brought to the classroom a metaphorical toolbox of materials and techniques, even if one may sometimes doubt the methodological value and motivational effectiveness of some of the contents.

It is a complex business finding causal connections or other forms of correlation between the natural inclination and motivation to learn mathematics- variables known to influence the learning process- and strategies that organise and shape the process of learning of mathematics in the reality in which both parties-children and teachers- find themselves, i.e., the classroom.

We can say that teaching provision that should facilitate math learning is only partly able to respond adequately to the changing needs of virtual anthropology[1] (Levy P., 1994). The environments children grow up in are already vibrant and sometimes conflicting mixtures of the real and the virtual. As ever the case when innovations upset the established paradigms, it becomes necessary to reanalyze the underlying structures and harness the potential of change (Fregola, 2003). Or society is based on paradigms that are linear, certain, deterministic, where everything is reduced to the smallest detail, and these can only partly help us understand the changes in progress. It is, therefore, essential to search for more suitable models of analysis and interpretation of daily life and this implies recourse to paradigms involving simultaneity and uncertainty, situational paradigms, and the ability to reconstruct an overall vision, starting from the need to manage processes of communication, production and development that characterize complex systems to be determined or defined (Gandolfi A., 1999).

In order to deal with the consequences of this profound paradigm shift, primary school math, besides counting and measuring, should also develop competences that contribute to personal growth and supply pupils with the tools to deal with complexity[2].

What is clear is that the theme of prospective methodologies has been left open and there is little trace of references to learning and teaching models that take into account the consequences of recent changes that have involved children, adults, the interrelationships and their respective roles[3] in different contexts of life.

For this reason, it becomes essential to reflect on certain aspects of math teaching: "Math has a specific role in the development of the general capacity to operate and communicate meanings in formalized language, and to use this language to represent and construct models of the relations between objects and events. In particular, math provides the tools for a scientific description of the world and for tackling problems of daily life; moreover it contributes to developing the ability to communicate and discuss, propose arguments, in a correct manner, to understand the different points of view and arguments of other people"[4].

The construction of learning environments can take these elements into account by using, as a foundation, the awareness that: "the construction of mathematical thought is a slow and progressive process in which concepts, skills, competences and behaviors emerge, interweave, consolidate and develop though various stages; it is a process that also involves linguistic difficulties and requires the gradual acquisition of mathematical language"[5].

Nevertheless, if we consider that math education "contributes to the formation of various aspects of thought: intuition, imagination, projections, assumptions and deductions, checking, and therefore verification or rejection, and that this tends to develop, in a specific way, concepts, methods, behavior geared to produce the ability to order, quantify and measure real facts and phenomena and form the necessary skills to interpret critically and intervene consciously upon reality"[6] math teaching in elementary school should set educational objectives that take account of the evolution of "reality" and also of the development in educational psychology and neuro-science. The teaching of mathematics in nearly all countries of the world is directly orientated toward the acquisition of concepts and structures; yet the vast experience acquired has shown that it is not possible to arrive at mathematical abstraction without following a long course that links observation of reality, mathematization, problem solving and the conquest of the initial levels of formalization. Through careful analysis of the cognitive and meta-cognitive processes involved in math learning, the most recent research has revealed the complexity and gradual growth and the uneven lines of development lines of development. It has also been demonstrated that calculus and the study of geometric figures have an educational importance that far exceeds their practical applications that once justified their insertion in the syllabus. It is interesting to note that in the 1980s the development of information science and the spread of electronic calculators reopened the demand for knowledge and competence of applied mathematics that had revealed hitherto unimagined potential[7].

These conquests have only been partly incorporated in educational systems. However it is up to teachers and educational researchers to take the didactic decisions that will overcome the limits of innovation in schools, supply the resources necessary for developing learning environments equipped to face daily reality, provide synergies and find the right balance between everyday and virtual reality.

A GLANCE AT THE LITERATURE

In the 1980s and 1990s international research into the process of learning mathematics began to pay more attention to the specifics and complexity of this discipline, and set about constructing stable and reliable concepts to be used for the identification, understanding and resolution of problems (Pellerey, 1999).

These research directions took shape within a general perspective founded on a complex and problematic vision of the teaching and learning ambit, characterised by interdependence between learners and their cultural contexts in the process of the development and construction of knowledge (Semeraro, 1999).

From this point of view, the role that both conceptual and procedural knowledge- and the quality of their internal organisation- play in the process of problem solving assumed fundamental importance: in particular, the function of self-regulating structural skills and the incidence of environmental, affective and motivational components as well as the preconceptions regarding the learning of mathematics.

Other research, albeit from different standpoints, converged towards the same basic conviction. In particular, according to these schools of thought, mathematical concepts can only be constructed on the basis of pre-existing concepts (Anderson, 1983). These concepts form a network on which both the single pieces of information and their interrelations are embedded, thanks to the specific link with meaningful and shared experiences with teacher support to enable the learner to grasp their underlying purpose (Resnick, 1987). These experiences can be perceived as authentic and connected to an emerging need (Dreyfus, 2008; Sfard, 1991). In the creation of learning environments, the ways in which the concrete and operative aspects are approached are crucial (Piaget, 1973; Dienes, 1971); these are defined not only in terms of the physical characteristics of the real world, but also on the basis of meaningful connections that can come to light and/or be applied by relating them to other mathematical concepts or situations. With reference to this, it is important to mention the studies of Fischbain (1992), Vergnaud (1992) and, more recently, Fregola (2003), as well as the work of Laeng (1991), Sfard (1991) and Gagnè E. (1989); according to all these authors, the construction of concepts can be achieved in different and complementary ways, both in terms of processes and in terms of objects: in other words, the learner will become familiar with mathematical concepts by using them in processes and operations.

Much research, moreover, has highlighted the fact that common preconceptions can create obstacles in the subsequent process of constructing knowledge. Various authors have tackled this problem with different terminology, for example intuitive theories, misconceptions, synthetic models (see Gardner, Posner, Vosniadou on this), focusing on the need to render learners' initial acquisitions explicit for mathematical knowledge to progress. In order to be able to do this, however, knowledge acquired so far must be made explicit: this is essential both from the point of view of identifying and correcting any gaps or errors but also to guide the teacher whose role it is to intervene and support the conceptual change (Ausubel D.P., 1978; Novak J.D., Gowin D.B., 1984; Vosniadou, 2004). Awareness of one's own cognitive processes and the strategic competences relating to their control in view of the achievement of set objectives can bring about a marked improvement in a student's learning ability (Cornoldi, 1995; Lucangeli, 1999; 2003). Alongside the attention reserved for the description of cognitive mechanisms, research into the construction of mathematical concepts, analysed in relation to knowledge, contexts and individuals has shown how interaction with a context affects learners' personal convictions and their problem solving ability. Furthermore, it has been shown that interaction between previous learning experience, the pupil's perception of the usefulness of mathematics can be determining factors in performance (Pajeres, Miller, 1994). However, the commonly held view is still that the ability to learn mathematics is innate, in other words, you either have it or you don't, and there is nothing you can do about it. This widely held belief has always been an obstacle for those who wish to widen the boundaries of learning. However interesting it may be to monitor the research and discoveries in the field of neuroscience where, thanks to technological advances, new frontiers have broadened our understanding of learning mechanisms, we shall continue to follow our own line of research. Recently, Devlin (2007) published some work illustrating the existence of *a mathematics of various behaviours and different forms of thought*.

From the study one can infer that certain ways of thinking and certain mind sets operate by employing mathematical concepts and models. The question one can pose at this juncture is: but is the mind aware of this?

It is also the case that mental abilities codify this knowledge in mathematical language but it is necessary to be a mathematician or have a high level of math ability to grasp the structure which describes the structure itself. All this could help reinforce the belief that there are certain types of mathematical eggheads.

PLURALITY OF APPROACHES IN RESEARCH AND MATHEMATICS EDUCATION

It is worth noting that scientists from different disciplines often pursue the same research aims. For example, from the very beginning the International Commission for the Study and Improvement of Mathematics Teaching (in French CIEAEM, Commission Internationale pour l'Etude et l'Amélioration de l'Enseignement des Mathématiques) set out to study the state of the art at that time, and the possibility of improving the quality of teaching and learning of the subject.

The mathematician and philosopher of education Caleb Gattegno of London University, the French mathematician Gustave Choquet (president) and the Swiss Jean Piaget (vice president) psychologist and epistemologist, through a revision of mathematics teaching, tried to bring together three types of knowledge that, at that time, were evolving rapidly, in the hope of contributing to: "the achievement of a society whose members would be able to use mathematical reasoning and its instruments in order to act rationally and develop critical thought both as citizens and as future scientists. This humanistic perception of maths education should act as a safeguard both from the behaviour of technocrats and the folly of ideologies"[8].

In particular, Choquet brought to the debate the idea of a guided reform structuring the architecture of mathematics. Piaget presented the famous results of his research into cognitive psychology, opening up new prospects in the relations between the structure of mental operations and the scientific development of mathematics. Gattegno tried to link the new mathematical meta-theory to psychological research through a philosophical synthesis, and to establish relations with the teaching of mathematics in view of its overall educational importance. In the 1960s and 1970s mathematicians on the commission, such as Artin, Dieudonné, Papy and Servais, took up the cause of revising the didactics and the total restructuring of how mathematics was taught in schools "from infants to university" The, at times, controversial debate inside the commission became focused on the reformulation and reorganisation of the mathematical content of mathematical syllabuses or guidelines in accordance with the main ideas and methods of "Modern Mathematics". In the 1970s and 1980s the CIMAEM with the work of Anna Sofia Krygowska, a teacher and mathematician from Poland, Emma Castelnuovo, a teacher in Italy, Claude Gaulin, a Canadian teacher and Hans Freudenthal, a Dutch mathematician, tried to bring mathematics teaching closer to other sciences and to social reality within the context of an approach to teaching mathematics across the curriculum.

During the 1980s the debate on the subject turned to consideration of the contents and methodology of maths teaching, ever in the direction of issues of an epistemological, psychological and sociological nature, as well as to the question of technology. Among these greater attention was paid to the study of teaching/learning environments (interaction, evaluation, costs) and, in particular, the use of new technologies and their implication for the curriculum, besides their influence on the educational environment *per se*. Nevertheless, comparative international studies, such as TIMMS have underlined the loss of social esteem that has come with a widespread mistrust of mathematics and how it is taught.

More recently, an international commission chaired by Anna Sfard, from the University of Haifa, has been working on the redefinition of standards for mathematics teaching. A number of the conclusions highlight the difficulty in finding the right balance between the rigour of the mathematical language and the language to base teaching programmes on; let us read an extract (1998):

"I have tried to show the unsolvable nature of the dilemma that face those involved in the teaching of mathematics. In our efforts to improve the learning of mathematics we are always worried about two factors: concern for the student and concern for the quality of the mathematics taught. This is the very reason for the continuous tension that makes us go from one extreme to the other. However there is no possibility of ever being in a position to stop the swinging pendulum. If, on the one hand, we stick to our demands as regards the mathematics the results obtained from the students clearly demonstrate that we have not been realistic. If, on the other, we compromise on the mathematics we will quickly discover that we are hindering the learning process rather than helping it [....]. Thus, if we remove too many of the ingredients from the exquisitely structured system called mathematics, we may well find ourselves with a fairly insipid subject that leads nowhere".

One hypothesis that can be formulated is that mathematical language can be considered the arrival point of a passage over time through which the term "concrete" slowly evolves into a semantic network whose most efficient expression coincides with a mastery of the set of meanings of mathematical constructs. Furthermore, it can promote the acquisition of autonomy regarding what is referred to as "mathematical thought", understood as a repertoire of skills to manage mathematical knowledge in its widely varied fields of application and within a self-regulating system of the learner's own processes of acquisition. At the same time, when mathematical knowledge becomes the object of learning, the "field of creative effort" (Klein, 1976, p.16) that comes into play will lead to productive enquiry and the use of a mathematical language that is rigorous enough to avoid distortions and misunderstandings of concepts and structures and the consequent loss of overall meaning of mathematical constructs.

BUT ARE THE MATHEMATICAL CONTENTS TO BE LEARNT ALL OF THE SAME KIND?

The overwhelming majority of maths teachers agree on the distinction between the purely computational aspect of mathematics (algorithm, calculus, rules) and the conceptual aspect which is heuristic problem solving, i.e., concerned with understanding (Gagné E., 1989, p. 286). The most immediate consequence of this dichotomy is that the structuring of the learning environment brings into play different options that can depend on the process that develops on the basis of the nature of the object.

The didactic aims, therefore, take into account the specific characteristics of the content but both the aims and the content may require analysis in order to determine the conditions for the methodological decisions that will guide the construction of the learning environment.

Robert Gagné (1973) proposed a possible analysis of the objectives of learning that supports the identification of elements to structure teaching courses. For example, from the list of objectives proposed in Table 1, it is clear that there can be a difference between the activation of courses and the possible intervention strategies.

The objectives of the Table 1 can also be read as a sequence. One unusual aspect of learning is that the logical order proposed is not the same for every child. Moreover, by analysing the list one can recognise the requirement of different levels of abstraction involved in the single objectives. This implies that the ability to master the use of symbols can be attained regardless of a conscious understanding of the underlying meanings or of the awareness of concepts that are communicated via those symbols.

To give a full account of this question K. Devlin (2000) compiled a list, in which were indicated four levels of abstraction characterising the passage from the real to the mathematical world:

Table 1.

• Associate a specific name to a symbol
• Discover a concept which requires verbalisation
• Achieve the verbalisation of a construct that has been built
• Discover the rule hidden within a situation from the actions characterising a procedure
• Apply an already known procedure to a new situation or context

- 1st level: the objects of thought are real objects present in the surrounding environment and accessible to perception;
- 2nd level: the objects are real and familiar to the person who thinks but not directly accessible to perception;
- 3rd level: the objects are real, but have never been encountered in reality; or they are imaginary variants of real objects;
- 4th level: the objects are completely abstract; they have no link with the real world other than the fact they have been abstracted from reality.

The abstract is not a negation, it is the multiplication of the concrete, it is multi-concrete[9] (L.L. Radice and L. Mancini Proia, 1988, p. VI).

In order for formal words and phrases, that are meaningful in mathematical discourse, to be communicated it is necessary to have a conceptual map that is constructed through various stages of abstraction.

"In order to encourage the pupil's critical sense and stimulate inductive and deductive processes, teachers must concern themselves, not so much with transmitting notions but rather with building concepts and guiding the pupils' rediscovery of mathematics. Rediscovery, understood as the active appropriation of ideas, structures and procedures, implies the activation of two categories of mathematical thought: intuition and discipline. Learning through discovery, i.e., finding what someone else has hidden, like finding the Easter egg. With reference to the organization of teaching contents I would prefer to use the term discovery; however, for some time I have used the invention that incorporates at the same time form and content, finding out new things and invention". Freudenthal observes that the construction of mathematics is born from rich contexts, that then stimulate the interest of the learner and lead to the construction of cognitive procedures and algorithms. These mental objects are subsequently reinvented and consciously internalized, becoming part of the intellectual property of the learner which can be easily retrieved even when they seem forgotten." (Manara C.F., 1994)

REFERENCES

Anderson, J. R. (1983). *The architecture of cognition*. Cambridge: Harvard University Press.

Ausubel, D. P. (1995). *Educazione e processi cognitive*. Milano: Franco Angeli.

Ballanti, G. (1988). *Modelli di apprendimento e schemi di insegnamento*. Teramo: Lisciani & Giunti.

Bronfenbrenner, U. (1986). *Ecologia dello sviluppo umano*. Bologna: Il Mulino.

Cornoldi, C. (1995). *Metacognizione e Apprendimento*. Bologna: Il Mulino.

De Kerckhove, D. (1993). *Brainfraimes. Mente, tecnologia, mercato. Come le tecnologie della comunicazione trasformano la mente umana*. Bologna: Baskerville.

Devlin, K. (2007). *L'istinto matematico. Perché sei anche tu un genio dei numeri. Milano: Raffaello Cortina. Devlin, K. (2000). Il gene della matematica*. Milano: Longanesi.

Dienes, Z. P. (1971). *Le sei tappe del processo d'apprendimento in matematica*. Firenze: OS.

Dreyfuss, T., & Paola, D. (2008). New trends in mathematics education as a discipline, in (Mogen Niss editor) *ICME-10 Proceedings of the 10th International Congress on Mathematical Education, 4-11 July, 2004* (pp. 417-421). IMFUFA, Department of Science, Systems and Models, Roskilde University, Denmark

Fischbein, E. (1998). *Conoscenza intuitiva e conoscenza logica nell'attività matematica*. Bologna: Pitagora Editrice.

Fischbein, E., & Vergnaud, G. (1992). *Matematica a scuola: teorie ed esperienze*. Bologna: Pitagora Editrice.

Fregola, C. (1992). *I prerequisiti all'informatica*. Milano: Quaderni ENI.

Fregola, C. (2003). I livelli d'astrazione nell'apprendimento matematico attraverso i materiali montessoriani. In *Centro di Studi Montessoriani, Annuario 2003 – Attualità di Maria Montessori*. Milano: Franco Angeli.

Gagné, E. D. (1989). *Psicologia cognitiva e apprendimento scolastico*. Torino: SEI.

Gagné, R. M. (1973). *Le condizioni dell'apprendimento*. Roma: Armando.

Gandolfi, A. (1999). *Formicai, Imperi, Cervelli. Introduzione alla scienza della complessità*. Torino: Boringhieri.

Laeng, M. (1991). (Ed.). *Percorsi Didattici*. Teramo: Lisciani Editore.

Lévy, P. (1994). *L'intelligenza collettiva. Per un'antropologia del cyberspazio*. Milano: Feltrinelli.

Lévy, P. (1997). *Il virtuale*. Milano: Raffaello Cortina.

Lucangeli, D. (1999). *Il farsi e disfarsi del numero*. Roma: Borla.

Lucangeli, D. (2003). *L'intelligenza numerica. Abilità cognitive metacognitive e nella costruzione della conoscenza numerica dai 3 ai 6 anni*. Trento: Erickson.

Manara, C. F. (Ed.). (1994). *Hans Freudenthal, Ripensando l'educazione matematica - Lezioni tenute in Cina*. Brescia: Editrice La Scuola.

Meyrowitz, J. (1995). *Oltre il senso del luogo. Come i media elettronici influenzano il comportamento sociale*. Bologna: Baskerville.

Morin, E. (2001). *La natura della natura*. Raffaello Cortina.

Novak, J. D., & Gowin, D. B. (1984). *Imparando a imparare*. Torino: SEI.

Pajares, F., & Miller, M. D. (1994). Role of self-efficacy and self-conception beliefs in mathematical problem solving: A path analysis. *Journal of Educational Psychology, 86*, 193–203. doi:10.1037/0022-0663.86.2.193

Pecchinenda, G. (2004). *Videogiochi e cultura della simulazione*. Bari: Laterza.

Pellerey, M. (1999). Le conoscenze matematiche. In Pontecorvo, C. (Ed.), *Manuale di psicologia dell'educazione* (pp. 221–241). Bologna: Il Mulino.

Piaget, J. (1973). *La costruzione del reale nel bambino*. Firenze: La Nuova Italia.

Radice, L. L., & Mancini Proia, L. (1988). *Il metodo matematico nel mondo moderno. Per le Scuole*. Milano: Pincipato.

Resnick, L. B., & Ford, W. W. (1991). *Psicologia della matematica e apprendimento scolastico*. Torino: SEI.

Semeraro, R. (1999). *La progettazione didattica. Teorie, metodi, contesti*. Firenze: Giunti.

Sfard, A. (1991). On the dual nature of mathematical conceptions: Reflections on processes and objects as different sides of the same coin. *Educational Studies in Mathematics, 22*(1). doi:10.1007/BF00302715

Sfard, A. L. (1998), *Equilibrare l'inequilibrabile: gli Standard NCTM alla luce delle teorie dell'apprendimento della Matematica*. Retrieved from http://www.universityofhaifa.it/ Proposlals/Standards/Sfard-pap.doc.

Vergnaud, G. (1994). *Le rôle de l'enseignement à la lumière des concepts de schème et de champ conceptuel*. In M. Artigue, R. Grass, C. Laborde & P. Tavignot (Eds.), *Vingt ans de didactique des mathématiques en France* (pp. 177-191). Grenoble: La Pensée sauvage.

Vosniadou, S. (2004). Extending the conceptual change approach to mathematics learning and teaching. Special Issue on Conceptual Change. *Learning and Instruction, 4,* 45–69. doi:10.1016/0959-4752(94)90018-3

ENDNOTES

[1]   Levy (1997) adopts the term "virtual" to define the passage from reality to another ontological dimension and *virtual* represents a way of being, not what is false, illusory or imaginary, as the term is often used to mean in common language.

The term derives from the Latin *virtualis* that, in turn derives from *virtus* that is "force" or "power". Levy contrasts virtual and actual and possible and real, and the relation between these terms enables us to consider different ways of being, existing at the same time; furthermore, what is virtual exists without being materially present, i.e., without precise spatio-temporal coordinates.

"Virtual is a problematic node, because it contains within itself all the potential from which being can flow in its specific entity." Virtual is a human construct, since the human being has always lived in a virtual world, the world of language and the world of complex social organisation. The process of virtualisation or rather the current process of virtualisation is a creative process, in contrast with actualisation, and it transcends the object by inserting it in a problematic field with a wider relationship, whereas actualisation proceeds from a problem to a solution. Virtualisation passes from a solution to another problem. Present day information society provides instruments that have changed our relationship with consciousness, accelerating cognitive processes and the need for updating. There is a revolution in progress that is not just technological but also cultural, and the cognitive operations that derive from this can be also used to orientate ourselves in cyberspace, the World Wide Web, in other words, in a totally new environment conditioned by information.

2   On the theme of complexity see Morin E. (2001).

3   Reference is made to the ecological perspective of Bronfenbrenner (1986). For an interesting analysis of the consequences of the sense of identity and related matters, see Meyrowitz J. (1995) and De Kerchhove D. (1993).

4   These aspects were made explicit in *Indicazioni nazionali* published by the Italian Ministry of Education in 2007.

5   Cfr. Previous footnote.

6   Cfr Primary School program 1985.

7   Significant example is given by the hexadecimal system and the binary system as well as by Boole's algebra. At that time the problem was to find out about computer science's necessary abilities. (Fregola, 1992).

8   50 anni di CIEAEM: *Dove siamo e dove andiamo?* Manifesto 2000 for the year of mathematics

9   In 1977 I had the good fortune to attend the didactic maths laboratory at the Castelnuovo Institute of the Faculty of Mathematics at the Sapienza University of Rome, coordinated Lucio Lombardo Radice. In the lab we could observe and carry out projects that began from experience, from explorations in the piazzas, churches and, more in general, from the true laboratory of nature itself with the explicit aim of identifying situations, finding characteristics common and otherwise, and objects, facts and phenomena. Thereafter, it became necessary to bring them back to the laboratory in order to explore them more closely and understand, produce, reproduce and transform. The need to communicate these results led to the birth of *l'esigenza della matematica* (the need for mathematics); and slowly the language became more formal and evolved, the starting point based in realty, the concrete was pushed into the background. It is somewhat like what happens with children when the abstractions they are coming to terms with allow them to grasp the concept, the structure, the rule or model as invariant. Only at this point can variations in symbolic situations lead us through successive abstractions to the domain of awareness of more formalised expressions. In that ambit the mathematics of reality was a way of being alive, and the teaching courses that we managed to set up were also directed at ourselves. The most intense time of reflection that I remember was of the resistance I felt to leading the teaching courses to the, albeit complex, point of competence, then to smash that knowledge expressed in mathematical language in order to reconstruct it with the aim of anchoring it more strongly in the memory. Today I find a few more indications: the learning environments and materials, which require itineraries that involve time and means to throw off the concrete- in order to avoid a sort of dependence on it- can favour the construction of a mental place that can gradually sustain (among other possibilities) the growth of self-regulating processes. The final

goal is the mastery of mathematical language in its home territory in order then to connect with real objects, facts and phenomena on which to employ instruments, methodologies, models and schemata that cannot be expressed in other languages.

Chapter 2
Towards the Construction of a System of Maths Teaching

Daniela Olmetti Peja
Roma Tre University, Italy

ABSTRACT

The chapter sets out to identify the interpretive and structural criteria for educational innovation in order to find the necessary elements on which to plan the transformation (or to confirm the use) of instruments, means, technologies, learning models and schemata for the teaching of mathematics.

"Guy Brousseau was the universally recognised inventor of what is today recognised as mathematics didactics but, at the dawn back in the 1960s, it was only a mixture of clever intuitions, creation of ingenious and unstable devices, suggestions on the ways and contents often based on vague and wayward ideas." -Bruno D'Amore (2008)

INTRODUCTION

The defining of a system of mathematics teaching springs from the need that, in a classroom situation, each and every learner ought to be in a position to gain maxi-

DOI: 10.4018/978-1-60566-930-4.ch002

mum prophet from an experience designed and realised to match the pupil's level and background knowledge and the special characteristics of the subject. To put it another way, the need for interaction between the pupil and the suitable learning environment (Glaser, 1977). The concept of adaptation represents a key aspect in the learning process. A learning environment that is able to adapt changes socio-cultural conditions outside the school is certainly preferable to one that does not take into account the needs of the pupils attending the school. It is necessary, therefore, to identify the exact conditions that will foster the needs of all the pupils on the basis of their potential. The quality criteria for teaching decisions are based on an awareness of the pupils' abilities and the conditions that encourage the growth of internal processes in order to support, increase and stabilise acquisition (Fontana, 1996). As a point of departure, the educational setting must be adapted to the actual situation on the ground to guarantee an increase in knowledge acquisition. Teaching provision, therefore, assumes various guises, and the elements that define a given educational environment are the "learning devices" (Calvani, 1995); these make use of different types of artefacts, cultural and organisational contexts: multimedia systems, museums, libraries, laboratories, organised games... Simulation games!

Perhaps, the least familiar aspect of all this discourse on how to adapt the educational environment is the planning of cadenced times that leave room for experiences that render the process of learning fun. For teachers this commitment constitutes a necessary source of professional stimulus for the creation, projection and realisation of the times and spaces for learning that can be translated into group activities involving reciprocal exchange and hetero-control as well as direct guidance towards a desired goal.

In brief, mathematics teaching requires the ability to invent and experiment learning systems both in terms of educational psychology and methodology. At different times in the process of checking acquisition there is a need to activate strategies that can structure the forms and directions in order to bring out background knowledge and forms of thought on which mathematical learning is based. These, then, should act as a support for the development of the ability to connect the various concepts, rules, algorithms and solving procedures. The growing mastery that pupils acquire can guide the long process that requires, among other skills, the ability to:

- cope with ever more complex tasks;
- monitor learning in order to consolidate the underlying processes;
- incentivate self-evaluation through individual and group feedback;
- personalise the mode of intervention by integrating cognition, affect and emotion.

THE NEED FOR A SYSTEM OF MATHEMATICS TEACHING

Mathematics is increasingly present in all the fields of knowledge in various explicit and implicit forms, yet interest in its learning and teaching is in decline: international surveys on mathematical knowledge show not exactly sparkling levels among students, and the number of maths undergraduates is decreasing[1]. These findings lead us to imagine places in which we can bring together experience, expertise, good practice, learning and teaching models (Ballanti, 1988). In such environments we can work towards a definition of courses that will allow students to explore reality, arts and sciences in order to embark on an internal voyage of discovery towards knowledge and the relationship between knowledge, reality and our reasoning potential. Play, imagination and art become, therefore, the ingredients of a new approach that provides the motivation to learn mathematics (Boscolo, 1997) and a sense of self-efficacy (Bandura, 2000).

In a work whose aim is to study and define a system for mathematics teaching we have identified two key questions in particular:

- to what extent does the learning of mathematics continue to be necessary for work or any other social context (mathematical knowledge in itself)?
- to what extent does the learning of mathematics develop our rational potential that otherwise would find no context (social activities, other disciplines and so on) in which to develop (mathematical knowledge for personal growth)?

These questions allow us to identify the need for a system for the teaching of mathematics that goes beyond the fact that mathematics permeates nature, social productions and organisations and daily actions, at times in an overt at others in a covert way, guiding the structuring and realisation of thought processes.

The shock that comes from the conquest of a mathematical problem reveals the concealed complexities of the logical structures behind the results. Nevertheless, it is not necessary to become a mathematician to discover and use many of these secrets, which unlock the door to such wonders (Conte, 2009)[2].

In order to understand these secrets and to make them our own, or at least explore them, they have to be inserted into a learning project coherent with the age of the pupils and their institutional environment.

THE NEED FOR A SYSTEM

In order to develop the skills and competences to utilise scientific methodologies in the learning-teaching process we assumed that it was no longer possible to propose learning contexts in the classroom with groups of children, leaving in the background mathematical convictions and widespread misconceptions, and adopting models that do not produce tangible and unequivocal results: as regards this it is appropriate to pose two questions in particular:

- to what extent does the teaching of mathematics create conditions that can be used to build a sense of mathematical knowledge in a communicative environment that can stimulate curiosity and a desire for knowledge of real phenomena (*how can mathematics communicate with non mathematicians*)?

These questions re-enforce our conviction of the potential of a system mathematics teaching that can give birth to a collective work on the reorganisation of the knowledge contents, and the discovery of suitable methodologies on which to base the preparation and use of instruments, technologies and strategies under the overall guidance of the evolving study of learning psychology in particular, and educational science[3] in general.

A POSSIBLE SYSTEM FOR MATH TEACHING

The issue of mathematics teaching has given rise to an important debate, involving contrasts, methodological convergence and a search for a common framework (covering different disciplines) orientated towards the rediscovery of mathematical concepts and structures. On the basis of this framework an on-going work of reflection has been searching for, and testing teaching practices geared towards furthering the development in children learning mathematics of competences, such as intelligent play (Gardner, 1987), sensitivity, taste, imagination, creativity, and curiosity.

A willingness to investigate and a desire for knowledge are defining characteristics that allow and encourage an internal intellectual dynamic in the process of learning mathematics, and the use of mathematical language allows learners to embark on a voyage of discovery in which imagination combines with logic to explore the world. As regards this, Courant and Robbins (2000) write: "As an expression of the human mind, mathematics reflects active willingness, contemplative reason and the desire for aesthetic perfection. Its fundamental elements are logic and intuition, analysis and construction, generality and individuality. Different traditions can shed light on different aspects, but it is only the reaction of these antithetic forces and the struggle for their synthesis that constitutes the life, utility and the supreme value of mathematical science."

The review of the construction of a teaching system for mathematics, therefore, stems from a need to examine different approaches to scientific disciplines that, confirmed on the basis of direct personal experience, allow the activation of processes of construction of mathematical language and facilitate the acquisition of the basic concepts of logic, arithmetic, and geometry.

A systematic approach to teaching, even if this may seem a contradiction in terms, implies recourse to ever-relevant basic educational principles, in particular, individualised teaching and the consequent focus on each pupil's learning needs.

From the quantity criterion of methods and good practices, we search for the quality criterion of the most appropriate and expedient teaching decisions:

- The individual characteristics of each child;
- Mathematics as a discipline;
- The ability to communicate mathematical knowledge that comes from mastery and practice though the deliberate use of its language.

The adoption of individualised teaching methods involves overturning of the traditional perspective; hence, it is not the pupil who must adapt but rather the interventions must be designed in accordance with the real and proven needs of the pupil, and from this basis the teaching decisions can be taken on the design, organisation and realisation of learning environments.

Research into learning has thrown light on the wide range of individual differences, for example the differences in level of readiness, in attitudes, needs, interests, behaviours, motivation, willingness to dedicate time to learning, concentration span, speed and accuracy of acquisition, cognitive learning style, application, readiness to take risks and so on. All this seems to us to open the possibility to explore *fields of potentiality* that have nothing to do directly with the substance and form of mathematics (Pellerey, 1994) and *a priori* existence of mathematical processes in the minds of individuals.

For these reasons the realisation of the individualisation of teaching needs constant improvement: the treatment of the individual learner's needs must balance organisational restrictions with the specific times of the learning process of the pupil who has not yet found confirmation or validation of the concepts in question. All this can be reinterpreted in the light of the micro and macro interactive processes between the various contests in which the process of learning takes place (Bronfenbrenner, 1986).

On the basis of personal observation, every teacher is able to produce a variety of teaching proposals differing as regards ways and means, and set a clear goal in order to progress and develop the current situation. The right procedures for the realisation of learning environments lead to teaching practices based on a concrete awareness of given situations and not merely on the uniform application of theoretical norms dictated from other experiences and situations. This, therefore, is the setting of the organised task in which " teachers have the role not only of applying, but also of choosing, adapting and applying the rules, in the infinite variety of situations they experience together with their pupils" (Ballanti, 1988, p.12).

In mathematics more then in other disciplines the passage from a uniform style of teaching in which the contents and methods do not vary, to a quality approach requires as a starting point a profound awareness of the various teaching theories (interpretive models) with the teaching methods deriving from them (applicable schemata); the latter need to be contextualised, and decisions taken on priorities and modifications[4] in order to translate them into specific teaching and learning opportunities. The entire process can be summed up in the experimental teaching plan, divided into three areas in order to make the information accessible, in a practical sense, and readily available when required. In practice, past elements are examined as well as internal aspects of the process and factors resulting from it, since it is expected that there will be a need to access information *before, during* and *after* the project, albeit in different ways and with different aims. In other words, the most relevant data, therefore, to be found upstream, *before,* are the anticipations or assumptions teachers formulate when programming teaching interventions; *during*, in the divers forms of scholastic work carried out in class interacting with the students; and finally *after*, in the documentation of the various strategies derived from the teaching of mathematics (Laeng, 1991). It is clear that these forms are connected with the teacher's way of working, both on the professional and the cultural level (Pellerey, 1994; Vertecchi, 1993).

THE NEED FOR MATH

With reference to the aforementioned learning needs Sfard (1998) identified the following:

- understand the meaning
- grasp the structure
- carry out repetitive (and non repetitive) actions
- feel able to tackle problems
- meaning and relevance of learning
- social interaction
- verbal interaction
- clearly defined discourse

- belonging
- balance between intention and action

The needs identified by Sfard can be found in many other situations besides math teaching. It can be noted that each of the aforementioned needs corresponds to growth strategies that lead every child to develop the emotional and cognitive skills for learning and, in the case of math, provide the necessary tools for understanding.

The need for a specific language, in math acquisition in particular, becomes apparent when the child realizes that the code he/she is gradually acquiring when faced with math problems has a practical use; whereas it is often claimed that such a need arises from external stimuli and a competent teacher.

On this point (as Sfard writes: "There is no right answer but there is no way back") it is not a question of replacing one approach with another. It is rather the case of identifying innovative teaching criteria so as to find efficient tools, means, technologies and learning models.

The integration of innovations with tradition and the transformation of tradition wherever necessary represent two necessary evolutions required to make teaching today's children relevant. Each teacher needs the right tool kit, but it must be based on a coherent system.

REFLECTIONS ON A POSSIBLE SYSTEM

The issue of math teaching has long been discussed by experts and much has been said and written on the best way to teach mathematics. Now, however, it is time to reflect and shift focus towards developing teaching environments where sensitivity, imagination, creativity, curiosity become the requirements for the development of math knowledge.

The use of mathematical language in various ambits can encourage learning processes in which imagination combines with logic in order to explore the world. This exploration may give rise to unexpected solutions but, in any event, it is a process that leads learners toward the conquest of concepts, rules, procedures and mathematical structures.

Our conviction of the potential of math teaching has encouraged us to search for more appropriate methodologies, strategies, means and tools, and to put our research intuitions to the test in the classroom.

We asked a question: To what extent today is math teaching necessary for developing necessary skills in the workplace and elsewhere?

For us the answer is obvious: math permeates nature and social relations, sometimes covertly, sometimes overtly, guiding thoughts through its structure and effects.

Just think for a moment of the wonder that a math result can generate or the complexity of the logical structures that lie behind such a resolution. That said, it is hardly necessary to become a mathematician to discover and make use of these secrets. In order to unlock these secrets and make use of them, all that is needed is to participate in a coherent teaching program, adapted for the age range, which has a clear design founded on a sound methodology.

A complex system of math teaching should:

- Put forward experimental learning contexts
- Be based on controlled educational procedures that enable pupils to develop freely
- Try out new courses and test the effectiveness of experimental methodologies
- Adopt an interdisciplinary approach.

Our mission is provide intellectual adventures to whet pupils' curiosity and bring out emotions that can be a resource, to teach children to read between the lines by exploring the codes of mathematical language, and to construct learning models that are made to measure.

Method, intuition, experience, creativity, teaching theory and math knowledge become interconnected and generate discovery.

One can assume that there is a need for a methodological approach that brings into play intuitive thought, divergent and convergent thought in order to guide the didactic decisions and determine the methods that can stimulate the development of strategies that can be structured as meta methodological phases that enable the learner to:

- prefigure an overall learning development plan and its phases
- carry out teaching activities with greater awareness and provide teaching direction and autonomy to the teaching schemata that characterize the mathematization process in current teaching
- estimate the consequences that could flow from the activities, coherent with the specific stage in the various environments characterizing the *real*
- monitor the consequences and link the results to the actions that arose from the results themselves; to the context conditions and to the process that develops itself in the various environments characterizing the *real*
- confront the process with the overall teaching schemata and gradually redefine and re-orientate itself
- emphasize the importance of the result to underline the activities that produced it

- reiterate the discoveries induced and place them in the context of the evolution of mathematical thought.

REFERENCES

Ausubel, D. P. (1978). *Educazione e processi cognitivi*. Milano: Angeli.

Ballanti, G. (1988). *Modelli di apprendimento e schemi di insegnamento*. Teramo: Giunti Lisciani.

Ballanti, G. Fontana, L. (1989). *Discorso e azione nella pedagogia scientifica*. Teramo: Giunti Lisciani.

Bandura, A. (2000). *Autoefficacia: teoria e applicazioni*. Trento: Erickson.

Boscolo, P. (1997). *Psicologia dell'apprendimento scolastico. Aspetti cognitivi e motivazionali*. Torino: UTET.

Bronfenbrenner, U. (1986). *Ecologia dello sviluppo umano*. Bologna: Il Mulino.

Calvani, A. (1995). Manuale di tecnologie dell'educazione. Pisa: ETS.

Carroll, J. B. (1963). A model of school learning. *Teachers College Record, 64*, 723–733.

Courant, R., Robbins, H. (1971). *Che cos'è la matematica*. Torino: Bollati Boringhieri

D'Amore, B. (2008). Prefazione. In G. Brousseau (Ed.), *Ingegneria didattica ed Epistemologia della Matematica*. Bologna: Pitagora.

Fontana Tomassucci, L. (1996). Aree e strategie di intervento individualizzato . *Cadmo, 10-11*, 29–40.

Gardner, H. (1987). *Formae Mentis. Saggio sulla pluralità dell'intelligenza*. Milano: Feltrinelli.

Gardner, H. (1991). *Aprire le menti. La creatività e i dilemmi dell'educazione*. Milano: Feltrinelli.

Glaser, R. (1976). Components of a psychology of instruction. Toward a science of design. *Review of Educational Research, 46*, 1–24.

Laeng, M. (1991). Percorsi Didattici. Teramo: Lisciani e Giunti

Pellerey, M. (1994). *Progettazione didattica. Metodi di programmazione educativa scolastica*. Torino: SEI.

Sfard, A. L. (1998). *Equilibrare l'inequilibrabile: gli Standard NCTM alla luce delle teorie dell'apprendimento della Matematica*. Retrieved from http://www. universityofhaifa.it Proposlals/Standards/Sfard-pap.doc.

Vertecchi, B. (1993). *Decisione didattica e valutazione*. Firenze: La Nuova Italia.

ENDNOTES

1 Personal conversation
2 On this matter Ellen Gagné (1989) writes: while technology (and mathematics its silent companion) becomes ever more important in everyday life, the level of consciousness of students, rather than increase, seems to decline even further (p. 285).
3 With reference to this, see Visalberghi, A. (1978). *Pedagogia e Scienze dell'Educazione*. Milano: Mondadori.
4 In view of the attainment of the assumed goals, teaching action must be *adaptive*, that is to say, able to modify where necessary the preordained operative sequence on the basis of indications arising from the interaction.

Chapter 3
Simulation Games:
Ontology

Carmelo Piu
University of Calabria, Italy

ABSTRACT

This chapter develops a reflection on the theme and the different meanings that simulation can assume in applied research ambits, and deals with the problems connected to the lack of a specific ontology shared by the scientific community. In this context, after the reflections on the interconnections between simulation and reality with a view to integrating rather than superimposing one on the other, we propose a classification for simulation in the educational field that takes the didactic, social and political literature into account and underlines the need to construct an ontology that can overcome the semantic ambiguity and support a scientific debate, with particular reference to simulation games seen from the perspective of the ecology of human development.

INTRODUCTION

The spectrum of the term simulation covers many different meanings, each of which assumes a particular significance depending on the use made of it, the context the objective and the scientific ambit in which it is used. The hypothesis is to be able

DOI: 10.4018/978-1-60566-930-4.ch003

to construct and elaborate an ontology on the theme and meanings of simulation, with reference to a classification that takes into consideration the current literature- scientific, educational, cultural and political. Our aim, therefore, is overcome the semantic ambiguity that has dogged the concept of simulation, and provide an overall synthesis in terms of classification, description and interpretation, that can lead towards a unified and accepted theory. To do this it is necessary establish close and symbiotic relationships between the two domains of simulation, i.e., simulation, object of analysis, and the *ontology*, the meanings that generally attributed to it, in order to provide clarification. In other words to build on the semantic plane a shared hypothesis which combines the two terms.

ONTOLOGY AND SIMULATION

Despite its original setting that was eminently theoretical in nature, ontology is assuming an ever-increasing practical relevance. Recently it has been used in the field of Artificial Intelligence and of *representation of knowledge* and thus for a variety of ends amongst which inductive reasoning, classification (concept repertoires) and various techniques for problem resolution (Wikipedia, 2008), as well as facilitating communication and information exchange. There is a need to create general and defined schemes to develop data sets to provide a coherent description within the domain under inspection, in this case simulation. In this sense, ontology is essentially taken to indicate an attempt at formulating a clear conceptual scheme. Such conceptual schemes are "to have value", Paparella (2007) notes, "not just as *principles*, but as rigorous points of reference, justified, appropriately motivated, carefully documented, and thus usable as control criteria" of the very discourse of simulation. In general, it is a question of creating a *data structure,* which contains the relevant entities, the relations existing between them, the rules, the axioms and the specific constraints, from which grades of freedom of ideation, creation and planning of simulation games may be derived. It is important to create a structure formalized through semantic language, linked on the basis of a formal logic. This is a *foundational and formal ontology* to be used as a glossary or as a database, i.e. a conceptual scheme for classification, which also includes the semantic relations in order to describe the ways in which the concepts are interrelated (Bottani, Davies 2006; De Monticelli, Conni, 2008). Varzi (2005) maintains that the objective for ontology is to *classify* what already exists, and that as you cannot classify something without knowing what it is, the task of ontology is to "draw up a sort of complete and detailed inventory (at least in principle)" (Varzi, 2003) of all that is known of a certain scientific domain.

Ontology has a clarifying and classifying function with respect to the data from the scientific research on the theme of simulation. "An ontology is, fundamentally, a *conceptual organizer of the scientific discourse* and thus a heuristic facilitator, and for this same reason, a formidable support for the hermeneutic work" (Paparella, 2007). The relationship, insofar as it is realized between ontology and the sciences is resolved in the function assumed by the former of organizing and classifying what is discovered through the sciences. It follows from these assumptions, therefore, that there is a *descriptive* and *formal* ontology; the former is concerned with gathering data in scientific domains, whereas the latter, the formal one, addresses the working of data on the basis of ontological-formal categories such as thing, process, substance, form, etc. From this perspective, the term *simulation* can be an ambit and a field of enquiry of great value, "ontology being able to offer credit and credibility to the epistemological frameworks" (Colazzo, 2007), continuity to the research and sense and meaning to the community of those who fuel scientific research. This result can be obtained through the completion of a conceptual classification and the possible construction of a sort of taxonomy, as a shared basis specific to a certain domain, especially if this domain has, as in the case of simulation, a vast semantic range, or in other words it presents diverse and numerous collocations. Despite the epistemological weaknesses, it has nevertheless given rise to a period of significant interest both in theoretical reflections and innovative practices and settings; and this development has not only characterized the ambits of business, technology, informatics, and mass media, but also education; thus the need for a terminological clarification, in order to trace the limits of the semantic field and understand the variety of contexts and meanings. Such plurality highlights the semantic ambiguity of the term, caused by the vast use that is made of it in different contexts, in many disciplinary ambits and also in the field of technological training. In the e-learning sector it almost always refers to software carried out with programs where the mouse controls movement on the screen and it is used with forms of representation of reality itself, or more generally, to indicate virtual worlds. Furthermore, simulation is often confused with games, such videogames and the like. Hence the need for constructing an ontological structure on the theme of simulation, whose objective is to organize and structure a scientific field which is ambiguous, pluri-semantic and difficult to define.

THE MANY MEANINGS OF SIMULATION

Before entering into the construction of an ontology of simulation, the first clarification to be made concerns the different meanings it conveys in everyday, legal, bureaucratic and scientific language and and the different meanings and uses of simulation in the educational field.

In the current language, the term generally indicates "the reproduction of a behavior which wants to make what is in reality not true appear true". In fact, the majority of Italian language dictionaries give the term the meaning of "fiction" "deceit" and also "imitation". All these terms refer to a behavior generally employed for negative ends with the intent of deluding, deceiving or lying, albeit with inventiveness and creativity. The examples provided by the dictionaries, highlight this negative aspect. Thus, the very expression *simulation of offence*, used in the juridical ambit, refers to a false or improper declaration or to an invented fact or event; in the same way another expression of a juridical nature, *simulation of contract*, refers to a fictitious agreement, which is a juridical negotiation falsely stipulated and declared as really having taken place, between two parties, whereas in reality no agreement was stipulated or if it were it was different from the one declared.. A similar expression, *simulation of illness* or *physical infirmity*, used in medicine, refers to a behavior which tends towards the recognition of an illness or infirmity, through the declaration of invented or imagined symptoms, with the aim of procuring the certification of a false or indeed non existent pathology.

In the technical-scientific language, on the other hand, the term assumes meanings different to that of deceit, falsification and illusion, present in the common usage, although it conserves in a broad sense the previous connotation of reproduction of something that is presented as real whilst being constructed artificially. Shannon (1975) specifies that simulation is a process that is able to plan and construct a hypothetical model of a real system, on which to carry out experiments to explain and comprehend the very behavior of the system and to verify various strategies to operate on and within the system.

What this means is that technically, simulation is the ability to carry out enquiries on phenomena conducted through the dynamic of a *model* isomorphic to reality, with or without electronic assistance. Nor is there a clear or univocal meaning, as each discipline, in using the term, gives it a different meaning. With reference to this Taylor (1976) attributes this ambiguity to the lack, in the academic field, of a universally accepted lexicon, due partly to the fact that the term assumes a specific meaning closely related to the discipline in question, and partly to the complexity of the problem, linked to the growing amount of research undertaken in each discipline in an autonomous and often isolated manner. Over time, an undifferentiated and unclear use of the term has developed. The development of a terminology, which presents itself at the same time rich and confused, is determined by the necessity of each discipline to use the concept of simulation in a diversified manner from time to time, giving it a specific role, so that a there is proliferation of meaning, both specific and specialized, which cover a vast range of possible uses.

SIMULATION BETWEEN MODEL AND REALITY

Between these two settings, which represent the term in an ambivalent manner, one can nonetheless arrive at a unitary meaning, as if the term had two souls or was the two faces of the same coin. These two families of meaning, in fact, are not entirely divergent from each another. In both cases if simulation is intended as fiction, deceit and lie, or if it is intended as imitation, representation, reproduction, it remains a fictitious representation of reality, the former indicating "false" behavior, and the latter proposing a reconstruction which is not real. In both cases there is an ambiguous relationship between language, reality and behavior, thus between the virtual world and the real world, between the representation or reconstructed model and reality. The relation with reality, is always mediated through a certain language that is called to on simulate, to represent what is the reality under examination, so the term simulation can be understood either as the elaboration and construction of a model and subsequently as verification of its functioning, or as provisional and predictive inquiry, in other words an instrument for prediction and interpretation, although these two meanings are often interrelated and one is propaedeutic to the other. In both meanings, however, simulation is always characterized by the construction of an interpretative and representative model with respect to a certain reality, so it becomes the result of a synergic interaction between a theoretical hypothesis, which leads to the realization of the model and its application. In this view, simulation can lead, on one hand, to the formulation of a scientific hypothesis regarding an unknown reality (Derossi G., 1976), and on the other, it can be a tool for prediction and interpretation of reality.

There are, however, a number of problems which require clarification, linked on one hand to the interconnection between simulation and reality and, on the other, to the real/virtual relation, in other words to simulation in the virtual ambit. The first problem, regarding the relation between reality and simulation, is somewhat difficult to define, as simulation is an attempt at reproducing reality, whilst conscious of the fact that reality cannot be entirely reproduced. In effect this is a paradox: we use simulation to copy reality but are conscious of the undoubted difference which, in the end, will result between reality and its reproduction (Santilli, 2002). Parisi (1999) maintains that simulation aims at understanding reality by reproducing synthetically in an artificial system, so reality and simulation remain different and distinct, but alike and analogous. The study of a system is carried out by constructing a model which is then manipulated in such a way that, depending on how the model behaves under different conditions, it becomes possible to evince the behavior of the real system in analogous conditions (Piu A., 2002). Simulation always operates on its representation, as it is based on the reconstruction of a real situation which recalls and postulates necessarily the realization of a significant model of the reality to be studied, so it needs to refer to the concept of the model. This can be defined as "a representation of a real situation through an ensemble of data and elements analogous to it", thus the model needs to be *isomorphic* to the system as it has an abstract and symbolic "similarity" with it, i.e., the model has the role of "mediator" and "operative interpreter" of the reality under examination. Such similarity is based not so much on the ontological nature of the elements in the model but on the structural *analogies* between its properties, the relations and the functions of the reality that is to be modeled. The model is an instrument which gives an analogical image of a particularly heuristic effectiveness, without departing from the phenomenon itself; it is a fiduciary construct of a special mediator of the process of knowledge; in other words, although artificially constructed with different elements from those which make up the phenomenon under examination, it is a reliable means for studying that phenomenon (Paparella, 1984).

Despite the above-mentioned difficulties, simulation can be defined as a "series of dynamic representations which use elements substitutive of reality, such as models, obtained through a process of abstraction, in order to facilitate the study, comprehension and management of reality itself". This definition, despite being generic, is shared by many scholars, as it is rooted in the common way of thinking through *systems.* Systemic thought represents a cognitive and interpretative method which considers reality as a complex entity, made up of a series of interacting elements, seen as an organically structured ensemble or *unicum*, as it is characterized as the sole *system*. Within this framework, it becomes possible to hypothesize and propose a definition of the concept of simulation, with more definitive criteria and variables. Shannon (1975), thus, sees simulation as a process which is able to plan and construct a hypothetical model of a real system, on which we can carry out experiments with the intent of explaining and understanding the behavior of the system itself.

Figure 1. Simulation between model and reality

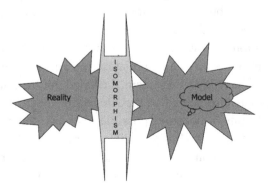

The second problem is related to simulation in the virtual ambit. The very definition of virtual reality leads us to an initial differentiation, based on whether it is analyzed on the technological level (Beretta, 1998)[1], as simulation of the physical world, or as a likely and imaginary representation of reality (Fini, 1998)[2]. To synthesize the two positions, a simulated environment is an artificial space in which one is immersed in order to explore the environment and construct models within which (environment-model) one can navigate, interact and verify the consequences. The salient characteristics are, therefore, immersion, navigation and meaningful experience.

Immersion is related to the perception of being within the artificial space, of being able to experience it as real, whilst knowing that it is a reconstructed and imaginary reality. Navigation, on the other hand, refers to the perception of moving and interacting within that environment. This experience is linked to the fact that it enables one to receive multiple inputs or feedback in response to the actions engendered thanks to the manipulation of the controls (Piu A., 2006). In all these situations, however, the user always has the perception of acting and establishing a relationship with reality, whilst being aware, on one hand, of being in an environment which identifies itself with reality, but is simulated and hypothetical as a partial and not total reconstruction or reproduction of it, and, on the other, of acting in an environment which surpasses and excessively enlarges reality itself, so one can act freely and creatively within it and hypothesize possible worlds or models of "poietic" reality.

It is on this distinction and on the relationship that lies between the real and the virtual that simulation- games, videogames and computer simulation and so on- are to be framed and explained. A faithful reproduction of reality would not make sense in the same way as an invention of reality (Santilli, 2002). Within this paradox between identity and difference simulation makes sense, as it is not real but it seems real; it is not mere invention and fantasy but it refers to a real phenomenon. In fact, different but analogous worlds, with which one can interact in real time, are created in these environments. Participating in a virtual simulation means essentially "to find oneself immersed in a reality that presents characteristics analogous to the reality of reference, within which we can interact and verify the consequences of our actions" (Piu A., 2002). Virtual environments, however, do not intend to and, in fact, cannot offer true living reality, but rather establish a *relation* with reality.

In a simulated environment, however, regardless the type of simulation, the experiences are useful insofar as the subject can interact and intervene to modify, verify, confute or validate the behavior of the variable and monitor the results obtained. In this way we can *practice* and *exercise* our intellectual, heuristic and investigative capabilities in an operative, albeit simulated, environment (Wynn, 1987). In other words, the partial reproduction of a phenomenon acquired in the artificial environment can be subsequently used in the real environment. This passage, which is concretized through a transfer of knowledge, allows us not only to achieve a better understanding of the specific phenomenon under examination, but also to investigate different areas, as it raises new questions, which can open and activate further fields of inquiry, making possible, through the additional information it produces, an increase in knowledge which leads to a higher degree of comprehension, interpretation and management of reality itself. The model in simulation, therefore, has a fundamental role, as it makes the reality to be studied more accessible and comprehensible, in the sense that the elements of the real situation to be taken into examination become, in a sense, visible even if we do not have an accurate and systematic description of that overall reality. In this way it is possible to interpret, predict and monitor the behavior of the system under examination scientifically.

In the research field, simulation can be considered a valid method of inquiry, or rather, a procedure for discovering reality that is closely linked with the methods of inquiry and procedures of experimental research, whilst in the educational ambit it can take on different meanings in relation to the different uses proposed. Experimentation manipulates reality in a direct way, i.e. it operates on a system, which corresponds to a sector of reality or a sample of it, whilst simulation does not operate directly on reality, but rather on a representation of reality; its aim is to reproduce elements or parts of reality and subsequently to intervene on this representation. In this way useful bits of knowledge about reality are acquired through simulation, without directly intervening on reality.

Within this framework, after the reflections on the interweaving between simulation and reality with a view to integration and not identification and superimposition, attention will be given to the construction of an ontology on simulation in the educational field, with particular reference to simulation games, considered from an ecological perspective of human development.

SIMULATION IN THE EDUCATIONAL AMBIT

In the educational ambit the relation between model, simulation and reality and the cognitive processes that can be activated, in relation to the possibilities of action of the subject within the model and the environment generated on the basis of the model, can lead to an important distinction. Often the term simulation is used in an undifferentiated manner, particularly with the proliferating of technologies today that offer numerous simulation environments. The proliferation of technologies and their widespread use has modified the relation with the external world and with knowledge itself. It has introduced elements which radically redesign both the models of communication and distribution of knowledge and the strategies and methodologies of acquisition for learning and constructing competences (Piu C., 2006).

The use of new didactic methodologies, linked to the use of technologies and of virtual environments and contexts of learning, allows for the setting up and organization of the optimal conditions of climate and relation, both of communication and training, in order to develop the cognitive potential and the critical faculties of the students to the full. Through the new virtual and on-line environments it is, in fact, possible to acquire, construct and share competences, by exchanging information, discussing, reflecting, comparing and contrasting, and negotiating meaning. The knowledge of reality, in the simulated context of a virtual world created by information technology is not handed down but rather experienced and lived, as simulation is both the modality of application of thought and knowledge of reality and the regulating principle of the action (Piu A., 2008). The main function of the methodology of simulation is that of representing guidelines for action, as it traces the principles through which the action itself has to be developed as it hypothesizes a path which is to be constructed, in a motivated and methodologically organized manner, i.e. in its creation and unfolding. Knowledge, in other words, is enacted not only in the *declaratory* form and expressed in *propositions*, but is presented and used within *actions*, i.e. as *procedural knowledge* and realized in a multiplicity of contexts and through a multiplicity of languages. This double dimension of knowing, defined in the English speaking world as *know-how* and *know-that,* i.e., the *how* and *what* of knowing, characterizes every area of learning. The simulation activity, therefore, is both a strategy for, and a method of learning. In fact, simulation is closely bound up with planning and workability seeing them as fundamental resources for learning, so it is both a strategy and method aimed at developing a sort of *cognitive apprenticeship* that, on one hand, privileges laboratory and hands-on activity for the realization of tasks and for the resolution of concrete problems and, on the other hand, develops the autonomy and cognitive flexibility of the learners.

Starting from these concepts, one can form a basic distinction in the educational ambit between the meaning and use of simulation. In the ecological conception of human development (Bronferbrenner, 1986; Bateson, 1976), simulation puts the subjects in the conditions of knowing and immersing themselves in *models* of reality and acting and intervening in an environment wider than the factual one, contingent and immediate and thus of a broader scope, incrementing and enriching their experience and projecting it in a more general and more abstract context: a global, spatial, holistic reality. That is, the immediateness is lost but its semantic dimension is increased. Learners become aware of finding themselves in a situation where they have to act, choose, make decisions, operate and experiment; this world, within which they move as protagonists and not spectators, is not real but artificial, i.e., analogous and isomorphic to reality (Pecchimenda, 2003). In this way the users experience and realize a sort of *cognitive apprenticeship*, taking responsibility for their decisions and actions. They decide on the *how* and *what* to keep or modify and review their actions and actions, as they observe the consequences of their decisions and actions (Parisi, 2005). In this way they think about and examine the critical points, make decisions and increase their capacity for autonomy and cognitive flexibility, having the opportunity of learning how to learn autonomously (Piu C., 2007). Within these simulated contexts, the learners not only acquire *knowledge,* by practicing it in a given situation, but also the *modalities* of *how* to learn, elaborating old and new bits of knowledge, reflecting upon the various critical points and developing their metacognitive skills.

THE CLASSIFICATION OF EDUCATIONAL SIMULATION GAMES

Simulation, as a learning strategy, was first used in the 1960s, although antecedents of the principal techniques go back to many years before that.

Forerunners will be examined through the various key stages of their development in the educational field in relation to the three main strands that is role play, simulation games and computer simulations, each of which have had a separate history and development. The classification we used is based on Taylor and Walford (1979) who provide a general reference that highlights the differences on the historical and structural level, despite the interconnections they often find between the different strands. Role play, not having a well defined structure, is considered a more basic form of simulation; it involves participants reacting spontaneously to the situation they are placed in, whereas the simulation game is based on more formalized procedures and the relationships are more structured as the players must operate within a system of rules. Computer simulation, on the other hand, requires electronic means to process a large amount of information, and hence human participation is restricted to the initial development of the program and reaction to the results.

This long tradition has made it possible for simulation to have become in many countries today an established methodology, considered and used as a valid tool in the educational environment. This practice is reinforced by that fact that there is a rich body of literature in these countries on the subject and there are hundreds of commercially available games for every type of educational area.

We can add to this classification others[3] which are even more developed[4] that include these and other techniques presented in a closely interconnected manner. Among these that of Cecchini appears particularly interesting: it is based on a very elaborated definition of simulation that includes the aforementioned techniques and others in the expression gaming simulation, an expression used by the author not just to mean simulation games but also the whole range of techniques used in played simulation, i.e., "the simulation of the effects of decisions taken through the assumption of roles in a rule bound game" (Cecchini, 1987). The classification is carried out on the basis of factors that define the simulation techniques, with particular attention to the quantitative dimension that each fact assumes in the different techniques. In other words, the author tries to create "quantitative parameters for the various classes present in the category", which leads as the author himself admits, "to a slightly dizzy combination". The point of departure developed by Cecchini is that proposed by Giacomantonio (Giacomantonio M., 1984), who defines gaming simulation as a technique included in three dimensional space, with respect to the three points: role (R) simulation (S) and game (G) (Figure 2). This three dimensional space can become dynamic by assigning to each point a number on the basis of the relative importance of R, S and G in the simulation; hence one can draw the position that every specific technique assumes in the space on the basis of the intersection obtained.

Role-Play

Role-play is a simulation technique requiring the direct involvement of participants who, interpreting the assigned roles, are called upon to improvise situations based on the data provided before the representation. This was first born probably around the 1930s in the psychiatric field, as a intervention strategy and therapy for treating mental illnesses.

Jacob Levy Moreno uses role-play, creating the *theatre of spontaneity* and *psychodrama.* The first to exploit the creative and spontaneous potential of individuals and the second to develop capacity for free expression and interaction of his pupils and patients. Klein subsequently creates *Working with groups,* with the aim of improving personal relations through group work. It is Moreno himself who first transfers the role-play technique from the therapeutic to the education sector

During the Second World War, in the United States the technique was inserted in *programs of training* approved by public administration, as it was considered an effective learning strategy. Initially used in adult education it was subsequently

Table 1. Characteristics of the three simulation techniques

Role play	Simulation games	Computer simulation
• Unclear formal structure • Spontaneus action of participants in the hypothetical situation	• Defined formal structure • Action of participants included in an environment conditioned by rules and procedures	• Highly defined formal structure • Action of participants restricted by rules of programme

Figure 2. Three dimensions for simulation games

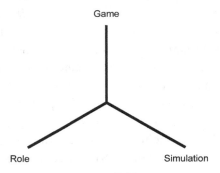

extended to many other sectors: for managers, for future trainers and teachers, for negotiators, trade unionists, politicians and so on.

In schools, the technique experienced a remarkable diffusion for the teaching and learning of oral language and history, structured around "medallions", i.e. centered around important historical events and heroic figures and it was then inserted in the framework of a *theatrical experience*, seen as a liberating means of self discovery.

It was subsequently also taken up by social organizations, particularly voluntary and community groups, with the aim of revealing the particular social situations of their members. In Italy, role-play as a learning technique is first used by Olivetti in the field of commercial training.

Today the technique is widely used in training programs, for personnel selection and in job interviews.

Simulation Games

Simulation games are considered "activities undertaken by participants whose actions are constrained by a series of specific rules and predetermined ends. Elements of the game constitute an accurate representation or model of a certain external reality with which the participants interact playing roles in the same way as they would with external reality itself". These are games and activities which involve groups of players, who need to make decisions in a given situation within certain constraints. Among such simulation games are *war games*, *business games*, *environment games*, *and urban simulation games*.

1st strand: *War Games.* These represent the first structured attempt at war simulation games made for military operations and conducted "using data, rules and procedures to represent an effective and presumed real situation". They are activities which must not be confused and with training in the field or the classroom or with forms of simulation which for centuries have represented the most effective form of "war school". It is not yet clear when, how and where military games originated, as their history, evolution and development is not well documented, although many scholars have underlined the evident similarity between war games, chess and other board games.

Among such war games are Wei-Hai (encirclement), of Chinese origins and dating back to 3000 years B.C. approximately; GO, a Japanese game. It is a game played out on a stylized board, with stones of different colors that identify opposing forces; after a series of alternating moves the winner is the player who manages to outwit the adversary; Chaturanga, an Indian game. This is another battle game, which is considered to be the precursor to chess, as it has very similar rules: it is played by four people on a map with military pieces and the roll of the dice determines the moves

In 1870 Helving in Brunswick invented the first war game; the Prussian officer Von Reiswitz adopts them institutionally and systematically in the Prussian army;

Subsequently, and in growing number, new and diversified games were invented, accepted and used also by the major states of Germany, Japan, Great Britain and United States;

After World War II, there is great simulation game activity partly in war schools in various countries, and partly in research centers and university, among which the *American Management* (AMA), the *Advanced Research Project Agency* (ARPA), the *Massachusetts Institute of Technology* (MIT);

This strategy is still used in the military field mainly through *didactic games*, in order to facilitate the acquisition of abilities, and conduct operations; *analytical games*, to experiment tactical and strategic plans and test criteria for the use of arms and tools.

In the professional sector the old models have now been replaced by computer games and other forms of electronic games; from electronic war games *videogames* were born.

Although with less complex and sophisticated procedures than the professional variety, war games are very popular with military history and war strategy enthusiasts and there are numerous associations in Italy and elsewhere which are dedicated to war games, for pleasure or for study.

2nd Strand: *Business games,* among this type of games is *Awele*, an African strategy game on the organization of agricultural work. The game uses pawns, which represent seeds, they are moved on a board composed of boxes, which represent the fields, and the game involves planting seeds and growing the harvest using the fields and rotating the seeds, victory is obtained by the player who manages this best; however, unlike capitalist games, you are not allowed to destroy your opponent; rather, the person who refuses to help another player in need loses the game;

Monopoly is considered the real founder of *business games,* capitalist versions of the African game; very simple and repetitive, it mimics the capitalist economic system. Such business games owe much to initiatives undertaken in 1956 by the American Management Association (AMA); AMA plans *Top Management Simulation,* for high-level managers, as a new way of entering the job market. It is also a useful training system in universities that carry out research in this field, and in industry and commerce to train young managers and public servants.

The attraction of this approach has led to the invention of numerous games which go from rather simple *decisional exercises* lasting a few minutes, to *extremely complex simulations.* Some games merely involve practicing techniques of production planning in the face of variable demand in order to economize on supplies; in others, on the other hand, the player is invited to make decisions in relation to the opportunity to invest in productive capacity, level of investment, sales organization, research policy and the management of prices and finance;

Even more interesting are the games where different groups of players compete with each other through the computer which simulates market behavior in response to their competitive strategies. Such games are used mainly in the US, where players of *business games* have a niche association called ABSEL (*Association for Business Simulation and Experiential Learning)* currently operating as a separate section of the main organization, the National Association of Simulation and Gaming (NASAGA).

3rd Strand: *Environmental games,* born from war games and business games move in increasingly intersecting directions: Diplomacy, a power game on early 20th century Europe; Risk, the game for the conquest of the world, played competitively; Polecon, which simulates the management of the economic system; Castellon, which simulates the socio-economic dynamics of a South American country.

4th Strand: *Urban simulation games,* which include all territorial games and qualify as "training techniques in urban planning for planners and administrators and as learning techniques for students and researchers". With these techniques, American urban planners tackle problems related to complex systems with a high number of unpredictable variables. In this game they are able to explore systems and processes of urban and social dynamics and through the interaction with other players who represent the various roles (social, political and economic) competing for the use of the territory affected by common issues such as town planning, conservation, re-development of urban areas and so on. Metropolis, one of the most significant games, was born out of the training needs for urban planning; New Town, a game dealing with the problem of the use of the territory and its development; City I and Telecity, directed to modeling, simulation and decision making on real urban systems; City II and Simuland, which provide a highly flexible scheme, which can be adapted to all urban systems.

Computer Simulation

By the expression computer *simulation* we mean the possibility of using a personal computer to simulate the evolution of a system described by a mathematical model, with the aim of dealing with a greater number of variables than what the human brain is capable of processing. Thanks to the capacity of the computer to treat the complexity of the system, it thus becomes possible to test the functioning of such models, determining the advantages and disadvanteages. Computer simulation is widely used in different fields of research. The use of the computer for teaching purposes has been common since the early 1960s in the managerial and commercial sector as well as in industry and education. Today this instrument has established itself in the world of *CBT*, as it offers high potential at low cost, flexibility, greater ease in programming and better visual impact in displaying results. Among the many ways it is used is the manipulation of a predefined model of computer program; this allows the user to control or vary the behavior of the key variables in the system analyzed and to measure the results obtained.

Albeit within certain limits, computer simulation can go beyond the mere manipulation of the model, by dynamically illustrating the repercussions of the decisions made by individuals or groups in a simulated environment. The game, with the aid of a computer or in competition with it, has in this case the advantage or rendering the exercise realistic, as the consequences are calculated in real time. The success of this form of simulation in the educational field, i.e. for teaching and training, can be considered a consequence of the development of *CBT* in recent years.

Computer based training, allows the user to work with complex variables and, for the first time, it offers the possibility of a tool, which enables the user to dynamically demonstrate the results of the simultaneous variation of diverse factors; Runoff is a simulation which shows variations in rainfall in the ecosystem, offering a useful aid to students of processes and systems evolving through time and space; Spread is a program which examines some of the factors present in the spread of contagious diseases and introduces pupils to the study of ecological processes, with particular attention to the concept of geological diffusion; Slick is a simulation related to a situation of oil pollution around the British coast, which helps students to learn how to control pollution; Poverty can be considered one of the many games that give students responsibility over a given territory, spurring them to use available resources in a rational way; Route is a program simulating the decision to build a motorway through an English town that introduce learners to techniques for the analysis of the environmental impact. This computer simulation encourages creative thinking and is used in many disciplines, in particular professions such as engineers, architects and environmental planners. In fact, such people can use the computer simulation to verify projects or to try out ideas without the risk of unpleasant consequences in the real world. In practice, this type of simulation is mainly used to acquire experience and practice in the professional sphere.

ONTOLOGY AND SIMULATION IN EDUCATION

A fundamental problem which characterizes educational research is that of representing knowledge in its function of communication and comprehension, acquisition and construction. In this sense ontology is inserted in systems of representation of knowledge giving it substance and making it manageable, recordable and available to the scientific community in order to be continuously enriched. It is a question of being able to generate, in the specific case of simulation, a web of conceptual elements by taking into account the relations and the connections between them through a subject-relation- (verbal) predicate structure. An ontology, Paparella (2007) claims, has the aim of *conceptually organizing the scientific discourse* and thus aims at a conceptual classification through the possible construction of a taxonomy or a wide conceptual map as a shared and specific basis on a certain domain and also as a scientific method of semantic clarification, especially if this domain presents, as is the case simulation, a multiplicity of meanings.

Thus, on the basis of the previous considerations, and restricting the field of inquiry to simulations in the educational field only, five correlated ambits have been singled out, on which a preliminary sketch and synthesis can be drawn up. This attempt can serve as a guideline for subsequent research and analysis. Thence, by observing the scientific production on simulation a pattern starts to emerge which takes account of the following factors:

- Educational ambits or other areas in which an educational perspective is used;
- There are conceptual and operative models, the first covers the principles, the theories inherent to the simulated systems and the second, the *operative* one, is more orientated more towards cognitive and/or non cognitive operations which can be applied to simulated systems (physical, artificial, hypothetical) with a more direct approach, i.e., encouraging, restricting, prompting etc.;
- The main trends and currents of thought, which have created the relative *techniques (role-play, simulation games, computer simulation)*, each of which has its own history and development;
- Modalities of use and their goals in the field of education and training;
- Societies, institutions, or organizations which produce and distribute numerous simulation games.

Within these sectors it is possible to collect and file all the contributions, the scientific productions, the various interpretations and settings. It is possible to start from one section before moving on to the others creating and developing self-sufficient and autonomous groupings. These sectors can be interconnected in order to create a unique logical-theoretical-empirical nucleus, in the sense that one can develop an ambit and complete it with all the necessary information, linked both to the relevant conceptual or operative principles, and to the trends or currents of thought on the use, production and supervision of simulation products. The same procedure can be followed in the other sectors.

Currently under the spur of the emergence of the new media and new technologies, simulation has become a widespread phenomenon, influencing every sphere of human activity. Thus, different types of simulation are used in multiple ambits ranging from the linguistic to the cultural sector; from economics to politics; from the science of education to psychology and applied sciences (chemistry, physics, biology, mechanics, architecture, medicine and so on) to the world of music and the arts. Simulation has also had a considerable influence on management and other forms of training and adult education, teaching of the social sciences; the study of international relations and military training; in the field of astro-physics and stellar navigation, as well as right across the curriculum at all levels of education; urban studies and architecture and the wide field of engineering.

There are many documented experiences, particularly in English speaking countries, of management training in the economic field, through the use of business games and simulation, founded on the *Theory of Games and Economic Behavior* by von Neumann and Morgenstern and on conflict theory; there have been similar experiences in the other fields mentioned above. It is in our interest to create links and references between these materials, in order to identify common or analogous elements or differentiated but innovative elements.

As to the models, it is appropriate to refer to the *conceptual model,* which contains principles and theories inherent to the simulated systems or to the *operative model* which includes sequences of cognitive and/or non-cognitive operations which can be applied to simulated systems (De Jong, 1998). Often the distinction between the two typologies is not clear-cut, as many simulations present the characteristics of both models. However, it is useful to specify that, whereas the former is used mainly to facilitate learners' understanding of the model underlying the simulation, the latter concerns instead the development of practical abilities, mainly to do with the acquisition of experience in the professional and working ambit. Within this set up, the real world can be represented through three different systems: physical, artificial, hypothetical. The physical systems, present in the natural world, given their remarkable complexity, are reproducible in an approximate manner; the artificial ones, on the other hand, being produced by human hand can only produce artifacts of situations; the hypothetical ones have no correspondence in reality, so they only serve to make predictions. Often simulation can be usefully employed, not as the only means for learners to acquire knowledge and skills, but as *value added* (Piu C., 2006) within the curriculum, as a support strategy. From this viewpoint the tools can be of a *directive* nature through suggestions and useful guides provided during the process, or at the beginning of the simulation; or *restrictive,* if constraints on the direct intervention of the pupil are envisaged; or *prompting,* when they suggest, orientate and guide the pupil during the simulation.

A further subdivision can be made in relation with three main currents or trends, each of which corresponds to a technique, i.e. *role-play*, *simulation game* and *computer simulation*, and has had its own history and development. *Role-play* is a technique which consists in a "scenic representation of a real situation reconstructed and acted in a simulated environment by actors who interpret real roles" (Cengarle, 1987). It is a technique requiring the direct involvement of the participants who, by undertaking the assigned roles and interpreting them in well-defined contexts, are called to improvise in situations on the basis of the data given to them at the outset. *Simulation games* are "activities undertaken by participants whose actions are constrained by a series of rules particular to that game and by certain predetermined ends" (Dorn, 1989). The elements of the game constitute a reasonably accurate representation or models of a certain external reality in which the players interact in the same way that they would in a real situation" (Dorn, 1989). The expression *computer simulation* is intended to mean the possibility of using a personal computer to simulate the evolution of a system described by a mathematical model, in order to deal with a greater number of variables well beyond anything that the human brain is capable of. Simulation is widely used in the field of research in different sectors and in the training ambit, both for acquiring knowledge and for constructing and mastering the competences with a view to *problem solving*.

Around the 1960s, simulation experienced its main development in the educational field: initially in the United States and subsequently, after the first half of the 1960s, in the United Kingdom and from there it rapidly spread throughout Europe and to all the developing countries, through a vast scientific production of monographic texts and remarkable contributions in specialized journals. At the same time, a number of organizations were formed to produce and disseminate simulation games, such as the *National Association of Simulation and Gaming* (NASAGA) and the *ABT Associates Inc.*, whose activities are centered round the creation of games for schools and training, and in England, the *Society for Academic Gaming in Education and Training* (SAGSET).

REFERENCES

Bateson, G. (1976). *Verso un'ecologia della mente.* Milano: Adelphi.

Berretta, G. (1998). Lo stato del virtuale. In Jacobelli, J. (Ed.), *La realtà del virtuale.* Roma, Bari: Laterza.

Bertelli Borsini, L. (1988). Nuove tecnologie educative: i giochi di simulazione. *L'Eco della Scuola Nuova* (44).

Bottani, A., & Davies, R. (Eds.). (2006). *L'ontologia della proprietà intellettuale. Aspetti e problemi.* Milano: Franco Angeli.

Bronfenbrenner, U. (1986). *Ecologia dello sviluppo umano.* Bologna: Il Mulino.

Calagno, C., & Camino, E. (1991). Giochi di ruolo nell'educazione scientifica per dare vitalità alla classe. *Scuola e città* (10).

Cecchini, A. (1986). Simulazione, giochi, giochi di simulazione. In *Enciclopedia di urbanistica e pianificazione territoriale.* Milano: Franco Angeli.

Cecchini, A. (Ed.). (1987). *I giochi di simulazione nella scuola.* Bologna: Zanichelli.

Cecchini, A., & Indovina, F. (Eds.). (1989). *Simulazione. Per capire e intervenire nella complessità del mondo contemporaneo.* Milano: Franco Angeli.

Cecchini, A., & Taylor, J. L. (Eds.). (1989). *La simulazione giocata.* Milano: Franco Angeli.

Cengarle, M. (1987). Role-play e dinamiche di contrattazione. In Cecchini, A., & Taylor, J. L. (Eds.), *La simulazione giocata.* Milano: Franco Angeli.

Colazzo, S. (2007). Abbozzo di un'ontologia pedagogica. In Paparella, N. (Ed.), *Ontologie, simulazione, competenze. Lecce: Amaltea Edizioni.*

De Jong, T., & Van Joolingen, W. (1998). Scientific discovery learning with computer simulations of conceptual domains. *Review of Eucational Research* (68).

De Monticelli, R., & Conni, P. (2008). *Ontologia del nuovo. La rivoluzione fenomenologia e la ricerca oggi.* Milano: Mondadori.

Derossi, G. (1976). *Semiologia della conoscenza.* Roma: Armando.

Domenici, G. (Ed.). (1989). *Conoscere, simulare, scegliere.* Bergamo: Juvenilia.

Dorn, D. S. (1989). Simulation Game: one more tool on the pedagogical shelf. *Teaching Sociology, 17,* 1-18.

Ellington, H., Gordon, M., & Fowlie, J. (1998). *Using Games & Simulations in the Classroom*. London: Kogan Page.

Fini, M. (1998). Il viagra elettronico. In Jacobelli, J. (Ed.), *La realtà del virtuale*. Roma, Bari: Laterza.

Giacomantonio, M. (1984). Gaming simulation e comunicazione educativa. *Quaderni di comunicazione audiovisiva*. 3.

Mulligan, K. (2002). *Metafisica e Ontologia* (p. 311). Aut Aut.

Paparella, N. (1984). Teoria dei modelli in pedagogia. In AA.VV. *Teoria dei modelli in pedagogia*, Trento: F.P.SM.

Paparella, N. (Ed.). (2007). *Ontologie, simulazione competenze*. Lecce: Amaltea Edizioni.

Parisi, D. (1999). *Mente. I nuovi modelli della ita Artificiale*. Bologna: Il Mulino.

Pecchinenda, G. (2003). *Videogiochi e cultura della simulazione. La nascita dell'"homo game*. Bari: Laterza.

Piu, A. (2002). *Processi formativi e simulazione*. Roma: Monolite.

Piu, A. (2006). La simulazione al computer. Prospettive educative. In Piu, C. (Ed.), *Simulazione e competenze*. Roma: Monolite.

Piu, A. (2008). *Il project work nella formazione*. Roma: Monolite.

Piu, C. (2006). *Simulazione e competenze*. Roma: Monolite.

Piu, C. (2007). Formazione e nuove tecnologie. In Curatola, A., & De Pietro, O. (Eds.), *Saperi, competenze, nuove tecnologie*. Roma: Monolite.

Santelli, R. (2002). Simulazione e apprendimento: un problema estetico. *Critica*, 32.

Saunders, D., & Smalley, N. (2000). (Eds.). *The International Simulation and Gaming Research Yearbook* (Vol. 8). London: Kogan Page Limited

Shannon, R. E. (1975). *Sistems Simulation: The Art and Science*. Englewood Cliffs, NJ: Prentice Hall.

Taylor, J. L. (1976). *I giochi di simulazione nell'organizzazione del territorio*. Milano: Franco Angeli.

Taylor, J. L., & Walford, R. (1979). *I giochi di simulazione per l'apprendimento e l'addestramento*. Milano: Mondadori.

Varzi, A. (2003). Ontologia. Dove comincia e dove finisce. *Sistemi Intelligenti*, *15*(3), 493-506.

Varzi, A. C. (2005). Ontologia. In *SWIF*. Edizioni Digitale di Filosofia.

Wikipedia. (2008). Retrieved from http://it.wikipedia.org/wiki/Ontologia%28informatica%29.

Wynn, M. (1987). La computer simulation. In Cecchini, A., & Taylor, J. (Eds.), *La simulazione giocata*. Milano: Franco Angeli.

ENDNOTES

[1]   For virtual reality is meant the set of instruments and technologies that allow us to operate in an interactive manner in real time in the virtual environment that can be modified through the effective intervention of the user.

[2]   Virtual reality simulates realty as a sort of tridimensional pantograph.

[3]   One classification often used is that of "format" carried out on the basis of the medium through which the technique is presented. The most important distinction is between manual exercises that do not involve the use of the computer and other systems that do (Ellington H. (2000). Games and simulations- media for the new millennium. In Saunders D. & Smalley N. (Eds.). The International Simulation and Gaming Research Yearbook. volume 8. London: Kogan Page Limited).

[4]   A more complete classification is that of "functions" based on the way in which the techniques are used. Ellington, for example, proposed the use of a Venn diagram to underline how these are closely interrelated. In his analysis he makes a distinction between pure techniques and hybrid techniques that derive from the interrelations between pure ones (Ellington H. (2000). Games and simulations- media for the new millennium. In Saunders D. & Smalley N. (Eds.). The International Simulation and Gaming Research Yearbook. volume 8. London: Kogan Page Limited).

Section 2
Theoretical and Methodological Aspects of Simulation Games for Learning Math

Chapter 4
Simulation Games for the Learning and Teaching of Mathematics

Angela Piu
University of L'Aquila, Italy

ABSTRACT

The chapter presents the educational perspective within which the simulation games for learning mathematics are presented, as well as a number of considerations on the implementation of teaching course and environments. The main decisions taken for the design of simulation games are introduced, whereas the methodological aspects will be studied in greater depth in later chapters.

"When I used to attend lower secondary school I was very good at doing expressions, a task which I greatly enjoyed. I carefully carried out the calculations in the right order and helped my classmates by inventing ways for them to solve problems. The question I always asked myself was: What use are these expressions? What advantage can be gained from them? The textbook we used at school claimed that an expression achieves… and/or …… but it provided no information at all regarding my query. Nor did my teacher who, being a graduate in biology, had no great love of mathematics and made no secret of the fact. I had no alternative but to search for an answer on my own and I'm still searching! However, I will tell you how I went about the task: I tried to think of situations or contexts in which that expression

DOI: 10.4018/978-1-60566-930-4.ch004

could have been useful, or I tried to think up possible situations... ... undertaking a mental voyage of discovery that, though I was still rooted at my desk, allowed me to visit other contexts of life and bring them back to the classroom, or simulate them in my mind. I set out, in other words, to reconstruct a context in which, by hypothesising problem situations it would become possible to manipulate numbers and find out the results, but without being in any sense oppressed, in which the mechanically resolved operations could acquire a meaning for me and my schoolmates, opening the door of the classroom on the world from which we had come, the daily life of each person with his or her bundle of experiences, and towards which we returned, in which the parenthesis told us something about our daily lives. I had the impression of working inside a greenhouse, in an environment that was not basically aseptic in which the mathematical contents could have a life of their own, but were at the same time protected, a place where I could nourish and cultivate my ideas by using the resources of the soil and the sun, recomposed according to the needs of the moment, within a systematic thought process, in order then to be able to take them to the fruit and vegetable market.... mathematical and otherwise."

INTRODUCTION

Unlike other species, aside from first order primates on rare occasions, human beings deliberately teach other human beings in situations removed from the contexts in which the knowledge acquired is put to use (Bruner, 1997). We are the only species, in other words, that teaches its young in a de-contextualised manner (Bruner, 1997). Such an organisation becomes possible, Bruner claims, by the use of language and by our predisposition for inter-subjectivity, i.e., the ability of human beings to understand through language, gestures and other means what others have in mind; this includes inferring the meaning from the context and negotiating meanings even when the words are ambiguous.

If it is the case that language enables us to transmit the contents of one culture to another and negotiate meanings in a de-contextualised context, it is nevertheless worth remembering that there are also other factors influencing the young that guide their learning process. Gardner (1994) has identified these: the need to conceptualise the world in terms of objects, space, time and causality; the internal limits to knowledge that enable us to define time and causality, and recognise objects in terms of broad categories- in other words, ontologies through which we group certain things together but not others; intuitive theories on the physical and social world, constructed thanks to our interaction with the world of objects that are destined to shape all our successive interpretations of people, events and concepts, inside and outside the classroom.

Besides the restrictions that apply across all cultures, we must mention those that differentiate one culture from another as well as individual differences within the same culture, both in terms of how the information received in early life is elaborated, and in ways of dealing with values within the different cultures.

Schools do not always take into account the tendencies and restrictions that emerge in children's first years of life, that will influence their future educational experience, and do not always create the right conditions or equip children with the necessary tools to help them overcome their innate predispositions. In other words, educational institutions do not always apply the resources, instruments or conditions needed to facilitate the construction of the self, or the adoption of the instruments and symbolic systems required in order to understand the world and participate in society. Nor do they provide the opportunity for pupils to become aware of the culture and make a contribution to it, i.e. how to join in and play an active role in society.

Rereading the work of Bruner and Gardner on these issues we notice, as the authors' themselves underline in different ways, how despite the potential of the human beings- schools all too often fail to achieve the main objects for their pupils, due to the manner in which they operate, even when they seem to be working well.

Gardner warns of the risk of not ensuring the students' full understanding, in other words making sure they have a sufficient grasp of the concepts, principles and skills to cope with new problems and situations; teachers must also check that their students' level of understanding is adequate for the task at hand as well as providing the means for further knowledge acquisition when required. Limiting the discourse to a strictly mathematical context, Gardner (1994) further claims, that the risk of not reaching a full understanding is mainly due to a lack of realisation that mathematics is a way of understanding the world, i.e., a way of highlighting a phenomenon, a type of conversation or enterprise in which young people need to feel involved, not just at the level of a rigid application of algorithms. Another factor is the contrast between intuitive type of mathematics concerning the sphere of real objects and the formal contents of mathematics that involve the use of a new type of symbolic notation. Moreover, there are differences in people's experience of being taught mathematics: in many cases the teaching has been highly successful, whereas in others mathematics was taught in such a way that the contents appeared remote and pointless, the systems of notation, the concepts, forms and structures impenetrable and the language and meta-language too refined and inaccessible.

Bruner, on the other hand, focuses his criticism on the lack of recognition of inter-subjectivity in the construction of knowledge in schools. In other words, the author writes, the so often proclaimed concept of reciprocity, providing children with greater insight into the how and why of learning maths, is rarely practised in schools.

EDUCATIONAL PERSPECTIVE

It is not the aim of this chapter to dwell too long on these issues, but rather to under-line the need to redefine certain elements in an evolving educational perspective, to which the research into simulation games belongs, in the light of changes in present day society and recent advances in educational psychology.

From this perspective we can assume an overall vision of the complex and difficult processes of learning and teaching, characterised by an inter-dependence between the subjects and their relevant cultural contexts, in development and construction of knowledge (Semeraro, 1999). Also the factors and variables regarding the type of cognitive and motivational characteristics of each learner need to be considered, but also the contextual variables, i.e., the cultural framework within which the particular interaction takes place. This event offers resources as well as imposing restrictions for the realisation and interpretation of knowledge and, in turn, it becomes enriched and modified by the actions and the words of all the participants (Duranti A., Goodwin C., 1992). For this reason, cognitive processes are considered in the light of continuous interaction between individuals and groups and the respective environments. This means taking into consideration not only the scholastic context *per se* but also all the other contexts in which the subjects live and the relations between the contexts which are becoming ever more open to exchanges. This broad perspective seeks to treat the characteristics of the individual learner, the environ-ment and the processes that take place within it as interdependent (Fregola, 2003). In this ambit learning is no longer considered a process through which informa-tion is passively absorbed, but rather a process of construction through which the new experiences, knowledge and skills of the individual learner are developed in a comparative teaching approach, i.e., the way in which each individual forms a relationship with the environment and transforms it (Kolb, 1984).

Recent research on the processes of construction of knowledge have moved at-tention away from the description of mechanisms to the internal cognitive processes of a subject in relation to knowledge, context and individuals (Pontecorvo, 1999), demonstrating that interaction with the social context influences the representa-tion each member forms to give meaning to the situations. Hence, the motivation and expectation of each subject in the context, the interpretation that each person constructs from the situation, the role of the individual and that of others, the aims of the interaction and the type of relationships that develop (Carugati F. Perret-Clermont A.N., 1999) and the epistemological beliefs, i.e. the convictions of a subject on knowledge and ways of acquiring it (Schommer M., 1994) can influence the processes of learning.

These considerations highlight the need for a framework for educational activity leading to the implementation of courses and learning environments in which such variables can become resources for the construction of knowledge (Semeraro, 1999). To put it another way, the task is to develop activities and utilise materials that can give a meaning to things, in such a way that the task acquires an importance for each individual and for their community that extends beyond the school and interacts with society as a whole.

This framework presupposes that certain indispensable conditions are realised that will be described below.

The first condition concerns the role of initial knowledge of the learner in the process of constructing knowledge: in fact, the more the initial knowledge is made explicit so that it can be reflected upon, both by the learner and the teacher, in order to spot any gaps or errors, and if required intervene to support the process of conceptual change (Ausubel, 1978; Novak Gowin, 1984). Thus, as much research has demonstrated, the learner's previous knowledge can represent obstacles to the learning process itself if there is no system in which erroneous conceptions or models are clearly brought to the surface and scrutinised (Gardner, 1994). As regards the mathematical ambit, the idea is to reach the discovery of that knowledge organised under the form of behaviours that conceal mathematical structures (Devlin, 2000) in order to implement a satisfactory organisation of the new knowledge, that can be an incentive for meta-cognitive awareness (Brown & Campione, 1994), i.e., the ability to change ideas and convictions with respect to what one already knows in such a way as to set in motion a process of knowledge restructuring. These processes can be activated only if approval is found within the learning community for testing the boundaries of knowledge. Reflection on the critical points and elements identified can lead the learner to develop critical self-awareness and enter the meta-cognitive domain.

The second condition concerns reflection on the significance that knowledge must assume not only in the immediate context in which learning takes place, but also in terms of social participation (Pontecorvo, 1999). It is insufficient, in other words, to pay attention only to learning contexts in which new information is contextualised, it is also essential to grasp the social and cultural meaning of knowledge acquisition. Hence, to contextualise information means to place the new information on the conceptual and cultural map so that it can be understood (Bruner, 1997). As regards this, the work of Resnick (1987) described well the differences between school learning and the context of daily life, highlighting the need to make scholastic activities meaningful. According to this research, activities that take place in school generally require individual tasks to be carried out without physical or cognitive support within a context that is, at times, aseptic, whereas in everyday life the tasks are of a social nature supported by help of every kind and the subjects clearly perceive the meaning and objective of their respective tasks.

The third condition concerns the interactive and inter-subjective dimension in learning contexts, in which all the subjects, though still in their respective roles (teacher and students) support each other, in turn, and supply the scaffolding to support others in the construction of a learning community, which privileges reciprocity in an educational setting where the protagonists carry out a process of intellectual, human, social and affective[1] growth together and the context itself evolves.

A MEANINGFUL BRIDGE BETWEEN DIFFERENT CONTEXTS

The term *game* is not new in the educational and psychological ambit where there is a long tradition of investigating and examining the phenomenon of games in all its aspects and functions from various perspectives.

The investigation of ludic activity has taken many directions, often with the help of other disciplines and a wide and far-reaching debate has given rise to a number of different explanatory models and classifications (Crisma, 1987). Recent studies, moreover, have sought to analyse not only the psychological characteristics of games (beliefs and aims) but also the environmental ones, i.e., the convictions in the mind of the subjects and their behaviours (Paglieri, 2002).

Today, in fact, there is no single definition of games sufficiently flexible to include the countless manifestations of the phenomenon and, at the same time, sufficiently precise to be of any practical use (Paglieri, 2002). The same word, in other terms, indicates activities and a set of elements and rules, that is to say an ongoing process and an abstract system. This ambiguity, that in the English language seems to have been resolved by using two separate terms, i.e., play and game, has never actually been all that clear cut or discrete. If this provides justification for the use of the term to refer to simulation games in the sense of a system of predetermined intrinsic rules, it does not, however, do justice to all the other aspects that could remain unarticulated regarding what actually takes places during the simulation game.

When we turn to the functions of games, a variety of positions can also be found that privilege the symbolic or representational aspects over the adaptive or evolutionary ones, or those that highlight cognitive aspects or mechanisms of social integration[2].

With this perspective in mind simulation games present features that offer the possibility to enlarge the phenomenological view of the learner within the school context; or to put it a different way, to introduce into the immediate situation elements of other environments (Piu A., 2006) on which it is possible to act within the limitations and rules of the game.

The simulation game creates a dynamic context in which the players are required to experience and question reality and take decisions on how to achieve the set objectives. Simulation games differ from other teaching strategies and practices in that they are configured as goal related activities carried out with other people over time that can help expand the conceptual boundaries of the learner (Bronfenbrenner, 1986).

In this way, aspects of real phenomena that lend themselves to mathematical interpretation (some never investigated, others investigated at other times and places) can be included in learning situations in school. They can find a place in guiding teaching decisions in relation to the structure and rules of the game and can become sensors of the initial acquisitions the learners require for the guided discovery of mathematical concepts and language.

Given the complexity and the processes of innovation described in the first chapter, there is a growing need to connect the macro and micro, the social world and the classroom, in a sort of contract between the two in which the environments and objectives learning are made explicit. Simulation games represent, in this sense, a meeting place between innovation and tradition and a model of integration between experience and methodological innovation in the field of educational psychology.

METHODOLOGICAL PERSPECTIVE

Within the research here presented the simulation game is proposed as a relational experience and a learning opportunity. This is achieved through reciprocity and sharing to stimulate learning processes, i.e. social participation and affectivity control, emotional modulation in order to intervene on these variables with *intentionality* coming from the structure of the game and from the relational environment that the rules, the procedures and the guidance of the teacher need.

The simulation games for learning mathematics here proposed are based on certain methodological choices (Piu A., 2002; 2006) that can be related to the definition of a simulation context that:

- allows students to experience situations where they are forced to analyze models of daily life and pay attention to the mathematical aspects (Dienes, 1971). In this way we try to stimulate the pupils and draw from the perceived reality of the simulation aspects that can be translated into mathematical facts in a process of guided discovery of mathematical concepts;
- can encourage exploration in conformity with the rules and objectives of the game where situations perceived as different have the same basic structure

that the pupil uncovers through manipulation of the materials. Through this activity the pupil can grasp the concept of the invariant;

- furthers the understanding of mathematical concepts by following a path that proceeds from the construction of symbols to the concept itself, slowly by abstraction to formalization. Thus the problem is not a question of "supplying the child with models", but to spark in the child a meaningful symbolic representation in such a way that the symbols evoke a meaning and the child comes to understand the importance of representation both for understanding and for communicaton (Vergnaud, 1994);

- facilitates the construction of a mathematical language through the definition of an intermediate zone between the language of the pupil and its evolution towards mathematical language through the process of transcoding;

- can at the same time give value to the cognitive, emotional and social aspects in the teaching process (Montuschi, 1987; 1993), favouring interaction with other children and shared exploration.

In this way simulation games can help underline progress towards mathematical knowledge through analysis of behavior before, during and after the game.

Seen in this light a simulation game can represent a knowledge sensor and a gauge of initial abilities since it focuses on the need to possess a repertoire of skills to launch participation thanks to the nature of the game that requires the completion of simple tasks that gradually become more complex as the game progresses.

The games structure provides the *scaffolding* and consequently can favor and support the discovery of concepts, rules and structures thanks to a process of construction, deconstruction and reconstruction of a language that is logical and mathematical through transcoding patterns. Moreover the understanding and utilization of concepts in different contexts leads to the conquest of abstraction, that we term in Italian *policoncretezza*.

**Cambiato un po' ->

In the end problem solving and decision taking are triggered and supported by interaction between the teacher and students in a shared experience, that includes reflection on, and evaluation of what has been achieved and integration of the mathematical discoveries involved in the process.

REFERENCES

Ausubel, D. P. (1978). *Educazione e processi cognitivi*. Milano: Angeli.

Bronfenbrenner, U. (1986). *Ecologia dello sviluppo umano*. Bologna: Il Mulino.

Brown, J. S., & Campione, J. C. (1994). Guided discovery in a Community of Learners. In McGilly, K. (Ed.), *Classroom lessons: integrating cognitive theory and classroom practice*. Cambridge: Bradford Books.

Bruner, J. (1997). *La cultura dell'educazione*. Milano: Feltrinelli.

Carugati, F., & Perret-Clermont, A. N. (1999). La prospettiva psicosociale: inter-soggettività e contratto didattico. In Pontecorvo, C. (Ed.), *Manuale di psicologia dell'educazione*. Bologna: Il Mulino.

Crisma, A. (1987). Giochi di simulazione e strategie didattiche. In Cecchini, A. (Ed.), *I giochi di simulazione nella scuola*. Bologna: Zanichelli.

Devlin, K. (2000). *Il gene della matematica*. Milano: Longanesi.

Dienes, Z. P. (1971). *Le sei tappe del processo d'apprendimento in matematica*. Firenze: OS.

Duranti, A., & Goodwin, C. (Eds.). (1992). *Rethinking context. Language as an interactive phenomenon*. Cambridge: Cambridge University Press.

Fregola, C. (2003). I livelli d'astrazione nell'apprendimento matematico attraverso i materiali montessoriani. In *Centro di Studi Montessoriani, Annuario 2003 – Attualità di Maria Montessori*. Milano: Franco Angeli.

Gardner, H. (1994). *Educare al comprendere. Stereotipi infantili e apprendimento scolastico*. Milano: Feltrinelli.

Huizinga, J. (2002). *Homo ludens*. Torino: Einaudi.

Kolb, D. A. (1984). *Experiential Learning: Experience as Source of Learning and Development*. USA: Prentice Hall.

Montuschi, F. (1987). *Vita affettiva e percorsi dell'intelligenza*. Brescia: La Scuola.

Montuschi, F. (1993). *Competenza affettiva e apprendimento*. Brescia: La Scuola.

Novak, J. D., & Gowin, D. B. (1984). *Imparando ad imparare*. Torino: SEI.

Paglieri, F. (2002). Credendo di giocare. Verso un'interpretazione cognitivista dei processi ludici. *Sistemi Intelligenti, 14*(3), 371–415.

Piu, A. (2002). *Processi formativi e simulazione*. Roma: Monolite.

Piu, A. (2006). Simulation, Training, and Education between Theory and Practice. In Cartelli, A. (Ed.), *Teaching in the Knowledge Society: New Skills and Instruments for Teachers* (pp. 205–219). Hershey, PA: IGI Global.

Pontecorvo, C. (1999). *Manuale di psicologia dell'educazione*. Bologna: Il Mulino.

Resnick, L. B. (1987). *Education and Learning to Think*. Washington, D.C.: National Academy Press.

Saunders, D., & Smalley, N. (2000) (Eds.). *The International Simulation and Gaming Research Yearbook* (Vol. 8). London: Kogan Page Limited

Schommer, M. (1994). Effects of beliefs about the nature of Knowledge on comprehension. *Journal of Educational Psychology, 85*(3), 406–411. doi:10.1037/0022-0663.85.3.406

Semeraro, R. (1999). *La progettazione didattica. Teorie, metodi, contesti*. Firenze: Giunti.

Vergnaud, G. (1994). *Le rôle de l'enseignement à la lumière des concepts de schème et de champ conceptuel*. In M. Artigue, R. Grass, C. Laborde, & P. Tavignot (Eds.), *Vingt ans de didactique des mathématiques en France* (pp. 177-191). Grenoble: La Pensée sauvage.

ENDNOTES

[1]   For further detail on social and other aspects see Chapter 5.

[2]   The multiplicity of these theoretical aspects notwithstanding, it can be confidently stated that the importance of games has been universally accepted in the field of scientific research.

Chapter 5
Simulation Games and Emotive, Affective and Social Issues

Cesare Fregola
Roma Tre University, Italy

ABSTRACT

This chapter presents a reflection on the subject of the skills teachers can use to intentionally influence the affective area so that this can positively influence the math learning process. Simulation games represent a learning environment in which the teacher's relational skills can be guided by models within the field of pedagogy, albeit also making use of insights from social psychology.

INTRODUCTION

One often hears it said that mathematics is a game but for most learners there is nothing to laugh about, especially those who have experienced failure. Such reactions bode ill for the future of math teaching. Emotions, feelings and states of mind often lead to frustration, and not the reorganization of behavior towards a planned commitment needed to achieve the learning objective in math. So fear, more than a resource for motivation, which should represent the emotion of *defense* from dangers and threats in the environment, and rage, which should represent the emotional

DOI: 10.4018/978-1-60566-930-4.ch005

response to those dangers and threats, increase the more widespread negative perceptions when learning math; thus three feelings about mathematics, math teachers and their teaching methods are commonly manifested:

- Inadequacy and incapacity, about onceself
- A feeling that math is something inaccessible
- A feeling that the teacher is inadequate or incompetent or both.

In the didactic relationship the above attitudes tend to perpetuate a vicious circle that has a negative influence on motivation for learning math. Certain indications on the emotions, on the believes and the behaviors caused by the *didactic relation's vicious circle in mathematics* will be described below.

The implicit assumption of our research is that the approach proposed in the Simulandia project can transform this vicious circle into a virtuous one through play and guided learning, protecting as well the learner from *racket* (Erskine.& Zalcman M., 1979). Indeed, simulation games by their very nature activate cognitive, social and affective abilities and help to build knowledge through a social process.

FEAR, CONVICTIONS AND BEHAVIOURS

Inserting in a research engine *fear of mathematics*, one can access an average of around 2,500,000 pages in which these words are found. Navigating various sites, you can discover that similar expressions used provide a sort of ranking in the intensity of fear, in which fear, as a feeling develops: anxiety, terror, anguish, panic. These reactions symbolise one extreme of the collective idea of learning mathematics. At the other extreme, you might expect to find expressions of joy as a reaction to success in learning whereas, instead, you find the syndrome of the masked man (Novellino, 2003), a syndrome that affects able students of mathematics, according to which they are seen as supermen, if not creatures from some other planet.

In the literature the theme of fear of mathematics has been the object of numerous studies inspired, in particular, reconductable to a negative experienced in an unsuccesfull occation. Tobias S. (1993) introduces the term *mathematophobia* to describe this phenomenon. Her analysis identifies fear of making mistakes as one of the most relevant factors, another is the way in which teachers rewarded or punished the partial results of learning obtained by students and again the myth that the capacity to learn is a *special gift* you have or you don't, that cannot be influenced by the way it is taught.

From the point of view of the process of social communication this causes the tendency for students, teachers and parents to adapt to a model of behaviour involving self-justification or resignation. For teachers it sometimes seems an easier option not to research into the possible teaching options or try out courses that could light a spark of motivation sufficient to sustain the objective difficulties encountered in the learning process, while parents become convinced there is little to be done, it is all down to an incapable child or incompetent teacher. The result of all this is that the majority of children-future adults- start walking with a wooden leg. A. Siety (2003) psychopathologist, who specialised in educational psychology of mathematics, focuses on the emotional aspect of mathematics and its consequences for the individual. A mental block in mathematics is not simply caused by lack of understanding of a subject or a problem, that could be resolved with some explanation and a little effort, but rather it is the entire universe of mathematics that remains closed and this can lead to panic or something deeper based on fear. The author claims that the origin of this fear in pupils is caused by their perception of mathematics as something unpleasant, incomprehensible because anybody who is not a boffin cannot be expected to understand it.

Simple reflection can lead to the realisation that when failure is ascribed to the fact that intervention is useless because the internal or external causes are intractable to any kind of intervention, the problem becomes depersonalised and from this we begin to lose faith in ourselves and in our ability to change. Another widespread conviction is that mathematics does not have a human face because it does not leave any space for the imagination and there is little room for self-expression as it is necessary to *stay rigidly within the rules* and should anyone stray from them by showing a little personal initiative they would fall inexorably into error.

According to constructivist theory convictions, that are the fruit of a continual process of interpretation of reality operated by children, develop with the implicit goal of giving sense to experiences through mathematics. More recently OpT Eynde (2002) describes pupils' convictions concerning mathematics as similar to those implicit or explicit subjective conceptions believed by pupils to be true. This influences their maths learning and ability to solve problems. Schoenfeld (1983) adds to the debate the importance of the environment in the generation of convictions; McLeod (1992) examines a categorisation that differs from that of Schoenfeld on account of the presence of convictions on the teaching of mathematics, rather than on the task of learning; Underhill (1988) takes into consideration convictions about oneself in the social context as well as those on the learning and teaching of mathematics. F. Lewis (1990) subdivides the categories on the basis of the ways in which they could have arisen; this latter category has certain problems because the same conviction could be found in different categories if held by two different people and it is not clear just who to establishes the origin of a conviction for not everyone is aware of it. It is evident that these convictions can have an influence on motivation and behaviour since *to do well* in mathematics and how to behave is defined by these. Nevertheless, nearly all the studies on convictions are based on the work of Bandura, in particular on his book Social Foundations of Thought and Actions (1986). The author states that convictions about oneself condition a certain form of control over thoughts and actions. Bandura also underlines the importance of, what he calls, *outcome expectations*, i.e., what the subject believes will be the consequences of his actions. More generally, he uses the term *theories of success* to refer to the convictions about success and about failure in mathematics. These convictions were the object of a psychological study leading to *attribution theory*. "*Attributions* can be defined as the perceptions individuals have on the cause of events that happen to them- auto-attributions- and to others- hetero-attributions" (De Beni R., Moè A., 2000). Another author, Weiner (1985), examines the internal attributions as a function of their role in success in the carrying out of a task; these can be divided into three dimensions:

- *locus of control* that distinguishes whether the causes are attributable internally, i.e., to the person per se, or externally. In this case different kinds of attributions can be made: "I was successful because I have ability" or "I wasn't successful because the task was difficult".
- *stability,* the causes, independently of the locus, can tend to be stable over time and different situations or unstable and variable depending on the context.
- *controllability,* the causes are, more or less, directly controlled by the subject.

The work carried out by Fennema (1985) highlighted that boys are more likely to attribute success to their own ability and failure to lack of effort. On the contrary, Schoenfeld (1989) found that, regardless of gender, the students who have less consideration for their mathematical abilities tend to attribute success to luck and the failures to their capability (or lack of capability). Schoenfeld focuses attention on a number of convictions held by the majority of students analysed:

- mathematics is an objective discipline that can be mastered;
- to do well in mathematics hard work is more important than natural ability. In the case of failure the reason is to be found in lack of effort.

Attitudes are understood as internal or mental states, with a direction (favourable/unfavourable) and variable in intensity, which are linked to predisposition to act (Zan, 1996). In the literature we can find two definitions that have generated different lines of studies of mathematics.

According to a more simple definition, attitude is the level of positive or negative affect regarding a given object. From this point of view, attitude towards mathematics is simply a positive or negative inclination (McLeod, 1989; Haladyna et al., 1983).

A more complex definition, however, divides attitude into three components: emotional reaction, convictions concerning the object and behaviour regarding the object. From this perspective, the attitude of a learner faced with mathematics is defined by the emotions associated with it (that can have a positive or negative outcome), by the convictions on the matter and by the behaviours the learner activates (Hart, 1989).

Thus, the attitude adopted depends on various factors among which we may include how learners perceive themselves, in particular their notions of self-efficacy (Bandura, 1993, 1997) and self-esteem (Convington, 1998).

In the research of Hackett and Betz (1989) attention focused on the fact that self-efficacy in mathematics precedes performance and results. The study of Schunk and Lilly (1984) highlights the influence of self-esteem on results in mathematics. They show that perception to be able to do a certain kind of job and confidence in their own abilities are critical factors in motivation and perseverance. Indeed, it is possible that perception of their own inability leads to a reduction of motivation and perseverance in learners of mathematics. Another study carried out by Norwich (1987) highlights similar results. According to the author, not only can a strong sense of self-efficacy be associated with high performance, but also the general attitude of pupils regarding the execution of a task differs according to their self-esteem: it is, in a sense, obvious that learners are more likely to be persistent if they feel they have a good chance of success.

To sum up, in learning, and especially in mathematics, the variables connected with both the discipline and with the learner's self-perception and its own belives on the external world, teachers and teaching, have a substantial influence on the *internal conditions* of the learning process.

RELATIONAL SKILLS IN DIRECTING EDUCATIONAL SIMULATION GAMES

Phenomena belonging to the person's internal world are involved in the learning process in general, and especially in mathematical one, although it is a difficult task to define these phenomena in forms that can be reduced to a mathematical theorem, to a poet's or a writer's life and it is not possible to discuss them and explain them as one can do for phenomena such as physics or biology once. Such factors generally stem from emotional components that, often, play tricks and relate to variables traditionally left untouched by the pedagogical studies being considered psychological in nature.

It is necessary that "students learn on their own to decline their communicative codes with an external reality- the subject with its own rules and alien codes, and *oneself other-than-oneself.* From this point of view also teaching a subject can be no more than indicative, it educates the learner to be able to make a choice by structuring situations in which subjects are not a series of certainties to be assimilated but rather problematic fields in which the students have to decide which direction to take, articulating theirown subjective world based on external information". (Blandino G., Granieri B., p261, 2002).

The lack of an affective alphabet does not compromize the resort to models that can orientate and facilitate the didactic action's influence on affective variables. In particular by deliberately employing teacher's relational skills it is possible to observe and deal with consequences, be they negative or positive, fuctional or disfunctional, of emotions, feelings, of states of mind which commonly arise within a learning environment, and orientate them so that a awareness development of the relationshp that each children have with his own learning.

In this context, teaching intervention during simulation games can influence affective aspects of the learning process provided that due consideration is taken of the fact that " affect is an educational problem in the sense that it is no longer considered in conflict with rationality but part of human complexity to be analyzed in its cognitive roots, its behavioral implications, for the position it assumes as an inevitable ingredient in the decisional dynamics of human beings (Montuschi, 1993, p.11).

There are terms and expressions frequently used in every day discourse that, for their intrinsic meaning or for the way they are spoken, reveal the emotional state behind the words. These emotional states are considered immutable or something nothing can be done about because "if that's the way it is, nothing can be done about it" or "math is not my cup of tea" or "me and math were not made for each other".

The communicative interaction in simulation games is guided by a series of exchanges in which cognitive emotive and relational aspects intertwine stimulating freedom of expression and creativity. The emotional reactions and states of mind that develop through participation in the rules and procedures of the game provide a protective terrain where children enter in the game or lose themselves in the game. Teachers can intervene by using their emotional intelligence and relational skills within a process that *allows each child to feel able to to learn.*

The most recent studies of emotions (Evans, 2004) agree on the four basic emotions: fear, anger, pain and joy. Each emotion has its biological aim and relevance for teaching action: each emotion can play a role in helping children to give their best, also when learning mathematics. By effective intervention on affective variables we can open up new prospects in the educational field (Fregola C., 2006).

REFERENCES

Bandura, A. (1986). *Social foundations of thought and actions: a social cognitive theory*. Englewood Cliffs, NJ: Prentice Hall.

Bandura, A. (1993). Perceived self-efficacy in cognitive development and functioning. In *Educational Psychologist, 28*.

Bandura, A. (1997). *Self-efficacy: The exercise of control*. New York: Freeman.

Berne, E. (1971). *Analisi Transazionale e psicoterapia*. Roma: Astrolabio.

Blandino, G., & Granieri, B. (2002). *Le risorse emotive nella scuola*. Milano: Raffaello Cortina.

Covington, M. V. (1998). *The will to learn. A guide for motivating young people*. Cambridge: Cambrige University Press.

De Beni, R., & Moè, A. (2000). *Motivazione e apprendimento*. Bologna: Il Mulino.

Erskine, R., & Zalcman, M. (1979). The racket system: a model for racket analysis. *TAJ, 9*(1), 51–59.

Evans, D. (2004). *Emozioni. La scienza del sentimento*. Bari: Laterza.

Fennema, E. (1985). Attribution theory and achievement in mathematics. In Yussen, S. R. (Ed.), *The growth of reflection in children*. San Diego, CA: Academic.

Fregola, C. (2006). *Sbrigati a fare quella divisione. Le spinte emotive in azione nella procedura di calcolo della divisione a due cifre*. Roma: IAT.

Hackett, G., & Betz, N. E. (1989). An Exploration of the Mathematics Self-Efficacy/ Mathematics Performance Correspondence. *Journal for Research in Mathematics Education, 20*(3). doi:10.2307/749515

Haladyna, T., Shaughnessy, J., & Shaughnessy, M. (1983). A causal analysis of attitude toward Mathematics. *Journal for Research in Mathematics Education, 14*(1). doi:10.2307/748794

Hart, L. (1989). Describing the Affective Domain: Saying What We Mean. In McLeod, D. B., & Adams, V. M. (Eds.), *Affect and Mathematical Problem Solving*. New York: Springer Verlag.

Huizinga, J. (2002). *Homo ludens*. Torino: Einaudi.

Lewis, H. (1990). *A question of values*. San Francisco: Harper & Row.

Marrone, G. (2009). *Giocattolando. Il bambino ludico: dal Gioco dell'Oca ai videogiochi*. Roma: Conoscenza Editore.

Mc Leod, D. (1992). *Research on affect in mathematics education: a reconceptualization*. In F.

Mc Leod, D., & Adams, V. M. (1989). *Affect and Mathematical Problem Solving*. Springer-Verlag.

Montuschi (1993), *Competenza affettiva e apprendimento*. Brescia: La Scuola Editrice.

Norwick, B. (1987). A Study of Their Relation. In *Journal of Educational Psychology, 79*. Self-Efficacy and Mathematics Achievement.

Novellino, M. (2003). *La sindrome dell'uomo mascherato*. Milano: Franco Angeli.

Op'T Eynde. P.& De Corte, E. & Verschael, L. (2002). Framing students' mathematics- related beliefs. In G. Leder, E. Pehkonen, & G. Torner (Eds.), *Beliefs: a hidden variable in mathematical education?* Kluwer Academic Publishers.

Schoenfeld, A. (1983). Episodes and Executive decisions in mathematical problem solving. In Lesh, I. R., & Landau, M. (Eds.), *Acquisition of mathematics concepts and processes*. New York: Academic Press.

Schoenfeld, A. (1989). Exploration of students' mathematical beliefs and behaviour. *Journal for Research in Mathematics Education, 20*(4), 338–355. doi:10.2307/749440

Shunk D. H., & Lilly M. V. (1984). Sex differences in Self-Efficacy and Attribution: Influence of Performance Feedback. *Journal of Early Adolescence*, 4.

Siety, A. (2001). *Matematica, mio terrore*. Milano: Salani.

Tobias, S. (1993). *Come vincere la paura della matematica*. Milano: TEA.

Underhill, R. (1988). Mathematics learners' beliefs: a review. *Focus on Learning Problems in Mathematics,* 10.

Weiner, B. (1985). *An attributional theory of motivation and emotion*. New York: Springer-Verlag.

Zan, R. (1996). Difficoltà d'apprendimento e problem solving: proposte per un'attività di recupero. *L'insegnamento della Matematica e delle Scienze integrate, 19*(4).

Chapter 6
Theoretical Reflections on the Construction of Simulation Games

Daniela Olmetti Peja
Roma Tre University, Italy

ABSTRACT

With the aim of studying the process of transcoding and identifying the meaning assigned to specific research variables described in the present work, a number of reflections are presented in this chapter that, apart from supplying the methodological background for the teacher, allow researchers to identify the main factors that distinguish the traditional classroom lesson and the experimental method represented by simulandia games. In particular, reference is made to the work of Bloom, Gagné and Gardner and Bandura's concept of self-efficacy.

BENJAMIN BLOOM'S TEACHING THEORY

At the end of the 1970s, Bloom elaborated the well-known Model of School Learning (1976) with the aim of drawing up a scientific procedure for studying the possibility, through numerous researches at micro-level as well as large scale longitudinal studies at macro-level, of using individualised teaching methods to modify aspects which, according to traditional pedagogical theory, were considered innate and, therefore, impervious to change. The goal of this research was to focus attention

DOI: 10.4018/978-1-60566-930-4.ch006

on learning conditions and on the quality of the teaching in order to offer all pupils the opportunity to reach the results aimed for by the teaching project and maximise their potential. Bloom considered four factors affecting each pupil's learning performance: family background, the level and kind of cognitive ability at the beginning of the teaching-learning process, the affective factors and the time taken by each pupil in the execution of a piece of work (time on task)[1]. This final variable was first analysed in depth by Carroll (1963) and later by Block (1972) and Anderson (1976); the main conclusion drawn from these works was that the time needed for a pupil to complete a task is variable. If, in fact, pupils are offered the help and the time needed to learn, then they not only become able but also manage to achieve the desired results in ever-shorter time spans. The research work of Bloom (1993), moreover, estimated the incidence and interaction of the three variables that the author considered sufficient to explain the learning results of any student, two of which refer to the learner while the third concerns the kind of teaching, i.e., the required knowledge and ability of each pupil, affective factors at the outset of the learning process, and finally the quality of the teaching:

- *Initial cognitive behaviour* This refers to the overall mix of different kinds of knowledge and abilities required to proceed with learning; in other words, the prerequisites which can be broken down into general prerequisites and specific ones: the former necessary for the learning of any discipline (general intelligence, reading ability, logical capacity, calculation speed and so on). The latter concern the knowledge and abilities required for the learning of a given task and are indispensable insofar as their absence would prejudice the possibility of carrying out the specific task with obvious negative implications in terms of performance and results. Specific cognitive behaviours at the outset of any learning process can be differentiated according to both the type of task and the didactic approach adopted by the teacher. While general cognitive behaviours are acquired and developed gradually over time, acquisition of specific ones may require rapid intervention by the teacher.
- *Initial affective characteristics* After an in-depth analysis carried out on learning in schools, Bloom claimed that pupils at the beginning of their school career, "... vary with regard to what they are emotionally prepared to learn depending on their interests and attitudes and the opinion they hold of themselves" (Bloom, op. cit., p 106). Bloom, therefore, wanted to highlight the fact that affective characteristics at the beginning of the learning process cover, together with the cognitive variables of the pupil and the quality of the teaching, a very wide area that has a profound effect on the final outcome. Affective characteristics concern many aspects such as: personal characteristics responsible for pupil motivation as regards learning in general and the subject in particular; emotional

attitude towards the school and formal education in general, and the pupil's opinion of self especially as regards learning ability. The emotional attitude of pupils towards a given subject is, in fact, determined by their perception of success and failure in the performance of related tasks. A feeling of confidence regarding a certain task clearly increases the likelihood that the pupil will apply him/herself to it. In the same way, the emotional attitude towards school and learning in general is determined by the frequency of approval received by the people the pupils see as important, such as teachers, parents and peer groups. Finally, pupils' behaviour towards learning is closely connected with previous experience inasmuch as, if pupils receive positive feedback on their scholastic performance, over a long period of time, both in terms of study and school in general, they will undoubtedly internalise that positive view. Conversely, the same will occur when judgements are negative and the more frequent such judgements the more this will be the case.

- *Teaching quality* As said before, it is essential that the teacher is able to modify the present situation when it is negative and/or to intervene quickly whenever the aforementioned affective prerequisites are inadequate or lacking. Bloom has shown that if the quality of the teaching is improved, if adequate checks are operated, if pupils perceive the subject as new and stimulating and if they are given the opportunity to fully understand the task, and finally if they are given the change to produce favourable results, it is possible to change negative attitudes towards subject, towards school and towards oneself. Thus, teaching at the start of the learning process can take account of two factors:
- Work so that that prerequisites are mastered;
- Present the learning environment in different ways, without diluting the level of complexity, so that it is within the reach of every pupil.

THE HIERARCHY OF ROBERT GAGNÉ AND LEARNING CONDITIONS

Introduction

When preparing learning environments to promote a quality learning process, it is a good idea to take into account a number of teaching strategies that can stimulate the ability to elaborate, integrate and, above all, make learning meaningful. Regardless of the disciplinary context, these are an essential part of the process that ought to be included in the syllabus or study plan.

To this end, it is particularly important to understand the contribution of Gagné, who identified the optimum conditions for learning to take place. In his model there are five categories or levels of ability to be reached with their corresponding behaviours that can act as a teaching guide.

Five Categories of Human Abilities

Within the ambit of learning theories Gagné's contribution is recognised for having provided a psychological systemisation of learning that has proved very fruitful in the field of education and teaching in particular. Based on experimental studies Gagné first elaborated a hierarchy of eight levels of learning, which show how each individual proceeds from simpler (signs, motor chains, stimulus-reaction etc.) to more complex forms of learning (verbal chains, multiple discrimination and so on) until the ability to conceptualise, apply rules and use experience to solve problems is attained (Gagné, 1985). Any teacher with knowledge of psychology, who elects to follow the hierarchy established by the author, which proceeds from the general and unintentional to deliberate awareness, can take advantage of the model in question and use it as a basis for teaching aims.

Gagné claims that, for each class of ability in his learning model, there are *internal conditions* regarding the individual and *external conditions* characterising the surrounding environment that have a significant bearing on the learning process. Every type of learning, therefore, has its own specific set of internal (prerequisites) and (external) didactic conditions. To simplify this, we can say that for any type of learning process, at whatsoever level, certain general conditions, such as motivation, developmental state and willingness to learn play an essential role, whereas with regard to the classification of the task the internal conditions are decisive. The latter are made up of skills previously acquired by the pupils that are required for a specific type of learning: should the pupils lack these skills they will have to be taught or reminded of them. Finally, in the management of teaching intervention we find the external conditions that can directly or indirectly influence the learning process. As we know well, in a specific teaching situation items of learning can be haphazard or carefully planned by the teacher. Since, according to Gagné (1985) external conditions mutate on the basis of the kind of teaching employed, it is necessary to identify and perfect the type of ability in question. The classification of the task seeks, therefore, to connect the work to the learning categories, i.e., to identify the kind of mental elaboration required by the task.

In a later work, Gagné proposed five categories of ability as the object of learning and linked each category to the desired teaching objectives: the first three refer to the cognitive area (intellectual skills, cognitive strategies and verbal information), while the other two are affective (behaviours) and psycho-motor abilities, respectively (Gagné, Briggs, 1990).

The intellectual abilities are indicated as procedural knowledge and enable the learner to put into operation symbolically controlled processes of execution. They constitute the fundamental structure of learning by making the learner competent. To acquire an intellectual ability means to learn to do something of an intellectual nature: the individual learns *how* to do something, not simply about something (for example, we learn how to write and how to do sums). To find out whether a pupil has learnt an intellectual ability, we observe his or her performance of tasks held to be a demonstration of the ability in question. These abilities, including discrimination, concrete concepts, definite concepts, rules, problem solving skills and so on, are hierarchically structured; in practice, they are disposed in an order of growing complexity in such a way as to make the simpler abilities progressively clear. These intermediate elements are part of a wider overall objective. It is worth underlining the fact that the purpose of the hierarchy is, above all, to provide a guide in the planning of a teaching programme or in the structuring or preparation of learning environments and the related sequences of the teaching programme[2].

Cognitive strategies usually bring to mind Bruner, to whom the term is attributed. Cognitive strategies are those skills that govern the behaviour of an individual in relation to learning, memorising and thinking and they allow learners to exercise control of their own thought processes. Some of these are specifically related to the subject to be learnt, whereas others are more general or rather transversal and can thus be employed across the board in diverse ambits.

Verbal information is defined as declarative knowledge, such as the learning of names, facts and, in a wider sense, general knowledge; this knowledge is organised and stored in the memory to be recalled at the right moment. This type of knowledge is highly important for later learning and for learning transfers from one situation to another. The skill corresponding to this type of knowledge is the ability to communicate the information learnt and transfer it to other contexts.

Behaviours, considered as internal states of the individual, influence choice of action. They mainly concern the affective sphere; they can be identified in the preferences that distinguish personal choice, and influence the predisposition of the individual towards external events. School can thus favour positive behaviours vis-a-vis external events, such as a flair for music, socialising, art and so on.

Motor skills are organised and regulated to carry out deliberate acts; they are, therefore, the easiest to observe (walking, jumping, climbing and so on).

It is by now universally accepted that the initial internal conditions of each pupil require greater attention, because it is those conditions that allow us to calculate beforehand the times, means and varieties of the learning process. According to the most recent studies, internal learning conditions are mental conditions, abilities within the individual about to begin a learning process that have been previously acquired. As we have seen above, Gagné deals with the internal learning conditions, identifying them in the information the subject already possesses, in the intellectual abilities, in the cognitive strategies or self-management skill that enables the subject to recall information to the mind and imagination, in motivation and the feeling of confidence and self-belief in the face of a learning situation and, in a wider sense, when faced with the learning opportunities of various levels on offer.

Types of Intellectual Ability

It is useful to highlight once again the fact that Gagné specifies the fundamental role played by the intellectual abilities through which the individual conceptualises and symbolises the surrounding environment; for example, numbers quantify the environment, words take the place of objects and place them in relation to each other, lines and curves represent spatial relations and so on.

Intellectual abilities can be categorised on the basis of their complexity regardless of the subject matter to be learnt. Starting from the ability to discriminate, which is the foundation of concrete concepts, we move on to the rules containing definite concepts that are the key to problem solving.

Discriminations are learnt when the individual is able to identify such defining characteristics of objects as form, size, colour structure etc. The subject must be able to respond in different ways to different stimuli. This is the first ability to be taught because it is the foundation of learning. In organising the teaching it is always worthwhile revising responses to stimuli by presenting the same or different stimuli with particular emphasis on their distinctive characteristics, offering a good number of examples and counter examples and supplying continuous feedback.

Concrete concepts are grasped when the individual is able to identify the properties of an object: it is a matter of putting objects in a class and responding to that class in the same way. The pupil must demonstrate, through words or signs, to be able to identify the properties that define objects as belonging to the same class. A subject, for example, can discriminate between a triangle and a circle, but this in itself is insufficient for attaining the concrete concept of a triangle. When, on the other hand, the learner manages to distinguish triangles that differ in terms of size and colour from a number of different objects, then one can say with certainty that the learner has grasped the concrete concept of a triangle. The external conditions for facilitating the learning of concepts can be served by providing as large a number of a class of objects as possible that differ in their less relevant characteristics and asking the learner to indicate and name them.

Definite concepts are grasped when the individual can demonstrate and not simply indicate the meaning of a particular class of objects, events or relationships. Pupils will demonstrate their knowledge of concepts through providing examples that fall within the definition and by a clear understanding of the inter-relations between concepts.

The rules are grasped when the individual is able to show how to apply them in concrete cases, thereby manifesting an understanding of the relations between classes of objects and events. A definite concept is a rule because it serves to classify objects and events; in other words, it is a rule of classification.

Problem solving is a learning process and as such it entails a sort of ability that can be observed when the individual is able to combine simpler rules and reorganise a synthesis that constitutes a higher order rule *per se*. In brief, problem solving involves the use of rules already learnt in order to resolve problems, and in this way new rules are produced that are more complex than the previous ones.

Gagné states that in the planning stage the five types of ability considered in his model are essential since they make it possible for the learner to carry out any type of task; all the categories can be inserted in the planning but, in his opinion, intellectual abilities occupy a central role. These have, moreover, a cumulative nature: they are built on one another; indeed, each one favours the construction of the next. The strategies, finally, are a certain type of intellectual ability to activate higher meta-cognitive mental skills that allow the individual to control, manage and monitor the lower level functions: this activity, in fact, implies reflection on one's own cognitive abilities that is not limited to those of a higher order but also focused on the strategies already used to decide on their efficiency and the need for change. Reflection and analysis of one's own cognitive dynamics allows the subject not only to become aware of their workings, but also and above all to manage them directly. It is clear that such a complex ability cannot be available to a child at the beginning of a school career: at this early stage there is just a trace of meta-cognitive ability and this is acquired gradually with the growth of knowledge. Children learning to read do not always immediately realise that they do not understand what they are reading and they certainly do not know how to go about remedying this situation; it is only by practicing this type of skill over a period of time that they will slowly manage to do this. The research has shown that learners must become able progressively in the use of cognitive strategies in order to improve their capacity for understanding and memorisation; moreover, in order to obtain the best result overall, they must learn to plan and organise their studies, as well as learn to complete their tasks within an acceptable time span. Finally, they must learn to monitor their thought processes constantly by assessing the effectiveness of their cognitive functioning.

Gagné's Events

Pupils at any level do not develop their knowledge and cognitive competence on their own; they need the continual support of and dialogue with a teacher or other competent adult. At the beginning of the process the need is stronger, while with growing confidence it becomes less evident and this fact in itself is a sign of the learner's growing autonomy and control of the acquisition process.

In order to put strategies and tactics into operation and in the choice of possible means to favour the development of the cognitive strategies, the most suitable teaching support material for each individual pupil's learning needs must be carefully selected, always bearing in mind the importance of calibrating the teaching to the ability level of the students.

According to the author, for each of the learning classes analysed, there are internal and external conditions guaranteeing the mastery of it. In other words, for any process of acquisition at whatsoever level, the primary influences are certain general conditions, such as motivation, state of development and willingness to learn; then come the internal conditions linked hierarchically to the complexity of the preceding level, and when it has not been adequately covered and understood, this lack needs to be addressed before continuing; finally, there are the specific conditions of various kinds to be prepared in order to build the appropriate learning environment.

In every case, with regard to the internal processes that, in the act of learning, move into action to elaborate and facilitate understanding, it is indispensable, in any learning context, to prepare the communicative functions that support the process. It is a matter, therefore, of identifying which communicative functions can be put into effect in the teaching process in order to choose the most appropriate medium.

With reference to this Gagné highlights nine didactic events he considers essential for a coordinated and variable intervention that can produce effective results. Thus in the teaching process the following actions are required:

1. Obtain and maintain the attention through the use of stimulation and reaction. Considered responses are a necessary step in the construction of the willingness to learn.
2. Communicate the teaching objectives in order to help the pupil recognise the importance and relevance of learning. In this way reasonable expectations are established and a controlled process of execution is put into operation.
3. Stimulate the memory of the prerequisites that have already been taught so that the previous learning acquisitions required for the next step are brought to the surface.

4.   Present different kinds of stimulus in relation to the abilities (and interests) of the individual pupils in the teaching content. Presentation must clearly underline the distinctive properties of the task to be learnt in order to ensure selective perception.

5.   Select the learning guide according to the level of complexity and difficulty of the material and the knowledge and ability level of the pupil.

6.   Elicit pupils' involvement by getting them to show what they can do with respect to the nature and level of the task at hand in order to generate organised responses.

7.   Supply feedback on the correctness of the responses regarding the acquisition of knowledge and skills with the aim of consolidating pupils' performance and motivating them to go further.

8.   Verify student performance by making space for opportunities for feedback with the tests to be completed at the end of each stage of the teaching process in order to give pupils the opportunity to develop self-regulation of their own learning progress with regards to the set objectives.

9.   Ensure the conditions for retention and transfer. For a start it is a good idea not to overburden the memory of pupils with nonessential information that might get in the way of more essential data; it is important to create meaningful contexts for the introduction of new material as well as constantly revise what has been learnt. As regards transfer it is of fundamental importance that the student learns to make generalisations from what has been learnt to find solutions to problems that develop the ability to utilise and apply the skills acquired in new situations that are new, yet at the same time comparable to the original learning objective (Gagnè, Briggs, 1990). Finally, it is also important to highlight the fact that the events are never used only once; one or more events may have been utilised as in previous stages of the learning programme and, for this reason, it may not be necessary to dwell on them (do not forget, for example, to clarify the objectives with the pupils).

GARDNER'S THEORY OF MULTIPLE INTELLIGENCES

Howard Gardner, who has for many years conducted studies into human abilities, highlights how for each individual there are different ways of learning, some of which take precedence over others. In his theoretical conceptualisation he emphasises, unlike in the theory of intelligence of a unitary nature, the existence of different types of intelligence with independent cognitive performances or, to put it in a better way, of competences with cognitive performances that could be developed if every individual were exposed to the right stimulus in a suitable setting.

The theory of multiple intelligences, therefore, pluralizes the traditional concept of intelligence, understood as the ability to solve problems or create products that are particularly valued in one or two cultural contexts (Gardner, 1987). At the base of this theory, there are studies that show the biological origin of the human capacity to solve problems, dealing only with the universal capacities of the human species in relation to cultural development. In every intelligence there must be a set of identifiable operations that is triggered by certain types of endogenous or exogenous information (e.g. musical intelligence can be activated by a sensitivity to different aspects of sound). Intelligence must be encoded in a symbolic system, i.e. in a culturally constructed system of meanings. Language, painting and mathematics are three universal symbolic systems, necessary for human survival and development. According to Gardner, individuals differ regarding the profiles of intelligence they were born with and these can vary in adulthood. Intelligences cooperate in problem solving and in the individual's attainment of different types of cultural goals, be they professional, recreational or something else. Every type of intelligence is a valid way of learning *per se* and should not be confused with talent, predispositions, attitudes or learning styles. Although everyone possesses all the intelligences, each one of these is distributed differently.

Each intelligence, at the beginning of its evolutionary development, appears in its raw state, as for example in the case of musical intelligence and the ability to discriminate between various musical tones. At the next stage, intelligence is manifested through the production of phrases and stories, music through song, the understanding of space through drawings, kinaesthetic intelligence through gesture and dance and so on. In this phase children demonstrate their ability in different intelligences through their possession of various symbolic systems. As it develops, every intelligence, together with the respective symbolic system, is represented by a notational system. Mathematics, drawing and reading of a map, the reading of a text, musical notation and so on are, therefore, symbolic systems of the 2nd order, in which the signs on the paper indicate the symbols. In our culture these systems of notation are learnt mainly at school. Then in adolescence and in adulthood intelligences are expressed through a wide range of professional and recreational activities. For example, spatial intelligence passes from the creation of mental maps in a small child to the operations required in design and systems of specific notation, to arrive later in adult mastery in specialised crafts such as that of navigator, chess player or professional biologist.

Pupils draw benefits from school teaching only if the teaching on offer is structured in a suitable way vis-à-vis their position on the intellectual evolutionary trajectory.

Even if all human beings possess, to some degree, all the intelligences, some are more promising in one in particular, i.e., they have a generous gift in terms of abilities in that specific area. Other individuals, on the other hand, are "at risk", vis-à-vis a particular intelligence; thus in the absence of support, these subjects will probably fail in performances that entail the use of that particular skill.

At school age, it is essential to acquire a certain confidence with systems of notation, but in the first years of school the identification of a favourable environment for personal discovery must not substitute or cause the learning of the necessary structure of specific systems of notation to be neglected, as in the case of algebra. With reference to this Gardner underlines the fact that the orchestration of the connection between practical cognition and cognition incorporated in systems of notation or symbolic systems is of critical importance.

In brief, the following is a summary of each.

Linguistic Intelligence

This form of intelligence includes mastery of and love for language as well as the ability to master other languages, the ability to read, write, speak and listen. Traditionally it is one of the forms of intelligence privileged in the scholastic environment. It has been held in great consideration because it corresponds to methods used in the past to teach and learn, for example, in face-to-face lessons the learning of certain texts or extracts by heart, the understanding of textbooks, exercises carried out and commented on at the board.

Logical-Mathematical Intelligence

This form of intelligence is strictly nonverbal in the sense that the solution to a problem can be intuited even before it can be clearly expressed in words. Together with linguistic ability, logical-mathematical reasoning supplies the basic principle for overcoming the standardised tests used to measure intelligence or to pass an examination. These tests may provide a reliable estimation of academic potential, but not of the greater riches of human potential. Nevertheless, logical-mathematical intelligence like linguistic intelligence enjoys notable esteem in the educational world. Its acquisition is encouraged by a learning environment and by systematic lessons that favour the construction of skills that will serve in the discovery of the relations between objects and abstractions, and it is useful for working out calculations and solving problems that experts can do in a short time.

Musical Intelligence

It is the intelligence of the structures present for example in songs, poetry, musical instruments, and sounds and rhythms from the natural world. It is manifested in the ability to recognise musical extracts, melodies and rhythms as well as in playing and composing music. It should be underlined that it is not just a matter of auditory intelligence alone but can, in fact include every other type of structure. Indeed, from the fact that mathematics is often referred to as the study of structures, this is also part of the domain of mathematics teaching.

Kinaesthetic Intelligence

The interpretation of kinaesthetic skill as a problem solving activity might seem less intuitive. Obviously the execution of a mime sequence or the skill in striking a tennis ball is not the same as solving a mathematical equation. However, consideration of examples of this kind of activity such as the ability to use one's body to express an emotion as occurs in dance or mime, for competition in any kind of sport, or to create a new product provides clear evidence of the cognitive contribution implicit in the use of the body. This form of intelligence is stimulated through physical interaction with one's own environment, both in minor and major motor activities, such as those that can be observed in practical sessions where manipulation activities are carried out, or in the laboratory with scientific experiments, in games and improvised drama. Dancers, athletes and actors are specialists in controlling and harmonising the movements of their bodies.

Spatial Intelligence

Spatial intelligence is the ability to perceive the various dimensions of the visual world, and to transform visual experiences by recreating them in the absence of the original stimuli. The resolution of spatial problems is necessary for navigation and in the use of a system of notation for the creation of maps and chats. Other types of resolution of spatial problems are involved in the visualisation of an object from different angles and in the game of chess. The visual arts also employ this intelligence in their use of space.

The right hemisphere has been shown to be the crucial site for the elaboration of spatial information. Besides the internalisation of external visual stimuli, this intelligence allows us to mentally picture concepts and solutions of problems before trying to verbalise them or translate them into practice. Spatial reasoning is helped by the use of diagrams, graphs, maps, tables, illustrations, works of art and many others beside.

Interpersonal Intelligence

This is the ability to understand others, their motivations and the way of working and discover, at the same time, how it is possible to interact with them in a cooperative manner. In its more advanced form this intelligence enables us to read the intentions and desires of others, even when they are disguised or hidden. This ability is employed in highly sophisticated forms by political and religious leaders, teachers, physiotherapists and parents. It can be stimulated though interaction with others; those pupils who are gifted with this kind of intelligence often need forms of co-operative teaching, in which they are free to ask questions, discuss and understand.

Intrapersonal Intelligence

This form of intelligence enables us to understand our inner selves, by helping us to distinguish, classify and finally draw conclusions from inner feelings and the whole range of emotions in order to understand and guide our behaviour. Thus, it is the ability to form a precise image of one's self and use this in our daily lives. Finally, as this intelligence is by its nature very private, in order to see it at work, the observer needs to look for evidence derived from other sources such as language, music and other forms of more expressive intelligence.

Natural Intelligence

This covers the study of botany, zoology and other sciences, which are carried on through a process of selection, classification and the creation of hierarchical structures. The use of diagrams and conceptual maps can, therefore, be very useful to develop this skill. The ability to recognise and classify natural objects is commonly found in the work of biologists and naturalists.

ACCESS FOR INTELLIGENCES

In the multiple intelligences theory, intelligence can serve both as a content of teaching and as a means to communicate that content, "…let us suppose that a child, not particularly gifted in the logical-mathematical field, is learning a mathematical principle. The child will meet certain difficulties. The reason for this is clear: the mathematical principle to be learnt (the content) only exists in the world of mathematics and logic, and should be communicated through mathematics (the means). This means that the mathematical principle cannot be entirely translated into words (linguistic means) or into spatial models (spatial means). At a certain point in the learning process, mathematics must speak for itself."

In the example reported by Gardner the subject, therefore, finds it difficult when access to the strictly mathematical problem is expressed in mathematical language; it is as if to say "learning mathematics through the medium of mathematics". The teacher, for this reason, will have to find an alternative medium that leads to the mathematical content, in other words a metaphor. Language is one of the alternatives; in other cases it may be more appropriate to use a spatial model or even a kinaesthetic metaphor. Gardner (1994) claimed he still had not conducted sufficient scientific verification in the gambit of educational psychology[3]. Returning to the previous discourse, however, we can say that his exposition obscures one crucial aspect with regard to teaching, that is the fact that the secondary route chosen belongs to another branch of intelligence, i.e., it is not translation *qua* translation, in the sense that one is doing mathematics in a learning environment that uses metaphors from other areas.

Teaching can find support in the theory of multiple intelligences in order to find different languages that can be used to carry the same contents[4].

SELF-EFFICACY

Self-efficacy is the faculty to generate action in order to achieve a given goal and consequently the ability to plan in advance the level of commitment required for success. It is based on the personal conviction of being able to use one's skills and knowledge in an efficient way, in other words the ability to become a transformative agent. The word "agent" refers to acts carried out intentionally and implies that individuals can influence what happens to them, by intervening on reality through their actions. What does all this mean? A bundle of skills and abilities that can be linked, in particular, to the ability to:

1. reflect on one's own abilities and resources;
2. self regulate in the course of an activity so it leads to the desired outcome;
3. decide on the right time to act, through an ongoing evaluation of results and re-orientation of successive actions.

This implies that, in each person's tactical repertoire, little or nothing is left to chance, in the sense that every action is accompanied by the awareness of covering an active learning role.

People who are gifted with strong self-efficacy have the tendency to visualize clearly and rapidly future situations and evaluate them by calculating the rapport between the necessary commitment and the desired result. On this basis self-efficient students decide on actions to be undertaken confident of achieving their goal with a given amount of time and effort. However, once embarked upon the course of action, each student is constantly checking the results against the objectives in order to take corrective action where necessary and stay on the right track. This operative competence involves the continual employment of a wide variety of skills- cognitive, social, affective and motivational.

There are three dimensions in particular that characterize self-efficacy: *willpower* that every person needs to overcome certain obstacles, *level*, established on the basis of the difficulty of the task to be undertaken and finally, *generality,* that refers to the ambit of the activity. From these characteristics one can deduce that self-efficacy is not a predetermined and constant ability belonging to the person involved, but can vary according to the different fields of application.

A student may feel self-effective, for example, when tackling problems of arithmetic and feel much less so what it comes to geometry. As regards the root of the perception of self-efficacy, Albert Bandura, who evolved this concept, reveals the existence of different sources of information the subject elaborates cognitively through a "complex process of self-persuasion".

The most important sources of information are represented by the results that each one of us achieves, from successful experiences of sharing a common objective with others, the so-called "vicarious experiences", encouragement from others as well as ourselves, emotional and physiological states. The results achieved by a subject constitute the main information on one's ability or lack of ability to master and influence a performance.

While the experience of success increases the sense of self-efficacy, failure, especially if often repeated, contributes to the growth of a feeling of inadequacy and incompetence. This scenario is a familiar one to math teachers.

The commitment accompanying the activity, linked to results, is of considerable importance when assessing self-efficacy in math but also in other areas of the curriculum. To be aware of having failed because of lack of effort is far less undermining to one's sense of self-efficacy than in the case where failure occurred despite great effort.

Moreover, vicarious experiences provide importance sources of information when judging personal efficacy. These experiences can come from people such as peers with the same or similar levels of ability as ourselves or from persons we look to as role models. Vicarious information is important both when learners have little experience of the task to be undertaken and when there are no clear criteria on which to base an evaluation of one's performance. Furthermore, the more our model is perceived as similar to ourselves, the greater the significance of the feedback. Another key factor in the construction of a feeling of self-efficacy is that of verbal persuasion. Expressions such as "You can do it", or "I'm certain you can make it" and so on can have a vital role in convincing a student of their own abilities, while negative judgments especially personal comments can have the opposite effect. In this area feedback during performance plays a vital role. The very concept of feedback is highly relevant and represents a process through which it is possible to keep track of the information provided by the results as they arrive that can be used as a sign that change is needed or confirmation one is on the right road. In particular, the evaluation from feedback is represented not only by the results themselves, but also from how they re interpreted on the basis of analytical criteria.

These processes develop in a silent way. The fact of being able to remove them from their immediate context and analyze them, also through questionnaires and check lists allows us to stimulate the underlying meta cognitive processes, thereby working on and enhancing the feeling of self-efficacy.

Having said that, it is also necessary to distinguish between different systems of reference: it is much more effective to praise a student who is carrying out a task successfully for their general abilities rather than for their effort. Another factor is the status of the person who provides feedback: the development of a sense of self-efficacy is in direct proportion to the credibility of the person who offers the praise; in other words, the more we value the person as a model, the more seriously we take the encouragement. The emotional and physical state of the learner during the task offer other important indicators for the evaluation of the level of self-efficacy. Anxiety and tension generally produce negative effects on the perception of one's ability to manage certain situations. It is worth noting that the sources of information considered here do not have a direct or automatic influence, in the sense that each person evaluates the information received cognitively attributing at different times greater or lesser importance to various factors. As regards the effects of the effects of the self perception of an individual's own ability, on the other hand, Bandura de-

Figure 1. Base structure of the math teaching system's elements

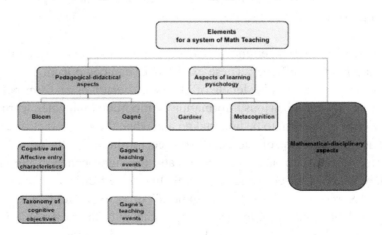

scribes three processes through which our thought, in the widest sense, can orientate our action: processes of choice, processes of motivation and cognitive processes.

An unrealistic evaluation of one's own competence, both in the positive and negative sense, can be counterproductive: this happens, for example, what the task to be faced is notably beyond the student's capacity to fulfill it, or when the choice offers too narrow a range of experience and does not allow the student to develop his/her potential. Motivational processes also contribute to the construction of a sense of self efficiency. This is revealed in the level of perseverance and commitment demonstrated in overcoming obstacles.

Finally, also affect is influenced by the conviction of self efficacy; in fact some studies have shown that people who do not believe in their own ability are more subject to stress and lack of initiative than others. This aspect can be seen quite frequency in the process of learning mathematics.

REFERENCES

Anderson, L. W. (1976). An empirical investigation of individual differences in time to learn. *Journal of Educational Psychology, 68*(2), 226–233. doi:10.1037/0022-0663.68.2.226

Bandura, A. (2000). *Autoefficacia: teoria e applicazioni*. Trento: Erickson.

Block, J. H. (1972). *Mastery Learning. Procedimenti di educazione individualizzata*. Torino: Loescher.

Bloom, B. S. (1993). *Caratteristiche umane e apprendimento scolastico*. Roma: Armando.

Carroll, J. B. (1963). A model of school learning. *Teachers College Record, 64*, 723–733.

Gagné, E. D. (1989). *Psicologia cognitiva e apprendimento scolastico*. Torino: SEI.

Gagné, R. M. (1985). *Le condizioni dell'apprendimento* (4th ed.). Roma: Armando.

Gagné, R. M., & Briggs, L. J. (1990). *Fondamenti di progettazione didattica*. Torino: SEI.

Gardner, H. (1987). *Formae Mentis. Saggio sulla pluralità dell'intelligenza*. Milano: Feltrinelli.

Gardner, H. (1993). *Educare al comprendere. Stereotipi infantili e apprendimento scolastico*. Milano: Feltrinelli.

Gardner, H. (1994). *Intelligenze multiple*. Milano: Anabasi.

Gardner, H. (1999). *Sapere per comprendere, Discipline di studio e disciplina della mente*. Milano: Feltrinelli.

Gardner, H. (2005). *Educazione e sviluppo della mente. Intelligenze multiple e apprendimento*. Trento: Erickson.

ENDNOTES

[1]   Time on task is the ratio between span of concentration and the overall time dedicated to a task

[2]   In particular, also simulation games require the activation of a process of analysis and planning. As regards this, see Chapter 11.

[3]   Within the applicative field many solicitations are used and they are based on Multiple Intelligences theory. Also the experimentation described in Section 4 refers to the experiences developed for the materials construction and research and strategies aimed at diversify teaching activities (McKenzie W., 2006).

[4]   Compare this with Chapter 4 of Section 2 (Transcoding)

Chapter 7

Methodological Proposals for Simulation Games:
The Transcoding Pattern[1]

Cesare Fregola
Roma Tre University, Italy

ABSTRACT

This chapter introduces the transcoding pattern, used in simulation games, to organize the language, the setting and the learning environment, defining the course of learning on various levels of abstraction. The aim is to facilitate the construction of a language that can be used in the processes of the mathematicization of reality and in math teaching in general. In order to give the reader a better understanding of the ideas and components of this process, an example of the transcoding pattern is provided before going on to describe the objective of our research the simulation game.

INTRODUCTION

In schools motivation to learn how to learn mathematics can be encouraged by an approach that orientates communication in such a way that it takes account of the real possibilities of children's abstraction, and teacher awareness of the meaning that children attribute to the words they use.

DOI: 10.4018/978-1-60566-930-4.ch007

Mathematical learning requires continual transition from experiential and informal codes used by children, to codes based on symbolic representations characterised by growing levels of abstraction and means of representation that become increasingly formal and complex.

From this perspective the design and realisation of learning environments can become a key element for the teaching of mathematics regardless of the different keys of interpretation that mathematicians, educational psychologists, educational experts, primary and secondary school maths teachers attribute to the learning process on the basis of theories developed within their respective disciplines, or with respect to the consolidated praxis used as a methodology.

Each discipline, in its turn, refers to a language characterised by a specific repertoire that requires an equally specific access code; it is difficult to organise the teaching of mathematics in a corpus starting from the ability to master different languages (at least, those of general teaching theory, educational psychology, science teaching and so on) that would allow us to organise learning environments on the basis of the specific and general learning needs of children, teaching strategies and the specific nature of arithmetical and geometric language.

In fact, mathematics continues to spread panic[2]; the number of mathematicians is declining and awareness of the educational value of mathematical learning is not very widespread. Here are, therefore, certain question marks underpinning our approach to the teaching of mathematics in primary schools:

1. How to introduce interface codes that are part of the process of stimulation, re-enforcement and organisational capacity of learning in order to tackle mathematical language when the conditions are developed for a dynamic and coherent process of abstraction and formal representation of concepts?
2. Can we accept *substantial rigour* of the language to be utilised in order to create the conditions in which motivation arises and maintain motivation when the complexity of formal mathematical language increases?
3. Which learning strategies can be stimulated in order to develop the construction of mathematical language in such a way that the necessarily less formal linguistic approach does not get in the way of understanding the concepts or introduce distortions in the use of a language (i.e., mathematical language) that does not allow for individualistic modifications?
4. Can we assume responsibility for the construction of a borderland between mathematical language and the meta-language that interprets the basic concepts in a way that is accessible to children?
5. Can we accept, for the time being, less *formal rigour*, monitored so that it does not prejudice the understanding of concepts and the future application of the rules and procedures of mathematical language?

The aforementioned list, based on experience of several research projects carried out in primary schools, as well as on an understanding of the literature, has led us to introduce the *transcoding pattern*[3] in our approach to the teaching of mathematics. From the didactic point of view, the *transcoding pattern* is used to organise the language, the classroom and the overall learning environment, by organising the processes on different levels of abstraction in order to facilitate the construction of a language that is both accessible and a sound basis on which to build a formal mathematical language (Piu A., 2002).

THE PROCESS OF TRANSCODING

Each communicative act utilises a specific semiotic register, which implies two abilities

1. **Codification**, i.e., the reduction of a determined schema, according to a determined code, of information; in the theory of information the operation is expressed in messages, data and instructions in code[4].
2. **De-codification**, i.e., the identification and understanding of the message, via a suitable code, on the part of the person receiving the message.

The two things work in tandem but activate different processes of elaboration. Indeed, it is by no means certain that the person carrying out the coding operation is able to decode the message or that the person who decodes the message is able to code it.

This dualism is particularly relevant when teaching students with learning difficulties, and the problem becomes much more acute when they are faced with the kind of mathematics teaching that privileges the aspect based on a formal concept, that places at the centre the form in which various mathematic propositions are expressed and the rules used to combine them (Pellerey, 1983).

It is difficult to integrate the coding and de-coding of mathematical language, which is highly abstract, synthetic and symbolic, in a competent and integrated manner. At the other extreme one can collocate a substantial concept of mathematics that privileges the meaning and reality underpinning the formulas or definitions: "in teaching we aim primarily at the substance of the discourse, at the meaning of the various propositions, at the content underlying the symbols: and this does not only apply to mathematics but also to other fields of application" (Pellerey, 1983, p. 25).

Mathematical language is based on a formal economic code for the representation of concepts, structures, and simple and highly complex theories but the processes of communication are based on the understanding that the sender and receiver manage to achieve through the use of a shared code.

If it is a mathematical code, both the sender and receiver must be able to master the code in order to communicate mathematically. In the teaching-learning relationship the teacher already possesses the means to do this, whereas the child first has to construct the code before engaging with the teacher in a dialogue, based on their respective repertoires and experience. This reciprocal process of communication is called transcodification.

In the process of transcodification the object of communication is preserved, i.e., its structure, the concept to be uncovered and formalised, the rule to be applied.

The code that presents the maximum level of possible abstraction possible for the receiver may not coincide with the specific code of mathematical language and the level of formalisation of the mathematical code may not be accessible to the child to the extent that he/she can knowingly express the underlying meanings.

And so, it is a matter of constructing intermediate codes that start from what is already known, preferably expressed in simple language and in ways of representing reality that are familiar to the child so that the meanings are susceptible to decoding; thus the codes themselves are in tune with competence and capacity for abstraction of the learner in the phase of developing mathematical thought.

This approach is close to the substantial conception of mathematics but does not overlook the fact that formal conception of mathematics must necessarily represent the point of arrival of the teaching-learning process.

One can state that *substantial rigour* is a necessary course to follow in the utilisation of an intermediate code during the process of constructing a mathematical language. The objective is that this code can act as a guide for the right approach to adopt in order to attain the *formal rigour* that characterises the codes that are the foundation of mathematical thought.

Transcoding helps to ensure that the *substantial rigour* introduced has, at least, two characteristics:

- provides minimum necessary to avoid introducing inappropriate levels of approximation in the use of intermediate codes;
- reduces the risk of producing partial learning based on misconceptions[5].

The process of transcoding finds an implicit reference in Montessori, when she proposed to construct objects and environments tailored for children. Transcoding can be defined, as a search for a working lexis to talk about mathematics so that the repertoire of words used ensures certain conditions until the child can:

a. feel at home when codes are used or constructed;
b. grasp the relationship between the words used and their meanings;
c. master the use of a code that becomes increasingly formal, ever closer to the mathematical one.

In teaching terms, therefore, transcoding is the task of the teacher: to construct environments that respect the three conditions indicated above, that must be accessible, challenging and favour the process of abstraction whose goal is the understanding and representation of concepts, rules and mathematical relationships.

With reference to classical communications theory (Shannon & Weaver, 1971) a good starting point for a definition of transcoding is the fact that each phase of the process of abstraction indicates a representation of reality, or its elaboration, and uses a specific semiotic register to construct and utilise, thereby deliberately creating the conditions until the field of communication produces an environment that facilitates access to learning.

Sadly, in most teachers' tool box there are no instruments, means, learning models and teaching schemes that can facilitate the unpacking of mathematical knowledge in order to then to reconstruct it in a processes of discovery.

From a exploratory study of teaching programmes for mathematics in the Faculty of the Science of Primary Education, it emerges that mathematics teaching privileges arithmetic, geometry and probability studies and does not identify methods recognisable as "tailored for children", that take account of the different phases of development[6] and the properties of learning processes.

Even when the teaching proposals are given practical application, the actual underlying methodology, based on research in the field of the science of education and educational psychology[7], is rarely made explicit.

Finally, another important aspect, which is beyond the remit of this work, is the relational components of classroom communication. In fact, the scientific evolution of social psychology has led to various studies and research works on the basis of which we are now able to intervene on a number of affective variables at work during the study of mathematics. Apart from the cognitive and meta-cognitive aspects, therefore, another important factor in the process of transcoding is the quality of the relational and affective dimension of teaching (Fregola C., Olmetti Peja D., 2007).

THE PROCESS OF "MATHEMATIZATION"

The process of applying mathematics to reality leads to the discovery of concepts, rules and structures, in a similar way to the representation of the complex concept of arithmetic and geometry and, in the right environment, it can find a variety of configurations. By integrating real and virtual environments within the confines of a particular task aimed at the discovery of concepts, rules, structures and the construction of representations in a code to be formulated gradually in a mathematical language, teaching courses can be developed that move from the real to the abstract and proceed through immersion in the learning environment where it is possible to interact through simulation of what is real which becomes defined in the light of the conquests of the knowledge acquired.

The identification and definition of learning and teaching models from the above can play a key role in the construction of teaching courses which provide an effective and motivating repertoire for the requirements of acquiring mathematical knowledge and the development of creative thought in the interpretation of such knowledge.

Certain processes, such as, for example, that of abstraction, coding, decoding, transcoding and the transfers involved in the acquisition of mathematics, can be found in these approaches, but they can also be reviewed in the light of the interconnections between the current state of mathematical knowledge, psychology and the science of education. The theoretical and practical concepts in the field of mathematical education, driven by the need to explore variable and invariable aspects of reality and to find an order on which to base a method, can initiate a process of construction and reconstruction of the linguistic code of mathematics and logic by the learner, within specific semantic fields that the learning environment and simulation exercises can encourage.

Such ambits can be defined as meeting places or interdisciplinary maps bringing together diverse perspectives, that can also be enriched by the learning experiences that the multi-media children have in other real and virtual places, fostering a sense of self-efficiency in the mathematical territory, a territory, one has to admit, even today is not very appealing or child friendly.

As we know the process of applying mathematics to reality represents initially the passage from the physical world and that of perceptive experience to its ideal and rational representation.

When the first elaboration of an abstract scheme in a concrete situation has been achieved, the abstract scheme, in turn, can be taken to a higher level insofar as the previous level has been mastered, i.e., it is now capable of manipulation and can be transferred to other contexts.

Within the context of the task one can consciously draw analogies or isomorphic structures from this schema, which gradually moves into action, in a direct but subtle way, and almost automatically becomes concrete; this indicates two reasons why we can speak of a process of "mathematisation": "first it concerns the construction of an abstract scheme of a relationship, after analysing a specific situation; second, the abstract schema can be framed at once, or later, without contradictions or other types of difficulties in a mathematical theory or a part of one" (Pellerey 1983, p.140).

THE TEACHING PROCESS

On the basis of the considerations developed so far it is now possible to amplify the references from educational psychology that utilise criteria that can support the decision making process of designing an appropriate environment for mathematical learning. With reference to this, Zoltan Dienes (1971, p. 11) proposed six steps for the development of the learning of mathematics: " We shall try to demonstrate how it is possible to bring the child, starting from free play, through the various steps to be described until the sixth step, in which the child will be able to play the demonstration game, i.e., manipulate a formal system".

Briefly the steps develop in the following manner:

1. first step (free play): the child is introduced to a predetermined environment provided with the mathematical structures to be abstracted; the child is free to play and explore the environment;

2. second step (structured game): exploration can lead to the discovery of rules that orientate observation and interaction with the environment during play. The games become associated with rules and a purpose. The situations in the game represent a mathematical situation and the manipulation of the game can bring about a manipulation in the mathematical situation. Manipulation in the construction of the game situation represents the construction of the mathematical situation as a learning factor;

3. third step (awareness): comparison between the game situation and the mathematical situation is encouraged through participation in the game the child has played;

4. fourth step (representation): "the structure is represented graphically or in another way" (Dienes Z.P., 1971, p. 61). The specific game is determined by specific states and operators; the child is now ready to carry out a gradual representation;

5. fifth step (formalisation): the level of abstraction reached with the representation has certain properties that are studied in this phase. The invention/construction of language is begun; the phase of formalisation is started through the proposal or construction of a symbolic code;

6. sixth step (axioms, demonstrations, theorems): "being set in a description all the properties cannot be defined, so it is necessary to take a minimum number of descriptions and invent a procedure in order to deduce the others. This minimum number of descriptions leads to the concept of axioms, and the procedure for deducing rules, propositions and so on from axioms leads to the concept of demonstration, and when properties and criteria are revealed we can obtain the primary idea of a theorem (Dienes Z.P., 1971, p. 61).

Manipulation of this system, which is a formal one, is the final goal of the learning of a mathematical structure.

One of the most important aspects of the work of Dienes is, in our opinion, it turned on its head the way mathematics was taught up till that time. In fact, the point of departure of a teaching syllabus was primarily that of a formal-symbolic type, i.e. coherent with the fact that the procedure was overwhelmingly functional gearing to the management of practical problems of daily life and the consolidation of learning was biased towards processes of calculus. Algebra and geometry were proposed within a frame of reference of applications of reality, interpreted through the lens of different jobs. The ultimate aim was to arrive at the demonstrative procedures of mathematics understood merely as a hypothetical deductive system for certain types of studies.

The students who obtained good results in mathematics were considered gifted as though they had innate gifts rather than a self-regulating competence over their own learning process. One of the most significant hypotheses of our research on simulation games is the construction of learning environments with a methodological rigour based on transcoding that can enhance motivation to learn even among those students who are overlooked and undervalued, not just the eggheads; in other words, stimulate learning processes of every child.

The way forward can be designed with reference to Dienes' (1967) four principles.

Constructive Principle

In children constructive thinking precedes the development of logical thought. Constructive understanding is to be favoured over analytical understanding. In other words, the construction of the concept precedes the symbolic construction that expresses the concept itself.

Dynamic Principle

Every abstraction is derived from experience. The formation of concepts develops along dynamic lines which teaching must encourage. From this stems the need to stimulate the analysis of real situations from the child's everyday life in order to focus attention on the aspects to do with mathematics.

Principle of Perceptive Variability

There is a need to provide situations that are perceptively different from the same conceptual structure. The common characteristics are the abstractions the child must become aware of. The teacher should provide situations with structural similarities to be used as a model of the concept to be learnt. The presentation of the models can be varied so that the approach is perceived as diverse and thus one arrives at the concept of the invariant.

Principle of Mathematical Variability

As regards the variation of symbolic situations that lead, through successive abstractions, to the "more formalised" expression, all the elements that are not essential to the construction of the concept are to be varied in order to bring out, as invariant, the concept thus highlighting the formal representation.

To sum up, the principle of constructiveness refers in particular to Piaget and later developments of his idea of isomorphism between mental structures and logical-linguistic learning (Chomsky, 1986). Vygotskij's (1990) concept of proximate zone of development illustrates the idea of the process of transcoding well. Moreover, recent studies in cognitive psychology on the concept of schema and representation do not contradict this approach, even if the perspective is widened to include studies of socio-cognition.

The dynamic principle represents the phase of "bringing out" from reality aspects that can be translated into mathematical facts. The principle of perceptive variability indirectly supplies practical indications from the didactic point of view and finds confirmation in the current research into multiple intelligences (Gardner, 1994, 1995). Finally, the principle of mathematical variability invites us to reflect on the importance of considering formalisation as the point of arrival of mathematics learning, and not the point of departure (Fischbein &Vergnaud, 1992).

STRAWS, UMBRELLA, BOWS, HAT AND GLASSES: AN EXPERIENCE OF TRANSCODING AT DIFFERENT LEVELS OF ABSTRACTION

Before going into the specifics of our research into the transcoding pattern, there follows an example of the application of the transcoding pattern to a sequential list or itinerary that exemplifies our approach to the design and realization of learning environments.

The aim has two aspects:

- to allow the reader to observe the proposed model in the light of an experience carried out in a school;
- to supply a key as to how the strictly mathematical contents are handled in our simulation games.

The effectiveness of the activity has been demonstrated a number of times in classes of infants, primary school children and with children with learning difficulties (Fregola, 1991). The aims of the pattern are as follows:

- favour the discovery and composition of the terms;
- manipulate them;
- encourage the process of codification with various codes at different levels of abstraction;
- propose representations that are increasingly formalised and abstract;
- encourage the process of transcodification by encouraging the children to reflect on the invariance of the concept with respect to its formal representation;
- underline the importance of using as many representations as possible in order to favour the processes of transfer and generalisation.

The most relevant aspect is found in the methodological value of the proposed direction. To sum up, the principles that guide our approach are as follows:

- The images indicate a representation of reality that uses an iconic semiotic register to stimulate visual-spatial capability;
- The sequence clearly shows the importance of the ability to discriminate and classify;
- The structure of the sequence implied in the analysis of the variations proposed in the succession of images promotes the need for words to bridge the passage from natural language to a more efficient and economical one that requires the ability to code and decode.

Learning the Mathematical Concepts Present in the Pattern

Regarding the underlying concepts in the pattern we should:

- highlight
- underline
- encourage intuition
- encourage discovery
- codify
- encourage understanding
- help the representation through a variety of means and codes
- help apply the concepts behind the sequence in order to reread it the light of the concepts themselves.

The Mathematical Concepts Present in the Pattern to be Learnt

- Terms
- Proposition
- Conjugation
- Logical implication
- Universal quantifier
- Sets
- Operations between sets

Procedure

The starting point of the procedure for the experiment proposed is natural language and, from there, the process gradually develops through the progressive introduction of stimuli to create the representation and the organisation of ideas required by the situation.

The work is developed in two modules, both of which unfold in a number of phases.

Now a game is proposed that consists in inserting the cups garnished with straws inside one fence and those with umbrellas in another.

The code utilised, that of the Eulero-Venn diagrams facilitates the abstraction of concepts, but it is not si useful when it comes to simplifying the combination of the logical terms.

However, when the terms based on symbols are introduced, and thus on a level of abstraction from the initial situation which we leave further behind a new phase in the use of language begins, and, therefore, in the relationship between the words and the discourse to be constructed.

Our pattern of transcodification entails a gradual and continuous move "back and forth" between the real situation, that is communicated in everyday language, and the search for code that slowly becomes symbolic and formalised, hence more abstract, until in the end the concrete is left behind. We have assumed, in the light of our observations of the children involved, that a process, requiring the mental ability to maintain *provisionally* the link with the concrete, while moving at the same time towards the symbolic, is activated in this way. "Provisionally", i.e., until the concepts[8] take shape in the mind and guide the learner in reinterpreting the original situation yet, also in developing an awareness that rises above the specific situation (Castelnuovo, 1979).

Figure 1. From the concrete to the abstract with two terms

SEQUENCE OF SUPERIMPOSED IMAGES	
First image	An image is proposed representing a set of ice creams; the semiotic registers used are those of colour and shape. - The children are asked to describe the situation in natural language - The children are encouraged through more focused questions, for example (What is there in the image? Are the ice creams of different flavours? How many flavours has each ice cream got? How many different types of container are there?)
Second image	Straws are added to the original image by superimposing a transparency. The new situation is discussed and a shared language is used to describe it. The relationship between the object "straw" and the object "cup of ice cream" can be expressed in various ways. One example is "cup of ice cream with straw". Now, to recognise all the objects that have the straw characteristic implies the formulation of a possible group. The fact of the straw being in the cup containing ice cream gives us the possibility to establish that, in the universe of cups containing ice cream, there are some with straws and some without straws. THIS LINGUISTIC FORMULATION describes in an effective way the variation considered.
Third image	Now umbrellas are added to the previous image in the same way as before. The new situation is discussed and a shared language is used to describe it. The relationship between the object umbrella and the object cup of ice cream can be expressed in various ways. One example is "cups of ice cream with umbrella." Now, to recognise that "all the objects have the characteristic of a umbrella" implies the formulation of another possible group. The fact of the umbrella being in the cup containing ice cream gives us the possibility to establish that, in the universe of cups containing ice cream, there are those with the umbrella and those without. THIS LINGUISTIC FORMULATION describes in an effective way the variation considered. BUT THERE ARE OTHER THINGS TO BE DISCOVERED IN THIS IMAGE.

Figure 2. From the concrete to the abstract with two terms (continued)

Third image continued	
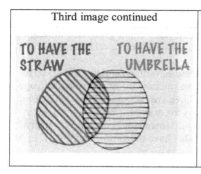	This representation requires a leap in abstraction and the use of a new code that "mathematicians actually call the Eulero-Venn diagram. There are a number of interesting discoveries that you can make from this representation. For example: the set, the collection of a group (the cups that do not have an umbrella but have a straw or the cups that do not have a straw but have an umbrella; the intersection between the sets (the cups that have a straw and an umbrella); the union of sets (the cups that have a straw or an umbrella, thus one or the other or both).

The most important aspect that can be extrapolated is that, at every level of transcoding, the concepts and structures that are the object of the pattern are conserved.

Moreover, the process of learning once activated allows the learner to move along the axis of the formal-substantial conception of mathematics observed in this chapter.

SIMULATION GAMES, LEARNING MATHEMATICS AND TRANSCODING

In the following section we shall present the transcoding patterns, tested that were created by our research group. The work has two aims:

Figure 3. From the concrete to the abstract with two terms (continued)

Third image continued	
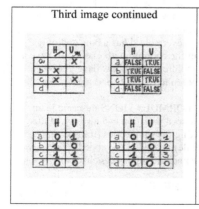	After introducing a table to represent the situations that have emerged, and that the Eulero-Venn diagrams have illustrated, we can now propose other codes. The table in the top left provides immediate information on the fact that the situation: a) describes cups of ice cream that have only an umbrella; b) cups of ice cream that only have a straw; c) cups of ice cream that have both straw and umbrella. The table in the top right provides information on the concert of "term" and of term composed with the conjunction "and". For example: situation a) tells us that it is *true* that some cups only have an umbrella and *false* they have a straw. Finally the table at the bottom left provides the same information but uses the symbol 0 instead of the term *false* and 1 instead of the term *true*.

Figure 4. From the concrete to the abstract and from the abstract to the concrete with three terms. Transfer and generalization.

First image 	An image is proposed that represents a group of children. The semiotic registers are social (group, schoolchildren etc.) - In this case as well the children are asked to describe a situation using everyday language - The children are encouraged through helpful questions for example (What can you see in the image? How many boys and how many girls? What have they in common?)
Second image 	A bow is added to every child by superimposing a transparency on the origin image. As in the first module the new situation is discussed together with the children in a shared language. The relation between the child and the bow has certain aspects that enable us to consider: -from the logical point of view, to the introduction of a universal quantifier "for every" (each child has a bow.... All the children have a bow) -from the point of view of the relations between the groups, to the introduction of biunique correspondence. (The language is enriched to describe the situation but displays, at the same time, redundancy).
Third image 	A pair of glasses is added to the image in the same way as above. As in the first module the new situation is discussed together with the children in a shared language. The relation between the object pair of glasses and subject child can be expressed in various ways, such as "children with glasses". Now, recognising that " all the objects that have the characteristic of wearing glasses implies the formation of another possible group and so other descriptions can be articulated: for example, every child has a bow and only some have glasses…but the children with glasses all have a bow, while not all the children with a bow have glasses….. or …… only some children have a bow and glasses but all the children have a bow. THESE LINGUISTIC FORMULATIONS describe in an effective way the introduced variation and already, at this point, we can start looking for similarities (transferring from the previous module) as well as the specific features of this new situation (launching the process of generalisation). IN THIS IMAGE TOO THERE ARE DISCOVERIES TO

Figure 5. From the concrete to the abstract and from the abstract to the concrete with three terms. Transfer and generalization (continued)

Fourth image 	A hat is added to the image in the same way as above. The relation between the object hat and subject child can be expressed in various ways, such as "children with hats". Now, recognising that " all the objects that have the characteristic of wearing hats implies the formation of another possible group and so other descriptions can be articulated: for example, every child has a bow and only some have hats…but the children with hats all have a bow, while not all the children with a bow have hats (and this formulation can be compared to the previous one with the glasses in order to grasp the regularity of the concept). THESE LINGUISTIC FORMULATIONS describe in an effective way the introduced variation but at this point there is an extra term, thus an extra set; therefore, does the Eulero-Venn diagram continue to hold for the three terms or it necessary to change something? Invent something?
Fifth image 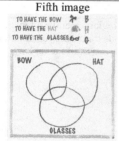	That's right! We need to add another fence, And so with this new representation we begin to see that the value of the diagram also stems from the fact that it allows us to go beyond natural language, in the sense that the schema can act as a guide to describe possible situations. The abstraction of the concept of *operation among sets* rather than representing an artificial device becomes therefore, a mental instrument to read, interpret and respond to reality in a better way.

- in the first place we can reread an "illustration" of our project in order to apply it, in a coherent way. We believe, in fact, that without this example we would have introduced the paradox of claiming that a concept must be expressed in a meaningful language the acquisition of which is already taken for granted; to this process of acquisition we have assigned the term *transcoding;*
- secondly, the search for a methodology to base the games project on involved us in a study of the contents of the units, which later became a guide for an analysis of the learning achieved in the classroom environment.

As regards the expected mathematical contents of simulation games in our research (and we believe this should hold for the use of simulation games in maths teaching in primary schools in general) the transcoding process represents a significant advance from the educational and methodological point of view insofar as it obliges the researcher to carry out a very careful analysis of the task with particular

Figure 6. From the concrete to the abstract and from the abstract to the concrete with three terms. Transfer and generalization (continued)

Sixth image	With this in mind, the children state the areas of intersection and list and describe all the other possible situations.
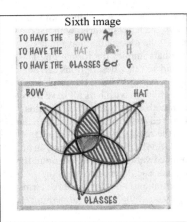	

Seventh image	In order to transfer from the previous module a table is provided that uses a further code that brings us to the final stage, as can be seen in the lower part of the table.

	B BOW	H HAT	G GLASSES
a	FALSE	FALSE	TRUE
b	FALSE	TRUE	FALSE
c	TRUE	FALSE	FALSE
d	TRUE	TRUE	FALSE
e	TRUE	FALSE	TRUE
f	FALSE	TRUE	TRUE
g	TRUE	TRUE	TRUE
h	FALSE	FALSE	FALSE

Eighth image The final level of abstraction	Any child who has not taken part in the process so far would find it very difficult, on reading the table on the left, to understand the group of concepts, schemata and structures, or to develop an awareness that could be abstracted, elaborated and expressed in a mathematical language; in other words, without going through the process of discovery it is hard indeed to develop forms of thought that can evolve into a system of learning and, simultaneously, the construction of a mathematical language.

	B BOW	H HAT	G GLASSES
a	0	0	1
b	0	1	0
c	1	0	0
d	1	1	0
e	1	0	1
f	0	1	1
g	1	1	1
h	0	0	0

reference to its complexity and universality. As regards this, the model used as a guide, especially in the design phase was that proposed by Dienes with a six step process of learning- teaching in the primary school classroom.

The phase follows a different order to the sequence where the 6 stages are described. We assumed the 6 stages represented a largely logical sequence as the skills that characterize each phase proceed according to a dynamic that is not entirely predictable but rather depends on the motivation and cognitive abilities of the children as well as on the specifics of the learning contents and the teaching objectives. Each stage has its own functions and characteristics but what does not occur is that each precedes neatly only when the previous one has been completed and so on. Indeed even the first part of the game has aspects that affect later stages. This makes it difficult to monitor the process of abstraction and formalization and for this reason the transcoding pattern from a sequential perspective envisages the application of a strategy that unpacks the contents into primary elements before they can be repacked according to certain learning rules. Thus we obtain within the teaching action the construction of a unit of consciousness (a concept, a rule, a structure, a procedure) with certain identifiable characteristics:

- the deliberate and meaningful use of terms starting from everyday language and graduating to a mathematical one;
- the ability to relate the meanings of the terms used to actions required by the game;
- the explanation of actions that characterise the application, construction or discovery of a procedure;
- reflection on the initial situation in the light of things learnt so far;
- a personal synthesis;
- communicate the units of knowledge through a mathematical language.

The way to deconstruct the contents has been supported by the application of Robert Gagné's taxonomy, that has shown itself to be a powerful instrument in the design of transcoding strategies insofar as the results of the task analysis filtered through the taxonomic levels have orientated our decisions in each phase of the game and in the overall learning process.

Thus each step in Dienes' model can be said to provide a metaphorical box to contain every communicative teaching action and, as this container has gradually been filled up, it has begun to reveal the relationships between the different ways of representing meanings and a growing awareness of the formal language in which the concepts are expressed by mathematicians.

Transcoding in Cartolandia

To illustrate this process Figure 7 describes the task analysis carried out to design the transcoding for *Cartolandia*.

For example, by observing the development of the game we found that the verb "apply" assumed various meanings over time which were not always the same for every child. Only at the end of the game and the debriefing was it possible to clarify the concept, the sequence of actions, the words that had become part of the group's identity (drag, shoot, let go, turn upside down etc.) and the words used to best describe the situation (move along a line, overturn) until we arrive at the mathematical words. Thanks to the application of the taxonomy the teaching objectives were defined with reference to Bloom's taxonomy and a study was carried out round the table to reflect on how to stimulate multiple intelligences from actions required to solve the game.

The results are reported in Table 1.

It is interesting to observe the notation of *isometry,* in the language of mathematicians who define it as a geometric transformation, i.e., given two points A and B, isometry corresponds to these two other points A' and B' so that AB = A'B'. Where a geometric transformation between the points on a plane is a biunique correspondence that associates, to every point P on the plane, one and only one point P' belonging to the same plan and vice versa.

The transcoding gap must appear clear before we can share such a definition so simple for those who know mathematical language, but so abstract and complex

Figure 7. Objectives of Cartolandia simulation game defined according to Gagné

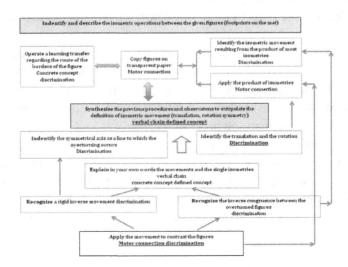

for anyone who is not yet equipped with all the knowledge required to decode the proposed definition and use it in a mathematical context and, above all with that awareness to be employed in real situations in which one can operate a transfer of

Table 1. Relations between multiple intelligences and teaching objectives from Bloom's taxonomy and type of learning according to R. Gagné[9]

Objectives	INTELLIGENCE (Gardner)	BLOOM'S TAXONOMY	VARIETY OF LEARNING (Gagnè)
1. **Apply** movement to contrast the figures	Kinesthetic Visual	Application Analysis	Motor connection Discrimination
2. **Recognise** a rigid inverse movement	Visual Logic	Analysis	Discrimination
3. **Recognise** inverse congruence between upturned figures	Visual	Analysis	Discrimination
4. **Explain** in your own words movements and single isometries	Verbal Logical	Understanding Synthesis	Verbal chain Concrete concept Defined concept
5. **Identify** the symmetric axis as a line where overturning occurs	Visual	Analysis	Discrimination
6. **Identify** translation and rotation	Visual	Analysis	Discrimination
7. **Synthesise** previous procedures and observations to extrapolate the definition of isometric movement (translation, rotation, symmetry)	Logical Verbal	Understanding Synthesis	Verbal chain Defined concept
8. **Operate** a learning transfer regarding the route of the borders of the figure	Visual Logical	Application Analysis Understanding	Discrimination Concrete concept
9. **Apply** the product of isometries	Visual Logical	Application Analysis Understanding	Motor connection
10. **Identify** the isometric movement from the product of the most axle symmetries	Kinesthetic Visual	Application	Discrimination
11. **Copy** the figures on transparent paper	Kinesthetic Visual	Application	Motor connection
12. **Identify** and describe isometries between the figures given (footprints on the map)	Visual Logical Kinesthetic Verbal	Analysis Synthesis	Discrimination
13. **Draw** on transparent paper symmetrical figures to the ones given	Kinesthetic Visual	Application	Motor connection
14. **Identify** points of symmetry of a figure intersected by the symmetrical axis	Visual	Analysis	Discrimination
15. **Draw** possible symmetrical axes	Kinesthetic Visual	Application	Motor connection

this knowledge and in situations where the learning content becomes a resource for the learner's own ability to reason.

Transcoding in the City of Percentages

In a certain sense, the analysis of the task to define the contents of the simulation game, called City of Percentages, was much more complex. Before continuing further, we would suggest the reader takes a look at Chapter 9.

The main issue here is the level of artificiality with which the concepts are defined and constructed.

The prerequisites (i.e., the necessary information to be able to access the content of the learning unit) are, in this case, of a higher level of abstraction insofar as the code to be used to express the concepts, describe the procedures and apply the rules already lies within the mathematical domain. Indeed, natural numbers, rational numbers, operations of addition, subtraction, multiplication and division with the relative procedures of calculation have already been tackled and should constitute the basis for action. Moreover, it is necessary to be aware of the fact that if whole numbers are placed in relation to operations of addition, it is difficult to imagine problems with the underlying concepts or insurmountable obstacles for the learners in reaching the final result. If, on the other hand, whole numbers are placed in relation to operations dealing with ratios, the situation, albeit more interesting, becomes more complex:

- it becomes more complicated from the point of view of algorithms insofar as one enters a world of decimal numbers;
- it broadens out, because neither whole numbers nor relative numbers contain decimals.

The formal way to express and represent, in mathematical language, the conceptual world of the relationship between numbers and size or magnitude has been one of the most fascinating chapters in the history of numbers and the mathematical edifice as a whole. Moreover, the value numbers have when they can be divided is lost when the numbers taken into consideration are not divisible, and we must introduce wider numerical sets which maintain some prerogatives but not others.

To this end we can, for example, find out what happens when the number 6 is divided by 2, by 3, and then by 4 and 5.

The following results are obtained:

$$6 : 2 = 3$$
$$6 : 3 = 2$$

6: 4 = 1,5
6: 5 = 1,2

If, instead, 7 is divided by 2, then by 3, by 4, by 5, by 6… there's a surprise:

7: 2 = 3,5
7: 3 = 2,333333333333333333…..
7: 4 = 1,75
7: 5 = 1,4
7: 6 = 1,1666666666…….

Finally, let's look at the result of 9 divided by 7:

9: 7 = 1,285714285714 … by continuing till infinity …285714!

So we discover regularity and irregularity, numbers that *after the point* do not have an infinite number of figures, or a sequence that is endlessly repeated.

To understand this better, think of the incommensurability between the side and the diagonal of a square for which the square root of the number 2 leads straight to real numbers.

Decimal numbers, in this sense, aside from expressing a part of an entire number lead us to explore the property of numbers, and this requires skills and instruments that are above the capabilities of primary school children.

The teaching of mathematics continues to mediate between giving children tools to deal with numbers in order to be able to *reckon*, and to help children become aware of the conceptual structures introduced by mathematical thought that relate constructs to reality in order to read and interpret it and to contribute to the possibility of transforming certain aspects.

The choice we made for the design of the *City in Percentages* was to develop a new programme to introduce rational numbers (Moss, J. & and Case R., 1999), that has as a point of reference an evolutionary theory for children's learning of rational numbers within a new model that was the object of the experimental programme. The first point was the percentage of a linear measurement divided in equal parts, understood as a calculating strategy. In the programme two figure decimals were introduced at a later stage, followed then by three figure and one-figure decimals. This choice was based on the consideration that the teachers do not always take account of the spontaneous efforts of the children to understand the meaning of rational numbers, thereby discouraging them from a deeper understanding and favouring, instead, a more mechanical approach.

Rather than an application of the rules and procedures, this simulation game has facilitated exploration of a learning environment and allowed the children to set in motion an analysis of the problem situation that can:

- grasp how the concept of percentages can be applied;
- supply hints and stimuli for the application of the algorithm so that, if the underlying concept is a guideline, it can be transferred to real situations;
- construct a model that supports intuition and leads towards abstraction.

In order to illustrate this process Figure 8 provides analysis of the design of the transcoding pattern in *City of Percentages.*

In this simulation game as well we have made use of Bloom's taxonomy for the definition of the teaching objectives, and carried out a joint reflection on how to stimulate multiple intelligences from the solution of the game.

The results are reported in Table 2.

TWO SCHEMATA FOR THE PROCESS OF ABSTRACTION

The most relevant aspect that can be extrapolated from the proposed courses is that, at every level of abstraction, the concepts and the structures that are the object of the transcoding pattern are conserved. The conceptual, theoretical and applied

Figure 8. The objectives of the simulation game City in Percentages defined according to Gagné

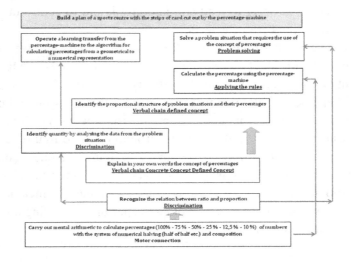

Table 2. Relations between multiple intelligences and teaching objectives according to Bloom's taxonomy and type of learning according to R. Gagné

Objectives	INTELLIGENCE (Gardner)	BLOOM'S TAXONOMY	VARIETIES OF LEARNING (Gagnè)
Carry out mental operations to calculate percentages (100% - 75% - 50% - 25% - 12,5% - 10%) of whole numbers with the system of *numerical halving* (half of half etc.) *and composition*	Verbal Logic Kinesthetics Intrapersonal	Analysis Synthesis	Motor connection
Recognise the relationship between ratio and proportion	Verbal Visual Logic	Analysis	Discrimination
Explain in your own words the concept of percentages	Verbal Visual Logic Kinesthetics	Understanding	Verbal chain Concrete concept Defined concept
Identify quantity by analyzing the data from the problem situation	Verbal Visual Logic	Understanding Analysis Synthesis	Discrimination
Identify the proportional structure of the problem situations and represent them in percentages	Verbal Visual Logic	Analysis	Verbal chain Defined concept
Calculate the percentage using the percentage machine	Verbal Visual Logic Kinesthetics	Understanding Application Synthesis	Application of rules
Solve a problem situation that require the use of the concept of percentages	Verbal Logic	Application Analysis Synthesis	Problem Solving
Operate a learning transfer from the percentage-machine to the algorithm for calculating percentages, from a geometric to a numerical representation	Verbal Visual Logic Kinesthetics Interpersonal *	Application Analysis	Transfer

characterizations examined are geared toward certain of the math learning goals entailing a process of abstraction and the learning that takes place enables the pupils to move towards the "formal-conceptual conception" of mathematics underlined.

The following two schemata represent the proposed structure and can be used to make generalizations to guide the abstraction process.

We underline the fact that " the abstract is not a negation, but a multiplication of the concrete, thus it is multi-concrete [1]." (L.L. Radice and L. Mancini Proia, 1988, p. VI).

The first one refers to the work developed in the first part of the present chapter with particular reference to the work with straws umbrellas hats and glasses. The

Figure 9. The process of abstraction develops in traditional reality

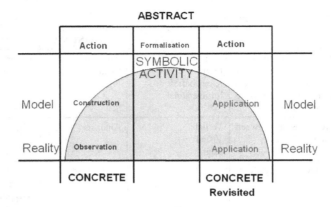

Figure 10. The process of abstraction that develops in ambits in which the reality is a virtual and multi-media one

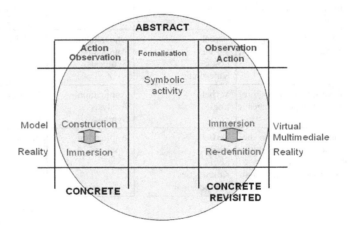

schema in Figure 9 starts from the concrete and returns to the concrete after various phases that lead to the formulation of mathematical language through symbolic activities. This follows a group of actions whose aim is to construct a model structured by the learning environment and the type of teaching used.

The environment is set up to facilitate the discovery of concepts, structures, processes and the application of rules and procedures. Once formulation has been achieved through the symbolic activities, the application of the model of the discoveries enables the learners to apply their acquired competence in similar situations.

The second schema represented in Figure 10 refers to our simulation games and stems from the assumption that children operate in a simulation environment and the term reality is redefined to include virtual as well as traditional reality. In these ambits there i san active process of immersion that can influence the process of abstraction

The circular aspect is highlighted in this schema since the process develops through immersion in an environment that activates processes of abstraction that, in turn, lead to a continuous redefinition of the terms employed, moving step by step towards formal mathematical terms.

REFERENCES

Castelnuovo, E. (1979). *Didattica della matematica.* Firenze: La Nuova Italia.

Chomsky, N. (1986). *La conoscenza del linguaggio: natura, origini e uso.* Milano: Il Saggiatore.

Devlin, K. (2007). *L'istinto matematico. Perché sei anche tu un genio dei numeri.* Milano: Raffaello Cortina.

Dienes, Z. P. (1967). *Costruiamo la matematica.* Firenze: O.S.

Dienes, Z. P. (1969). *Gruppi e coordinate.* Firenze: O.S.

Dienes, Z. P. (1971). *Le sei tappe del processo d'apprendimento in matematica.* Firenze: OS.

Dienes, Z. P. (1973). *Geometria elementare. Relazioni geometriche (schede di lavoro).* Firenze: O.S.

Dienes, Z. P. (1974). *La ricerca psicomatematica.* Milano: Feltrinelli.

Dienes, Z.P. (1991). *Apprendimento dei concetti di matematica e processi mentali.* Cosenza: AIAS.

Dienes, Z. P., & Colding, E. W. (1969). *La geometria delle trasformazioni (3 vol.). Firenze: OS. Dienes, Z.P. (1989). Psicodinamica del processo di astrazione.* Bologna: Cappelli.

Fischbein, E., & Vergnaud, G. (1992). *Matematica a scuola: teorie ed esperienze.* Bologna: Pitagora Editrice.

Fregola, C. (1991). Aritmetica vol. 3-4-5. Geometria Vol. 3-4-5. In M. Laeng (Ed.), *Percorsi Didattici.* Teramo: Lisciani e Giunti.

Fregola, C. (2003). I livelli d'astrazione nell'apprendimento matematico attraverso i materiali montessoriani. In Centro di Studi Montessoriani, *Annuario 2003 – Attualità di Maria Montessori*. Milano: Franco Angeli.

Fregola, C., & Olmetti Peja, D. (2007). *Superare un esame. Come trasformare ansia, emotività e studio in risorse strategiche*. Napoli: Edises.

Gardner, H. (1987). *Formae Mentis. Saggio sulla pluralità dell'intelligenza*. Milano: Feltrinelli.

Gardner, H. (1994). *Intelligenze Multiple*. Milano: Edizioni Anabasi.

Gardner, H. (1995). *L'Educazione delle Intelligenze Multiple*. Milano: Edizioni Anabasi.

Hill, W. F. (2000). *L'apprendimento, una rassegna delle teorie dell'apprendimento in psicologia*. Bologna: Zanichelli.

Montuschi, F. (1987). *Vita affettiva e percorsi dell'intelligenza*. Brescia: La Scuola.

Pellerey, M. (1983). *Per un insegnamento della matematica dal volto umano*. Torino: SEI.

Piu, A. (2002). Isoperimetria: un'esperienza didattica tra musica e matematica. *I problemi della pedagogia*, 1-3, pp. 157-173.

Pontecorvo, C. (Ed.). (1993). *La condivisione della conoscenza*. Firenze: La Nuova Italia.

Resnick, L. B., & Ford, W. W. (1991). *Psicologia della matematica e apprendimento scolastico*. Torino. SEI, Shannon E.E., Weaver W. (1971). *La teoria matematica delle comunicazioni*. Sonzogno: ETAS.

Vergnaud, G. (1994). Le rôle de l'enseignement à la lumière des concepts de schème et de champ conceptuel. In M. Artigue, R. Grass, C. Laborde et P. Tavignot (dir.), *Vingt ans de didactique des mathématiques en France* (pp. 177-191). Grenoble: La Pensée Sauvage.

Vygotskij, L. S. (1990). *Pensiero e linguaggio*. Bari: Laterza.

ENDNOTES

[1] Transcoding in our understanding of the term is drawn from an essay by Lucio Lombardo Radice published in Scienze in 1978 under the title "Un nuovo liv-

ello di astrazione: la teoria delle categorie". The subtitle goes on to state that mathematical progress is marked by the process of abstraction. For roughly a quarter of a century, the author claims, third level abstraction has acquired enormous importance.

2   Cfr. Chapter 5

3   The term pattern is rich in meanings: it can mean form, structure, rule, disposition, distribution, order, regularity, schema, model, design, configuration and also system. According to Devlin K. (2007) pattern indicates a basic motif that imposes itself on a series of phenomena.

4   The term code is defined in the Treccani dictionary as: a group of symbols or characters used, in a given system of the communication, recording or elaboration of information to represent, on the basis of assigned rules, the symbols or characters of another system of communication.

5   The misconceptions represent erroneous images that a child may adopt of concepts. In learning dynamics misconceptions can depend on the information received from the teaching input, rather than from models used in order to abstract a concept. This leads to a partial or distorted representation of the concept as a whole, i.e., in its completeness, correctness and all its formal complexity. When a misconception is formed apart from the wrong learning per se, it can lead to a prejudiced vision that can compromise the perception, intuition, the process of forming hypotheses and deductions and so on.

6   No explicit reference is made to developmental models, but rather to studies into the psychology of learning (Hill, 2000).

7   Cfr. D. Olmetti Peja's essay on the guidelines in the research to find a systematic approach for the teaching of mathematics

8   With regard to transcoding, it is interesting to reflect on the fact that various mathematicians have aimed to translate certain concepts in mathematical code. For example, on the concept of concept itself it is worth studying the observations of Gerald Vergnaud ((Fischbein &Vergnaud, 1992), who made a formula in which a Concept with the letter C with a tern (S, I, s):
S, the set of situations that gives meaning and from which concept takes its meaning;
I, represents the relational invariants the learner activates that are exposed to the activity or mental operation brought into play by the subject, i.e. the learner.
S, the significations, i.e., the symbolisation that from the natural language can cross various codes that aid linguistic understanding and favour the formal representation communicating with an internal representation the subject has constructed. For anyone familiar with this type of representation, Vergnaud's formula, its concision aside is extremely efficient. As for its efficacy this remains to be demonstrated insofar as the definitions proposed are syntheses

of constructs or other definitions requiring a contextualisation in the relevant theories of educational psychology. Vice versa, an educational psychologist who is largely unfamiliar with the typical formulations of abstract algebra runs the risk of not having the key for the combination and elaboration of the contents of knowledge so that such a person is unable to attribute meaning to the type of formalisation proposed.

[9] An important contribuition for this project has been given by Flavia Leonetti in her university tesi: "transcodification in geometry didactic processes" (Rome, 2007)

Section 3
Design and Conduct of the Game

Chapter 8
Design of a Simulation Game for the Learning of Mathematics

Angela Piu
University of L'Aquila, Italy

ABSTRACT

This chapter provides the theoretical and methodological background for the design of simulation games; within this context attention will be focused on the teaching model and the characteristics of the games that have been used in the research. Although aware of the fact that the process of acquiring mathematical knowledge is both complex and non linear, we present the guided stages of the work, in each of which we shall describe the teaching materials employed to help further the didactic aims.

INTRODUCTION

Planning a simulation game for the learning of mathematics in primary school can mean preparing an accurate representation or model of reality[1], presenting a problem situation, in which children can activate a process of discovery, guided by concepts, rules or mathematical structures. Interaction with the model takes place when players act out roles that require coherent behaviour within the context of the game played according to the rules.

DOI: 10.4018/978-1-60566-930-4.ch008

It is clear that, for the simulation game to achieve its learning and social aims, it must be tailored to the needs and level of the players. The various parts of the simulation, moreover, must remain within the logic and procedures of the game, and coherent with the learning aims and the psychological and educational theories (Ballanti, 1988) that supply the background.

The planning of simulation games is a complex task: to invent and produce a simulation game requires skills in syllabus planning in the mathematical field combined with the creativity necessary to ensure that the game is enjoyable, absorbing and instructive for the participants. Experience, moreover, plays an important role along with the knowledge of the main learning stages, the characteristics of the learners, and the practical skills required to ensure the game proceeds in the right direction.

Various skills play an essential role in creating a game and as it is difficult to find them all in just one person, the answer is to build a project team, with each member able to contribute their own expertise, their own creativity, their own knowledge and work together. Anyway, there is another good reason to set up a team: there is no single method on which to base simulation games for the teaching of mathematics, nor universally accepted guidelines on how to go about it.

Notwithstanding, the various situations and contests of possible learning, the multitude of characteristics of the participants of the game and the variety of contents that one can decide to explore in the simulation, it is possible to find a structure on which to base the game or, as some authors like to call it, a "grammar" for the planning of simulation games (Duke, 2007).

This grammar is the result of thoughts on theoretical and empirical processes and it is always necessary to use it to compare the participants' characteristics, the context in which the game is played, and the observations of games in progress.

Starting from these considerations, we intend to carry out a theoretical and methodological investigation on the projection of simulation games for learning mathematics in order to help the readers become competent in the planning of such activities.

This work, therefore, presents a theoretical and methodological frame of reference for simulation games that is the result of the work carried out by our research project, called *Simulandia*. The project concerns simulation games applied to the mathematic field, which involved linking the content and procedures of the games to the educational objectives of the project.

Within this context, the relevant models and the games that have been developed shall be discussed in detail. On the basis of the characteristics highlighted in the model, we shall present- ever bearing in mind the complexity and the non linearity of the activities therein- a clear and detailed guide to the project, divided into distinct phases for each of which there will be a comprehensive list of support materials that, we hope, will be of assistance to anyone who would like to become involved in such work.

A DESIGN THEORY

Given their complexity there is no overall design of simulation games that is valid for every circumstance. Nevertheless, despite the variations in learning situations, types of games and divers possible explorations, it is still possible to detect an architecture on which to base the design process or, as some authors prefer to express it, a *grammar* for the design of simulation games (Duke, 2007) and we would add a syntax of simulation games.

As can be seen from a study of the literature, many authors have identified structural elements and design phases; yet little attention has been paid to the process generated in the design and to its functions in relation to learners and contexts.

Certainly the structural aspects categorized into three areas- contents, context and process- help us to understand the overall structure of the game and its dynamic. At the same time the design phases allow us to take the right decisions in the course of the design of the three areas, supplying a prop for the designer in completing the project and maintaining coherence between the different processes involved.

However, certain aspects are not always rendered explicit:

- the close interdependence between the theoretical side, empirical aspects, the characteristics of the players and the context of the game;
- the process of structuring the project, given its lack of linearity, implies working though clues connected to methodological and theoretical ideas returning often to review the assumptions and even the goals in the light of the empirical results and observation of the game being played (Dick et al., 2005)

These considerations lead us to believe the reflective element is a constant in the design of games, from the start up till the successful conclusion, that can offer a mental map on which traces of the learning process take shape at various times.

THE MODEL AND THE METHODOLOGICAL CHOICES

In the planning of simulation games along with other types of teaching unplanned and ad hoc improvisation are to be avoided; to guarantee a more consistent and structured, and hence more fruitful result, the planning of simulation games must be based on the general educational principles covering such areas as intention, context and rationality.

Researchers, therefore, are required to set themselves a number of specific aims and to identify clearly the best way of achieving them, by combining the goals with the correct choice of technical solutions. Then, the social, cultural and anthropological coordinates in which the educational activity takes place must be studied carefully as well as the human resources and materials available. Finally, a logical scheme is necessary to guide the planning of the simulation from identifying the aims up to the procedures for checking the final educational results (Baldacci, 1994; Piu C., 2001).

Furthermore attention needs to dedicated to the specific elements of the model used and the relevant theories of educational psychology used as a point of reference for methodological decisions, as was the case with the *Simulandia* research project.

The definition of a model[2] allows designers to set up the conceptual architecture, that is to say, the educational orientation based on the concrete hypotheses to be developed through the design of simulation games. In other words, the model enables designers to identify the teleological core, i.e. the main teaching objectives and functions as a guide for the teaching praxis. We are not merely dealing, therefore, with theoretical speculation on vague educational aims and values, nor narrow didactic techniques for teaching, but rather with a conceptual framework in which the various educational aspects can be connected and ordered (Bertin, 1975, p. 77-78). If understood in this way there is no danger of producing a purely didactic technique in the narrowest sense since the project will incorporate both the specific teaching aims with overall educational objectives (Baldacci, 2004).

Figure 1.

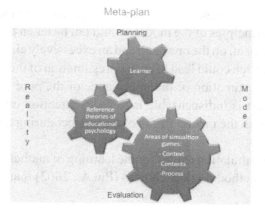

The identified model can be described as interactive-systemic[3] (Piu C., 2007) based on a complex and problematic vision of teaching/learning processes, characterized by an interdependence between subjects and the relevant cultural contexts in the process of the construction and development of knowledge (Semeraro, 1999). The teleological coordinates of this model are defined by the predominance of the "learning process" and that of the "learner", qua subject of learning, in the sense that- within the framework of this model the main aim is to stimulate the growth of higher cognitive processes and the development of the mental abilities of the learner (Baldacci, 2007) using an approach aimed at integrating the behaviourist vision with careful consideration of the internal mental processes that determine the conditions of learning (Gagné, 1973). Essentially learning is considered a work of transformation, a dynamic action on the objects of knowledge, through the communicative relationship between the teacher and pupil, between the pupil and the objects of learning, between the process of learning and that of forming relationships (Piu C., 2007). In this sense, we can talk of the entry of heuristic procedures into the model, that are not aimed at the transfer of pre-packaged knowledge but rather at training the student in the art of learning how to pose, analyze and resolve problems within specific fields of cultural activity.

Two clarifications are required at this point:

1.   We must not misunderstand the term "cognitive process". The aim is to find connections between the culture and the learner, and to harness children's understanding in order to build a bridge that allows the passage from spontaneous to scientific knowledge. The expression "cognitive process" should not necessarily be understood to mean cultural mastery of the symbolic world that helps us understand ourselves and the world around us. The products of culture, in other words, are not presented through codes defined by their conceptual system with the pretext of promoting a higher level of thought, but to launch the construction of these codes through the process of guided discovery;

2.   The guiding principles of the model should not be taken to extremes, if we are to avoid formalism, on the one hand and an excessively child-centred approach on the other, which could lead to an underestimation of the contents of learning and/or an overestimation of the importance of the pure efficiency of mental functions. What is indispensable is to focus attention on the relationship of the contents with the mental forms of the subject during the learning process.

The planning of simulation games for the learning of mathematics proposed here privileges specific methodological choices (Piu A., 2002) that:

- Enable pupils to have experiences that encourage them to analyze "models" of daily reality and to focus attention on the mathematical aspects (Dienes, 1971). In this way, students are stimulated to pull out from the perceived reality of the game the aspects that translate into mathematical facts to help their guided discovery and the formation of mathematical concepts;
- Could help exploration within the rules of the game and in relation to the aims to be pursued, where students are presented with situations perceived to be diverse but of the same conceptual structure. Thanks to these activities the pupil can grasp the concept of the invariant;
- Allow the development of comprehension of the mathematical concepts that proceed toward the symbolic construction that expresses the concept itself, through abstraction to its final formalization. The problem is not just to " give the child adequate schemes, but to launch the child on a search for a significant symbolic representation, in such a way that the symbols have a meaning and that the child can grasp the importance of representation both for understanding and for communication" (Vergnaud, 1994)
- Help the construction of mathematical language, through the definition of a *zone* between the language of the pupils and its evolution towards the mathematical language, giving life to intermediate codes between natural language and mathematical language, through a process of transcoding;
- Can simultaneously promote the cognitive, social aspects and affective aspects of the learning process (Montuschi, 1987; 1993), helping children's exploration and interaction with other subjects. We are resuming the subject widened in Chapter 4.

THE DEFINING ELEMENTS IN PLANNING THE SIMULATION GAME

A simulation game is based on various components that vary according to the educational intentions of the planners, on the dose of creativity and on the educational psychology models used as reference.

Notwithstanding the variety that can be found between different simulation games, they are all structured around the same basic elements, such as: the educational aims, the specific learning aims, the model, the scenario, the problem situation, the aim of the simulation, the roles, the timing, the materials, the documents, the rules, the debriefing, the evaluation system in the game and the overall evaluation.

1. *The goals.* They constitute the horizon of educational values, the general cognitive abilities and the appropriate attitude to promote and develop in the

pupils. These represent the frame of reference that orientates the choice and the definition of the learning aims related to the cultural contents, and facilitates all the other decisions regarding what is to be taught and how best to achieve the teaching aims.

2. *The learning aims.* These concern the pupils' cognitive performance with regards to the aims to be achieved.

3. *The model.* The definition of a model is a necessary basis for structuring the chosen simulation techniques. This, in fact, allows us to: determine the components that are quantified and linked to each other within the system; define the fundamental variables, their nature and their limits; define the working of the model itself in so that it presents valid analogies with the simulated process; finally, to identify the context in which the simulation activity takes place.

4. *The scenario.* The context in which the simulation is collocated, i.e., the setting in which the dynamics of the simulated system take place and the participants operate. It is used to mark out the space in which the action takes place, and thus contributes to defining the roles. It is in this context, in fact, that the protagonists can take on their new identity, on the base of which they can form relations with the other participants.

5. *The theme* or *problem situation.* It indicates the issue, i.e., the problem situation that is to be tackled through which the participants in the simulation will come together. The situation can be a dramatic situation or built up on the base of certain elements of confrontation that can occur in any group that can be developed into a small plot; other situations, a prepared activity that is close to a specific reality or based on speculation about group behaviour, or the learning needs of pupils. Its identification requires considerable attention and precision, because the activity involved in resolving the problem must be perceived as important and relevant by students.

6. *The objective.* This concerns the operative goal that the participants can realistically achieve through their action and the type and level of learning to be pursued.

7. *The roles.* The roles refer to the subjects as participants that have to identify with the simulation game. Depending on the situation, however, the roles and people that act them out can be identified by the group leader, by the members of the group or can be chosen in a random way through drawing lots. Thus, various types of roles can be played out in the simulation, roles that do not always coincide with physical people. The *actual* roles, that are part of the structured game, are acted by the participants. These can be *assigned*, i.e., defined rigidly by rules and goals at the outset, or *functional*, when they are defined during the course of the action, on basis of the general objectives, so they can be modified during the game. Moreover, other types of roles can

make an appearance in the structure of the game: virtual (pseudo-roles) and simulated. The former are invented when particular functions are requested, without influencing the structure of the game, because they do not depend on specific rules and on the overall management of the simulation. They are only used to make the game more dynamic, to clarify the roles by improvising, if necessary, rules on the spot, based on the situation in that specific moment. The coordinators of the simulation and anyone else who intervenes whenever it is considered necessary to help the interaction belong in this category. The *simulated* roles, instead, are inserted in the model, that is to say they participate in the dynamics of the simulation, influencing its structure and its outcomes, although often not impersonated, i.e., they are not acted by anyone.

8. *The documents.* Documentation is necessary for the participants to acquire the information they need; this provides the information about what roles to assume, on the possible existence of other roles, on the scenario, on the central problem and on all the other difficulties that can arise during the simulation. Moreover, further information can be given on how the participants should behave, what power they have, what strategies can be useful. Bambrough (1994) divides the documents used in simulation in: intrinsic and extrinsic. The former are present in the reality of the simulation world; for example, to establish the relation between two roles, a character could receive a letter from another, thanks to which it is possible to establish the role of the character, something about the player's functions or information about other roles. The extrinsic documentation, instead, is given to participants during the presentation of the activity, i.e., before it begins. They inform the participants who they are, what they have to do and so on and can be presented in the form of *role cards*, containing the identity and role of the character and other relevant information.

9. *The materials.* The materials for the simulation game are intended as an intermediary between reality and the mathematical world. Their purpose is not only to act as a concrete reference of the mathematical concept, but also to provide models that are more abstract than the perceived situation and less abstract than formal symbols (Dienes, 1970; Post, 1981). If the materials are not available, they can be created for the game. However, in the case where it is decided to create new materials, it is necessary to bear in mind the practical constraints in terms of time, expertise and human and economic resources.

10. *Materials for representation.* During the course of the simulation game support instruments can be used (maps, plastic cards, wall charts, tables and so on) to offer the participants all the necessary information through visual aids. They

can be used to visualize the scenario and, during the activities, to demonstrate the effects of different decisions taken during the game.

11. *Time.* It is necessary to establish the duration for the running of the simulation. This is always related to the objective and to the level of complexity of the simulation. It is generally preferable to avoid overrunning the allotted time span, but also curtailing or interrupting the game. This is because timing is a fundamental resource, especially when manipulation and material construction are the planned activities.

12. *The rules.* These define the possible actions and the circumstances in which the simulation takes place. They concern how the roles are played and are used to give the necessary information on the game's procedure; the rules set the cycles or stages of the game and the alternating sequences in the role play in every phase, the interaction in the game between the participants and the materials and also the ways in which the pseudo-roles can intervene and so on. The rules are a necessary element, particularly in all those games where there are no properly differentiated roles to act out, since every player operates in the same conditions, and there is no reality to present by analogy, but just a setting in which players make their moves, as for example, in the game Monopoly.

13. *The system of evaluation.* This includes the evaluation criteria, though which "points" are awarded to the participants for various results in the action. It is, in practice, a method to represent the results in competitive games or in those games that have a considerable number of constraints where rules have a predominant role.

14. The final discussion (or *debriefing*). This is the conclusive phase and the final synthesis. After the activity has finished the final discussion allows all the participants to view the simulation in the correct perspective, so that the experience is profitable and consciously understood and absorbed. The time set aside for the discussion represents a central element in the whole experience, because it enables the participants to discuss the results, exchange different opinions and analyze the outcome and the actions used, with the aim of analyzing, systematizing and arriving at generalizations regarding the contents and the mathematical processes presented during the game. The debriefing can be organized in many ways, from an informal discussion to a structured one and accompanied by other forms such as summaries or written comments on the experience.

15. *Evaluation.* This entails the collection and analysis of the data that will allow designers to establish whether, and to what extent, the defined aims set out in the presentation of the project have effectively been achieved, i.e., whether the modifications have really taken place (in knowledge, in attitude, in ability).

Evaluation implies forms of verification on the simulation process through check lists defining the indicators of the process regarding single items of knowledge, capacities and abilities that characterize the concepts, rules, structures to be discovered and coded in mathematical language. Finally, the affective dimension should not be overlooked, their motivational influence in terms of participation and involvement are also the object of the data collection and study.

THE PHASES OF THE PLANNING

The complexity of the simulation game itself (see the games presented in this text and used in the experiment) and the chain of decisions to be taken in the planning of the project require a series of distinct phases to guarantee their educational efficiency.

Creativity, moreover, as specified in the introduction, plays an important role in the planning activity and has to be combined with technical skills and experience gained over time. In other words, it means to follow a path, to use the analogy of the painter when planning a work of art, who proceeds from the sketch to the painting, from the initial idea to the final stage. We do not want to overestimate the artistic dimension of planning simulation games, but simply mark the complexity of a non linear process, where the designer returns, time and time again, on the basis the empirical results, to review the aims and how to achieve them (Dick et al., 2005). In spite of a certain lack of continuity involved in the planning process, it is possible to distinguish five distinct phases that, following the analogy of the artist, are presented below.

- Phase 1. *The sketch.* The first ideas are jotted down from which the single components will take shape to become the work of art.
- Phase 2. *The lights and the shadows.* The details of the work are defined using the appropriate techniques to create the right atmosphere in a coherent framework.
- Phase 3. *The final brushstrokes.* Modifications are made to improve the final product.
- Phase 4. *The painting.* Reflection on the work as a whole, after considering the modifications to the completed work.
- Phase 5. *The user.* Advice is given on the right setting of the work to guarantee a suitable environment in which it will be used to its full advantage.

The Sketch

It is the initial phase of the planning of the simulation game during which the first ideas are mapped out in relation to the aims, around which a coherent background of planning principles and relevant psychological theories will be filled in. It represents the most creative phase of the planning process, when the drawing of the plan starts to take shape; the sketch, to continue the analogy, will guide the implementation and construction of the following phases and will be the basis on which the game's effectiveness will be assessed.

In spite of the fact it is the most crucial phase of the entire planning process, and provides the scaffolding of the simulation game, it is the least understood and most underestimated. The authors of the game, in fact, often jump over or pass around this phase and start directly on the construction of the game that, as a result, becomes more costly, less efficient and less effective (Duke, 2007).

In this phase there are many questions that need to be addressed and planning principles to be decided upon, all of which can be expressed in a coherent way in a concept report.

This represents a permanent outline of the characteristics of the game to be developed and a record of the reasons for the choices made at the beginning of the operational phase (Duke, 2007) starting from which an initial evaluation can be undertaken. In other terms, the concept report has two main aims:

- the drawing up of the project to guide the construction and the implementation process;
- the base on which the final product will be assessed.

As a guide for the completion of the report, the Table 1 provides a series of questions, the answers to which can be used to fill in the document.

The answers to these questions can be reported in the concept report in various ways: written out in full using natural language or summarized in concepts and reported in conceptual maps or diagrams (Duke, 2007). Once this job is finished, and before starting the next phase, it is preferable to carry out an initial evaluation, essentially to verify if the design phase has been developed in a coherent and playful manner. The analytical categories for the evaluation of the concept report are listed and developed below in the Table 2.

If the evaluation on the *concept report* is not positive, it is preferable not to proceed further but to reflect on the answers in the report; otherwise- if the feedback is positive- the simulation game can begin, and we can proceed to the following phases.

Table 1.

Stimulation questions for the elaboration of project	
Aim	What is the aim of the game? Educational, training, recreational.?
Intentions	In what context is the game played? Is the game planned to be used in an educational environment? Which disciplinary fields does it cover?
Educational objectives	What are the educational objectives?
Problem situation	What problem situation is proposed? Which and how many solutions can it have? How is it proposed?
Reference theory	Which theory is used as reference for the construction of the game? What is its role in guiding the planning decisions?
Model of reality	What are the defining characteristics of the model considered? What is the isomorphic relationship between the model and reality, in terms of structural extension and level of detail? What scenario is derived from this? How are the above related to the components of the game?
Symbolic structure	How will the rules, concepts and principles be tested in the simulation game? How will they be encoded and decoded? What language and symbols will be used?
Type of game	What type of organization is envisaged for the participants? Individuals, groups, teams? Will competition or cooperation be the guiding principle? What will be the rules and the restrictions?
Characteristics of participants	What age are they? What level of competence is required? What is the optimum number of participants?
Roles	How many roles are envisaged and what are they? What are their characteristics? How do they interact?
Evaluation (in the game)	What goals will participants aim for? How will it be decided when they have been achieved? How will points be scored and recorded?

Table 2.

Analytical Categories	
Overall coherence	This refers to the coherence between the underlying psychological theory, the main aims and the model of reality in which the methodology and operative aspects can be played out.
External coherence	This refers to the isomorphism between reality and the model on which the simulation game is based.
Internal coherence	This refers to the coherence, interdependence and between every component of the simulation game in the defined model of reality.
Playability	This refers to whether the rules help to make the game an enjoyable and instructive experience. (Duke, 2007)

This is made up by the following headings: educational goals, requirements, specific aims, scenario, problem situation, aims of the simulation, running phases, rules, materials, documents, debriefing, evaluation system and evaluation of learning. (For a full description of each case we refer you to the fourth paragraph of this chapter, while for a concrete example see Chapter 9.)

Light and Shadows

The analogy used to give a name to this phase is efficient and to the point. The light and shadows that we can appreciate in a work of art, especially in a painting, in the art of painting, represent the correct balance between the artist's talent and the successful application of the technique the artist chooses to express the inspiration. To move outside the analogy for a moment, this means that this phase represents the meeting point or node between the idea of how the simulation game should develop, that has already been established in the previous phase, and the real collocation this can have in the process of learning/teaching mathematics. Thus, this phase represents the implementation of the game itself in didactic terms and the complete assembly of all the components that will make up its final shape. For this reason it requires more precision for the development of the game on the base of the chosen model and the decisions taken in terms of all the educational processes involved; thus the importance of careful attention to detail.

The decisions to be taken relate to the specific aims of learning and to the processes and didactic procedures used in the game. Such decisions, that can be made through reference to the questions provided in the report, will help the user complete the phase by filling in the uncompleted parts. (Table 3)

After answering these questions it is possible to finish filling in the documentation. Once the project in all its parts has been completed it is possible to proceed with its revision, using the following analytical categories. (Table 4)

At this point we are in possession of the project of the simulation game. Before starting the next phase it is important to compare the initial concept report of the simulation game and the project itself to check the congruency between the reasons for the choices made and the implementation of the game, using the analytical categories of the sketch. In the case that significant differences arise it will be necessary to go over the previous phases and use all the support instruments again to check the project and/or the concept report. In the case where there are no notable differences, it is now possible to proceed to finding the materials, or to create them if necessary, and to the elaboration of the documents to be attached to the game.

In this way the construction and the assembly are also completed, so that the planners themselves can "enter" the game situation and put the operations into action; and take the decisions required for the game to be played correctly. This involves identifying with the simulation game so that the participants fully enter their roles, thereby providing another test for the planners.

Final Fine-Tuning

Once the previous phase has been completed the next step is to play the game; this begins by introducing the game to a group of suitable participants. Returning to the analogy of the artist, this may mean making modifications to improve the overall

Table 3.

Stimulating questions for elaboration of the plan	
General/specific aims	What are the general aims? What are the specific aims?
Requirements	What knowledge is required by pupils to be able to undertake this learning activity successfully?
Construction of mathematical concepts and problem situation	What is the problem situation proposed? Which mathematical aspects will be focused on? Which audio-visual aids and materials are required in the game to help the formation of mathematical concepts, the discovery of rules and invariable structures? What degree of formalization of mathematical language is to be developed? Are intermediate codes between the natural language an mathematical language included in the plan?
Definition of Space and Time.	What spatio-temporal configurations are assumed? How is space delineated? How is time defined in the model? How does it act in the game? With respect to the time dimension, are there any precise references?
The roles	How are the roles and their characteristics explained? What is the interaction between the roles and the scenario? What is the contribution of each role to the solution of the problem situation?
Materials	What type of materials do you intend to use? Are they commercially available or do you have to create them? What principles will they be based on?
Rules, instructions and warnings.	Which rules and what information do you intend to give? Is it necessary to give any warnings?
Running of the game	How is the game to be managed? Which and how many phases are envisaged?
Documents	Are documents necessary to inform the participants on the details of the game? Which and how many are needed?
Feedback	What type of tests are to be used? What is to be verified? Process and /or product? When is assessment to be carried out? Which instruments have been chosen to verify the achievement of the aims? Which instruments are to be used for the evaluation of affective and motivational aspects?

Table 4.

Analytical categories	
1. Coherence of the didactic planning	
a. Internal coherence.	This refers to the connections between the parts. It means verifying if: the goals, the main and specific aims, the requirements and the contents are closely interconnected; the goals, the general and specific aims can be attained for every role defined in the project; the contents can be discussed by the pupils depending on their age .
b. Conformity of every component with the participants	This refers to the "do-ability" of the problem situation and to the scenario in which it is set with respect to the attainment of the general and learning aims. In other terms, it means verifying if the problem situation is a suitable vehicle both for the game itself and the learning aims.
c. Coherence in the running of the game	This refers to the coherent running of the game in all its phases, with the methodology, the goals, the main and specific aims and the materials.
d. Validity and reliability of test instruments	This refers to the coherence between the instruments of verification and the specific objectives to be verified, and involves assessing whether the tests, chosen or made for the purpose, are capable of assessing whether the objectives have been met, and whether the test procedures perform in a reliable manner overall.
2. Clarity of the language	This refers to assessment of the language used in the game plan.
3. Completeness	This refers to assessing the definition of the detail in all the components of the game.

effect of the work of art, i.e. to perfect the painting by some final fine-tuning so that the viewer or user can appreciate the work to the full.

To realize this goal careful observation is required of the participants while playing the simulation game in order to test its functioning, in terms of:

- verifying of the running of the game in all its phases to identify particular problems that may lead to communication breakdowns or interruptions;
- calibration of the materials used, in particular those found or created for the hands-on activities;
- verifying the appropriateness and the clarity of the rules;
- verifying the level of participation;
- recording the timing of the game.

Table 5.

Check list for the management of the game	
1. Running of the game	Verify the execution of the game with respect to the points listed as follows, for every single phase in the project.
a. Constructing the phases	Verify the completion of every phase of the simulation game
b. Participation of the pupils in each phase: -interaction -use of materials and resources	Identification of participation in the single phases of the game, involvement and interaction (in terms of number of interventions, the participation of every player and the quality of the interaction) and use of materials and resources (by whom and how often).
c. Use of space in each phase	Verify the function of all the spaces used.
d. Running time: total and for each phase	Recording the timing of each phase and of the total time
e. Briefing	Timing of the briefing and identification of difficulties.
f. Debriefing	Timing of the debriefing, identification of the difficulties and feedback from players prompted if necessary by group leader.
2. Application of the rules	Keeping track of how the rules have been applied and of the difficulties found
a. Instructions	Comprehension of instructions, and identifying misunderstandings
b. Rules	Verifying the application of the rules
3. Achieving the aims of the game.	Recording the achievement of the aims of the game.
4. Identification of roles.	Participants' identification with their roles.
5. Materials: easy to use.	Problems arising with use of the materials.
6. Understanding the documents.	Adequate comprehension of the language used.

Numerous problems can arise during the running of the game, which can, given its complexity, pass unobserved at the time. For this reason it is essential to prepare very carefully for the observation that should continue throughout the entire length of the game and, to this end, a checklist, reported in detail in the Table 5, has been proposed.

At the end of the feedback the data is analyzed with the aim of signalling problems found during each phase of the game, which are then analyzed in light of reports by the observers and by the participants, i.e., by the pupils and by the teachers/leaders themselves.

Wherever the employment of an assessment test is envisaged, then an item analyses is made of the assessment test to verify the reliability of the test as a whole and on the functioning of the single items, using a big enough sample of pupils with similar characteristics to those for whom the assessment is made, in order to fine-tune its workings and produce a definitive version.

As in the other phases, if problems inherent in the running of the game emerge that cannot be solved by minor adjustments, being related to the structure of the game per se, it is necessary to revise the entire plan, by going through all the previous phases. If, on the other hand, there are no problems you can move on to the final fine-tuning.

The Painting

In this phase we look back at the overall progress of the project, that is carefully reconsidered with reference to the concept report; this involves, in other words, a painstaking examination of all the components of the game, i.e. a phase of careful retrospective analysis, to complete the artist's work, as in the analogy, by reflecting on what has been created.

This does not mean questioning the main scaffolding of the game, but a fine-tuning of each component.

In this phase whose main function is that of monitoring the overall structure in relation to every single component of the project, attention should be paid to the language used in the plan. It is desirable to check that it is not overegged with technical terms nor oversimplified with misleadingly imprecise terminology, but at a suitable level for the users.

The Users

The planning process does not end with the revision of the project but requires the subsequent development of an appendix that incorporates feedback on the conduct of the game, so that the goals expressed in the planning are explicitly related to the outcome of the game.

It is advisable to attach a document with the aims of the game and the context in which it is to be used, instructions and advice on its conduct, a description of materials as well as the necessary information on how the game should be played and how to apply the rules (for an example of such guidelines, see Section 1 and 2 of the Experiment Document - Chapter 12 - and the teacher's notes - Chapter 9).

One important note, moreover, concerns the set of suggestions and instructions for the management of unforeseen situations that can arise during the course of the game.

REFERENCES

Baldacci, M. (1994). *Insegnare a programmare*. Milano: Ethel-Gìorgio Mondadori.

Baldacci, M. (Ed.). (2004). *I modelli della didattica*. Roma: Carocci.

Ballanti, G. (1988). *Modelli di apprendimento e schemi di insegnamento*. Teramo: Lisciani&Giunti.

Bambrough, P. (1994). *Simulations in English Teaching*. Philadelphia: Open University Press.

Bertin, G. M. (1975). *Educazione alla ragione*. Roma: Armando.

Dick, W., Carey, L., & Carey, J. O. (2005). *The systematic design of instruction* (6th ed.). Boston, MA: Pearson.

Dienes, Z. P. (1970). *Costruiamo la matematica*. Firenze: OS.

Dienes, Z. P. (1971). *Le sei tappe del processo d'apprendimento in matematica*. Firenze: OS.

Duke, R. D. (2007). *Gaming: il linguaggio per il futuro*. Bari: Edizioni La Meridiana.

Fregola, C. (1996). *Pragmatica della progettazione didattica: Esperienze a scuola, nella formazione e in azienda*. Cosenza: Bios.

Gagnè, R.M. (1973). *Le condizioni dell'apprendimento*. Roma: Armando.

Montuschi, F. (1987). *Vita affettiva e percorsi dell'intelligenza*, Brescia: La Scuola.

Montuschi, F. (1993). *Competenza affettiva e apprendimento*, Brescia: La Scuola.

Piu, A. (2002). *Processi formativi e simulazione*. Roma: Monolite.

Piu, C. (2001). *Autonomia scolastica: un'identità da ricercare*. Roma: Ma. Gi.

Piu, C. (2007). *Riflessioni di natura didattica*. Roma: Monolite.

Post, T. (1971). The Role of Manipulative Materials in the Learning of Mathematical Concepts. In *Selected Issues in Mathematics Education* (pp. 109-131). Berkeley, CA: National Society for the Study of Education and National Council of Teachers of Mathematics, McCutchan Publishing Corporation.

Sacco, P., & Spataro, E. (1989). La progettazione di un gioco formativo di simulazione. *Osservatorio ISFOL*, 1.

Semeraro, R. (1999). *La progettazione didattica. Teorie, metodi, contesti*. Firenze: Giunti.

Vergnaud, G. (1994). *Le rôle de l'enseignement à la lumière des concepts de schème et de champ conceptuel*. In M. Artigue, R. Grass, C. Laborde & P. Tavignot (Eds.), *Vingt ans de didactique des mathématiques en France* (p. 177-191). Grenoble: La Pensée sauvage.

ENDNOTES

[1]   In general, it is well known that a *model* can be proposed as a theoretical scheme or as a prototype built with the aim of being studying a situation, an object, or one or more real phenomena. A *model of reality* makes it possible to reproduce elements of a specific reality that requires being studied, described, analyzed, and represented. Thanks to the characteristics of direct or indirect reproducibility of these objects, we can catch the structure of that reality, some of its characteristics or behaviors considered fundamental for the type of research carried out. In this way it is possible to make inferences on the functioning of the model and, thus, on the elements of reality, that we want to study. In this sense, the construction of a model can represent one key stage of the research methodology, applied, in our case, to the teaching of mathematics.

[2]   Numerous studies, each based on a different didactic phenomenology, have given rise to a considerable number of different didactic models, some of which are based on common considerations. The reasons for these differences depend on the ideology or the school of thought within the scientific community to which each researcher belongs.

[3]   The author identifies three distinct didactic models: rationalist-informationist, interactive-systemic, and socio-educational constructivist.

Chapter 9
Description of Games

Angela Piu
University of L'Aquila, Italy

Cesare Fregola
Roma Tre University, Italy

Anna Santoro
Istituto Comprensivo Statale San Giuliano Milanese, Italy

ABSTRACT

The chapter defines the criteria on which the choices for the design and realisation of the simulation games were based as well as the educational goals. Two simulation games are presented, one for geometry the other for arithmetic; these are supplemented by the relevant documentation, a description of the materials and the observation and verification instruments.

INTRODUCTION

The term "simulation" is commonly understood to be associated with virtual reality, such as video animation and computer games. In this work, however, we use simulation to refer to the simulation games carried out in the classroom; these games make use of every day materials and have meaningful goals. This choice was made because it was felt such games could creatively involve learners with the target subjects (arithmetic and geometry) in a primary school context.

At the outset the members of the research team established the criteria for the project, some of which were later redefined after the experimental phase. Numerous

DOI: 10.4018/978-1-60566-930-4.ch009

discussions were carried out before a final decision was made to leave to one side the more widely cited criteria from the literature relating to the fields of economics, the handling of money or probability.

Indeed, from the analysis of these games, a picture emerged of generally complex situations requiring problem solving and decision-making skills, through which it became possible to amplify the selected phenomena or the underlying structures. In this way the pupils could acquire, stimulate and improve competences and skills transferable to real situations that it would be difficult to study at the same place and time without the utilisation of a simulation game.

Apart from focusing attention on the appropriate conditions in which learning can take place, our research efforts were engaged in the pragmatics of learning/ teaching mathematics.

The research group chose, therefore, to design simulation games to further the construction of mathematical thought and to help learners develop a positive attitude towards mathematics (Domenici G. & Frabboni F, 2007). In other words the group decided to design games with the aim of:

- Launching the guided discovery of certain mathematical concepts and the gradual acquisition of mathematical language. The simulation games are specially designed for the purpose of achieving the aims laid down in the math syllabus in a sheltered environment; students are set mathematical problems, and through their resolution they begin to perceive the universality of mathematical concepts and develop the process of abstraction, defining symbols which can be used later to represent formalised concepts;
- Promote a positive image of mathematics as a worthwhile and important discipline, not just a set of rules to be learnt by heart and applied but rather to be "appreciated and used to set or tackle problems and explore and perceive the relations and structures in nature and human creations" (Domenici G & Frabboni F, 2007, p. 228-229).

When designing the games the research group was very careful to use the guidelines laid down in the literature studied at the beginning of the project and theories of educational psychology for the overall decisions on the rules and materials for each game.

Leaving aside for the moment the specific details of each game, which will be examined at a later stage, other decisions were taken relating to the type of game, its practicality and conduct.

In order to capture the interest of the children it was decided to start by clarifying the aims of the game to raise their curiosity and start them working on the problem situation. In the conduct of the game, a collaborative approach was adopted between children and teacher, i.e., a high level of interaction was a necessary precondition for a successful outcome.

In the design phase the research group decided to supply a highly detailed and structured guide for the debriefing with the aim of guaranteeing that in the final discussion conducted by the teacher close attention would be paid to the key mathematical concepts and processes covered. It was, moreover, decided to supply suggestions on how to manage the different phases of the game, the materials and the instruments for assessing the learning and the final results.

In the following sections two simulation games are presented that were designed especially for this research work: one in the geometrical field and the other mathematical.

The simulation game titled *Cardland* introduces the study of isometrics, while the other game, *The City in percentages*, introduces, as its name implies, the study of percentages.

For each game, the following sections will describe not just the design of the game with relevant documentation, but also the materials and the instruments used for testing and observation.

CARDLAND: A SIMULATION GAME ON THE INTRODUCTION OF ISOMETRY

Requirements

Define in your own language the meaning of:

- Equality
- Distance
- Movement
- To be able to cut out shapes.

Specific Aims

- To identify direct and inverse congruent shapes.
- To define the concept of isometry.
- To identify isometric characteristics in relation to shape, direction and movement.
- To identify direct and inverse congruent shapes using translation, rotation, symmetry or by combining translation and rotation.

- To invent and use an economic "code" shared by the group to communicate isometric characteristics.

Scene

"Cardland" is a relaxed little town where millions of card-inhabitants live out their lives peacefully. One day a deafening noise of crumpling paper, continuous and unstoppable, suddenly awakens the card-inhabitants. It is the sudden movements of the card investigators, that are circling round town. –What has happened?- The inhabitants ask themselves- A horrible theft!- Who was it?- The inhabitants ask themselves- We definitely must find the culprit and have the geographical map back! So the search starts, while the crumpling noise gets even more deafening.

Problem Situation

How can the players go about achieving their aim? And who will be in charge of the investigation? The card-investigators are consulted, and given the task of carrying out the investigation; they immediately rush to the scene of the crime: the card-museum. They close the main door, to avoid tourists entering; then to conduct the investigation they start to collect:

- a series of different sized footprints on the floor of the room of the card-museum;
- a camera, situated on the wall on the right of the map, that takes pictures every time someone gets close to it and records them in the form of shapes;
- a camera, situated on the wall on the left of the entrance of the museum.

After searching for all the evidence the card-investigators along with the isometric experts examine minutely all the material listed in the card-lab.

Aims of the Simulation

- The return of the map.
- Search for the thief on the basis of the evidence available.
- Communicate to the card-general how the investigations have been conducted in the card-lab.

The aim of the game, therefore, is to be able to find the geographical map and search for the culprit on the basis of the evidence available. Once the guilty party is found, he will have to hand back the map; to be certain the investigations have been carried out in a rigorous and scientific manner, it must be demonstrated that the alleged culprit really is the guilty party. For this reason all the different steps in the investigation must be submitted to the assessment of the card-general, in the card-lab, in the special "isometry" section.

Phases

1. To start with you can analyze the mat with the footprints and identify those which have "crossed" all the mat. This can be done within the card-lab, by following all the instructions on how to use the instruments available and the rules.
2. Once the footprints have been identified, if they belong to different characters, you can proceed, to be sure not to be mistaken, by analyzing the photographs (that will be handed out during this phase), i.e., compare the shapes of the photographs taken in front of the map with those taken at the entrance of the museum. At the end of the game the participants, before declaring who is guilty, have to say how the investigations in the card-lab have been undertaken.

Rules for the Card Lab

To be able to carry out the work in the card-lab it is necessary to stick to the following rules.

After copying the footprints and/or the shapes on the transparencies, superimpose them and see if they match. This operation can be done in different ways:

1. You can "slide" sideways, forwards and backwards, the footprint or the shape pictured on the transparency, without lifting the sheet from the surface
2. You can "rotate" the picture by placing a drawing pin on the corner of the transparency
3. You can "overturn" the transparency maintaining the same distance from the border of the sheet of the pictures (footprints or shapes)
4. You can "slide" sideways, forwards and backwards, the footprint or shape pictured on the transparency and then rotate it by placing a drawing pin on the corner.

It is not always possible to use all these methods to compare the pictures, so the players need to discuss the different possible ways to proceed in every single situation. Every time the methods discussed are used (points 1, 2, 3, 4), moreover, participants need to note briefly on a piece of paper what has been done in order to be able to report it to the card general. One or more symbols can be invented to remind you what has been done and what has changed on the footprint or shape after the work with the transparency.

Number of Participants

6/7 children

Documentation

Letter from the Mayor for the Card-Investigators

Letter of the Mayor

Welcome to "Cardland"…
Hello my friends, I am Mr. Castor Rino, the mayor of Cardland.
Have you ever been to Cardland?
It's an extravagant little town shaped like a tree, situated on Cartoon island, where nature is preserved and its inhabitants live happily.
But something has broken the peace of this town: a horrible theft!
Yes, you have understood properly, an actual theft.
It's happened in the Cardland museum.
The inestimable Map of the town has been robbed.
Unfortunately it's not a normal map,
But the FIRST MAP,
Precious symbol of the town, that our ancestors made with a very rare golden bark paper.
Who is the thief?
Ooh…this is a MISTERY!
Straight away I called in my faithful Card-police,
But they are working in the dark and
Really don't know how to solve the case…
NOW IT'S UP TO YOU!
I've sent you this letter because
I believe in your enormous investigative skills.
Are you ready?
Well, I award you the title of CARD-INVESTIGATORS!
Good work…but most of all…GOOD LUCK!

Materials

- 1 photograph of the map
- 1 photograph of Cardland
- 1 mat: a long piece of paper on which the different footprints are drawn
- 3 photographs (shapes) taken in front of the geographical map
- 4 photographs (shapes) taken at the entrance of the museum
- transparencies; markers for the transparencies; drawing pins, blank sheets of paper

Roles

Card-Investigators
Card-General

Debriefing

The following provides suggestions on how to conduct the discussion that the teacher will lead at the end of the game. These can be used as a guide for a comprehensive and exhaustive discussion, that could begin by the teacher inviting the students to give their impressions of the game. After, the students will be encouraged to talk about the game in more detail, in order to bring out all the elements related to the learning units. The following list provides the main mathematical contents of the game and questions to be used for their systemization and generalization. The parts in brackets represent possible answers that the teacher can refer to during the discussion:

1. **Congruency.** During the game you have superimposed many footprints and shapes. Were they all the same or congruent as mathematicians say? When can we say two pictures are congruent? Try to remember the footprints of the thief! (If two footprints, shapes or pictures overlapped perfectly! That is if we are able to match two pictures in every point). For the moment this is good enough!

2. **Direct and inverse congruency.** To superimpose the footprints what movement did you use? Did you use the same movement to superimpose the right footprint with the right one and the left one with the right one? What differences did you notice when you made the superimposition? (For example, to superimpose the footprints of the right foot you have to drag the transparency or you have to rotate it, while to superimpose the footprint of the left foot with the footprint of the right foot you have overturned the picture on the transparency. Therefore, in the first case you have superimposed the two footprints

of the right foot by a surface movement, while in the second case you have superimposed the right footprint with the left one with a spatial movement). Well done! So in the first case we can talk about direct congruency, and in the second case about inverse congruency. Now let's try to make a geometrical picture! Which one do you suggest? What happens in this case?

3. **Direction and surface.** Which differences have you noticed as regards the surface after making the movement? And what about the distance of the path? (The direction of the path and the surface do not change in the case of a direct congruency but rather in the case of inverse congruency).

4. **The symbols of the code.** Mathematicians, when they speak among themselves, often use symbols to be precise and to make their discussions quicker. What symbols have you used to describe all these changes? How have you chosen these symbols? Let's compare and discuss them together! Mathematicians call the "dragging" translation; for rotation they use the same word and they refer to overturning as symmetry.

5. **Isometric definition.** So far we have analyzed what varies and what does not after moving the footprints. So, what does not change? (The pictures remain the same after the movement: the dragging, the rotation and the overturning. In particular, the distance, "metry" (metros) from the word isometry, between the points of the pictures remains the "same" (thus, iso). For this reason mathematicians have decided to call the movements that maintain the same distances between points of a geometric figure isometries).

6. **Summary.** Now let's sum-up what has been said so far! And…thank you for your attention!

Figure 1.

	Translation	**Rotation**	**Axial symmetry (with an external axis)**
The direction of the path covered on the border	Remains unchanged	Remains unchanged	Changes
The surface of the shape	Remains unchanged	Remains unchanged	Changes
The movement	Occurs on the plain	Occurs on the plain	Occurs in space
The shape	Is not distorted	Is not distorted	Is not distorted
Inside the shape	The distances between its points remain constant	The distances between its points remain constant	The distance between its points remain constant

Duration

Explanation
65 min
Debriefing

Evaluation

The methodology takes into consideration, not just the planned verification but also intermediate and final testing strategies aimed at achieving the results through the simulation process.

Figure 2.

Learning...	Pupils									%
	1	2	3	4	5	6	7	8	9	
Recognizes congruent shapes										
Distinguishes inverse congruent shapes from direct congruent shapes										
Defines in his/her own words the meaning of isometry										
Distinguishes examples of isometry										
Identifies the characteristics of translation in relation to direction, side and movement										
Identifies the characteristics of rotation in relation to direction, side and movement										
Identifies the characteristics of symmetry in relation to direction, side and movement										
Identifies isometric differences										
Produces symbols to represent isometric characteristics										
Uses the symbols of the "code" decided by the group										
Uses procedure to verify isometry										
Verifies isometry, using the correct procedure to address a problem										
Observations...										
....										
....										
....										

Notes for the Teacher (Who Conducts the Simulation Game)

Some necessary information is proposed for the management of the game, please do not tell the students about it during the running of the game, in order not to invalidate its outcome. This information can be made explicit to the students, in the case it has not emerged spontaneously, only at the end of the game and it can be used exceptionally as suggestions and not as detailed information, to guide students only if they have difficulties. In this case please write down what the problem was and what type of suggestion was made.

Description of the Mat

The mat presents footprints belonging to certain characters, and some random footprints, positioned as follows:

- 3 routes are directed towards the location of the map, i.e., they pass by the site where the robbery took place;
- 1 route goes in another direction;
- some footprints are scattered on the mat and do not follow any route. In other words these are distractions.

Application of the Rules

The Mat (Phase 1)
The routes of the alleged robbers, revealed by the footprints, correspond to the three routes directed towards the location of the map. All three of them are possible: in fact, they are all verifiable by using isometry (translation, rotation, symmetry, or by using a combination of these). The students, therefore, have to verify, footprint by footprint, that have used at least one of the rules. It is essential that attention be paid to the process of recognising isometry by following the rules on the "cardlab". We underline the fact that the aim is not to arrive quickly at the end of the route but rather to carry out all the comparisons before going on to the next phase.

The Shapes (Phase 2)
After the analysis of the mat, the identity of the thief can be uncovered by comparing the shapes of the three characters, whose shoe has a similar shape to the footprint. In other words every single shape photographed in front of the stolen map has to correspond (by symmetry) to the shape photographed at the entrance of the museum. But through symmetry we can verify that the shapes are the same for just one of the three characters, that is for the thief.

Figure 3. Cardland

Figure 4. The first map

Figure 5. Mat's structure

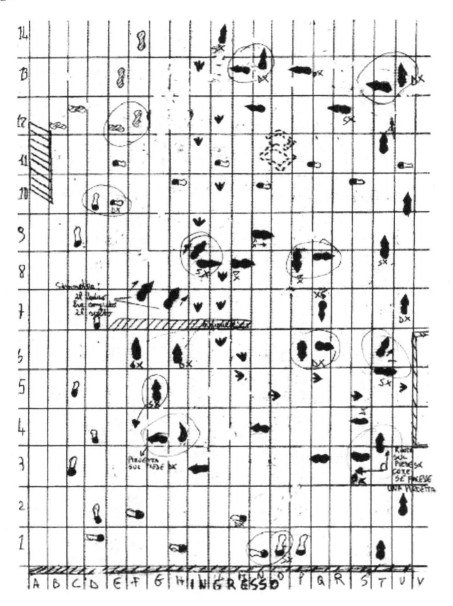

The reason is the following:

• the photographs in front of the map were taken a week before the theft;

Figure 6. The shapes

• the photographs at the entrance of the museum can only belong to the day of the theft.

This means the thief must be one of the characters photographed the day of the theft at the entrance of the museum.

Figure 7. Verification test

Look at the figures and put a tick in the right box	
1. Are the two figures congruent? 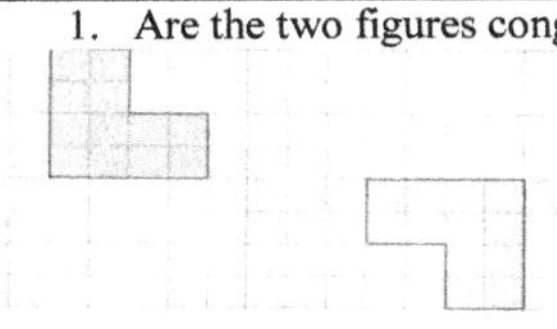	☐ yes ☐ no
2. Are the two figures congruent? 	☐ yes ☐ no
3. Are the two figures directly congruent? 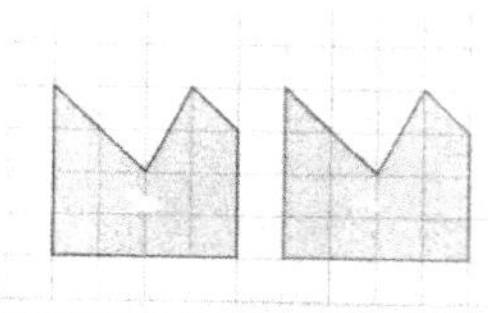	☐ yes ☐ no
4. Are the two figures inversely congruent? 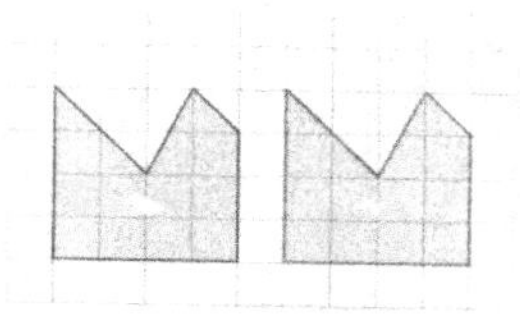	☐ yes ☐ no
5. The figures are 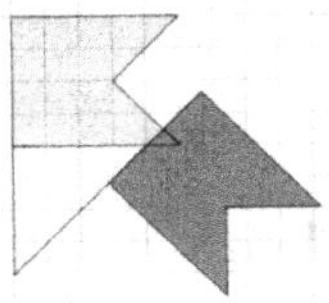	☐ inversely congruent ☐ translated/transferred ☐ not congruent ☐ directly congruent

Figure 8. Verification test (continued)

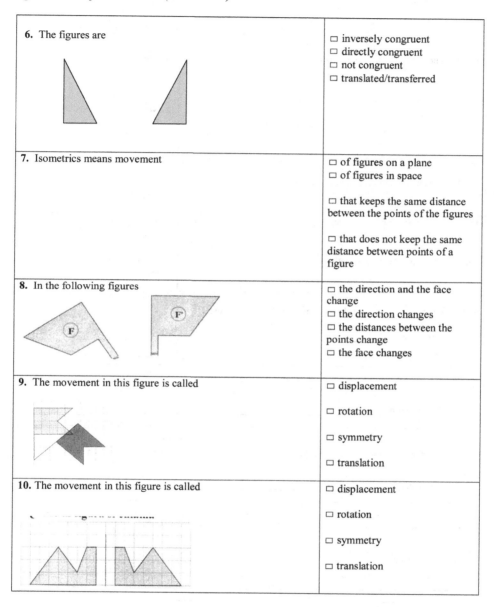

6. The figures are	☐ inversely congruent ☐ directly congruent ☐ not congruent ☐ translated/transferred
7. Isometrics means movement	☐ of figures on a plane ☐ of figures in space ☐ that keeps the same distance between the points of the figures ☐ that does not keep the same distance between points of a figure
8. In the following figures	☐ the direction and the face change ☐ the direction changes ☐ the distances between the points change ☐ the face changes
9. The movement in this figure is called	☐ displacement ☐ rotation ☐ symmetry ☐ translation
10. The movement in this figure is called	☐ displacement ☐ rotation ☐ symmetry ☐ translation

To identify the thief, reflect on the fact the thief is the only character you can see in the photograph in front of the map.

The thief has the same symmetric profile as the one in the photo in front of the map, the one that you are observing.

Figure 9. Verification test (continued)

11. The movement in this figure is called 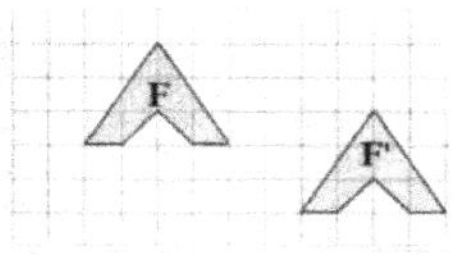 	☐ displacement ☐ rotation ☐ symmetry ☐ translation
12. In translation the movement occurs	☐ on the plane ☐ in space
13. In rotation the movement occurs	☐ on the plane ☐ in space
14. In symmetry the movement occurs	☐ on the plane ☐ in space

Now explain the meaning of these terms in your own words:

1. **Isometry**_____
   _____
   _____
   _____

2. **Translation**_____
   _____
   _____
   _____

3. **Rotation**_____
   _____
   _____
   _____

4. **Symmetry**_____
   _____
   _____
   _____

THE CITY IN PERCENTAGES: A SIMULATION GAME ON THE INTRODUCTION OF PERCENTAGES

Requirements

Pupils need to possess the following skills:

- Count from 1 to1000
- Add and subtract whole numbers
- Divide and multiply by two
- Explain in their own words the meaning of surfaces
- Identify what changes and what remains unchanged when comparing the surfaces of geometric structures
- Round up or down a number and explain this in their own words

Specific Objectives

- Identify the proportions of items in problem situations and represent them in terms of percentages.
- Carry out mental operations for the calculation of the percentages of whole numbers (100%....) with the system of numerical halving[1] (half of half etc.) and composition.
- Carry out mental operations for the calculation of percentages (200%- 150%- ...).
- Provide rough estimations for the result of the calculation of percentages.
- Carry out mental operations for the calculation of the percentage rate (100%.....)

Scenario

Your city is made up of high buildings with many families, two schools and lots of shops, but there is no place for teenagers and children to meet. To enable kids to play, get together and do sport, certain building companies decide to contribute to the realisation of a *sports centre* by donating material in percentages with which the local kids themselves will be able to build their ideal centre.

Problem Situation

After consulting their engineers and architects the administrators of the building companies tell the kids the quantity of material (strips of card) that they will supply and invite them to come to their building depots to collect the material. So it is directly up to the kids to supply themselves with the building material because the workers at the company site are busy working on other buildings outside town.

In order to give the kids a hand, however, the workers leave them indications contained in the paying cards on the percentage of materials that they can take and the workers invite the kids to use the percentage machine (Sheet 1) to work out the calculation.

At the second stage, after the centre has been built, three other companies decide to contribute to the construction of other sporting facilities. These companies show the material they have available and ask the kids to request in terms of percentages the quantity they will need to complete these facilities.

Aims of the Simulation

Construct a plan of the sports centre with strips of card with the *percentage-machine*.

Phases

First Phase

1. Explain the functions of the *percentage-machine.*
2. View the percentages of the materials donated by the building companies (see cards with information given by the companies).
3. Prepare a large sheet of card on which to attach the strips of card as they are obtained from the *percentage-machine* for the realisation of the sports complex, using a rough sketch.
4. Identify the percentage of each material (blue for the swimming pool, green for the tennis court etc.) and cut out each strip using the *percentage-machine.*
5. Construct the sports complex on the lines of your project.
6. Inform each company the quantity of material taken in terms of card surface.

Second Phase

1. Decide which facilities to design with the material from the companies.
2. Identify the quantity of material needed for the realisation of the new facilities to be communicated to the companies.
3. Inform the companies of the quantities of material required expressed in percentages.
4. Complete the sports complex with the new facilities and draw the outline of the sports fields.

Figure 10.

Sheet 1. The percentage-machine

The percentage-machine is an instrument used in the game to calculate the percentages with the system of numerical halving and composition. It allows the players to visualise 100% of the required quantities and to carry out from this, the calculation of the percentages by looking at the strips to find a result that can be visualised.

The machine is constructed of a vertical piece of sticking tape divided into four equal parts that can be stuck on the desk.

At the top of the tape is a roll of transparent and coloured paper.

The procedure for calculating the percentages is as follows:

1. Place the card alongside the vertical sticking tape making sure the margins and angles match accurately.

2. Find the percentage required.

3. Let the role of transparent paper flow over the card in correspondence with the notch that represents the required percentage.

4. Trace a horizontal line on the card with a pencil in correspondence with the right notch.

5. Cut the card along the line drawn with the pencil.

Documents

N° 3 playing cards with the communications from each company (Each card contains information about the company, the percentage rate, on the size in cm 2 and

the colour of the strips of card that each company intends to donate)
N° 2 communication

Materials

N° 1 photograph of the city
N° 1 *percentage-machine*
N° 1 large sheet of card for the plan
Sheets of coloured card
2 pairs of scissors
2 tubes of glue
Colouring pens

Roles

Builders
Percentage-machine operators
The roles can be exchanged at the teacher's discretion so that each player can have
a go with the *percentage-machine*. It is advisable that the roles should be acted
out according to the rules of the game.

Players

6/7 pupils

Debriefing

Here follows an outline on how to conduct the final discussion that the teacher will
lead at the end of the game. This is only an outline to be used as guide or check list
to help the discussion which should be as thorough and exhaustive as possible. It
should start with the students giving feedback of their overall impressions of the
game. Then the students will be invited to describe the game in detail, so that all
the elements in the learning objectives are well covered. The following list contains
an outline of the main mathematical issues dealt with in the game and questions
and prompts are provided for their systemisation and generalisation. The parts in
brackets indicate possible answers the teacher could use to move the discussion in
the desired direction only in the case in which they are not offered by the pupils.

1. **Initial intuition on percentages starting from use of the machine.** You used
    the percentage machine during the game. Did you notice what happened to

the strips each time you put them in the machine to work out the percentages? Every time the strips were halved. That's enough for the moment!

(It is advisable to take two strips of card of different lengths cut in half) When you cut the strips at 50% were the remaining pieces equal? In other words, all those pieces of card after you cut at 50 per cent, or as the mathematicians write at 50%, were they all the same size? Did they have the same surface area?
Let us try other examples with strips cut at 25% or at 75%.
(It is advisable to take two strips of card of different lengths at 200%) When you took 200% of the strips, were all the pieces equal? In other words, all the strips taken at 200 per cent- or when we write 200%- were they all the same size? Did they cover the same surface area? In general what do you notice? Can we say that the percentage depends on what you start with?) So if we have different quantities, is the same percentage of the two different quantities the same or different? Right, now we can conclude by saying that the percentage is not a fixed quantity but a variable one? In mathematical terms we call this relative quantity.

2. **Simple definitions of percentage.** So what is a percentage? How can we begin to define it? Right, now let's get a few ideas (Collect a few of the children's simple definitions). During the game we assumed that our strips, of whatsoever sizes, all started from 100...so ... . Let's see if we can come up with a more general answer! We can say that the percentage of a quantity is "as if every quantity starts with 100 and we take into consideration either a part of it or a larger part."

For example, when we consider half of the piece of card what percentage are we talking about? Right, 50%: in fact, 50 is half of 100. When, instead, we consider half of the half of 100, as you did in the game, what percentage are we talking about now? Right, 25%. When instead we consider 200%. Think about this.... Yes, we are talking about double the piece of card we started with. And if we consider 150%. Correct, we shall have to talk about a whole piece plus a half.
So now you understand why mathematicians use the symbol % to substitute the words per cent (cent means 100 in Latin) when they talk about percentages.

3. **Working out the percentage.** (Approach the percentage machine with a strip of card to illustrate what you are about to explain) Thanks to the percentage machine you were very good at finding 50% or 25% during the game, but did you find 75%? Right, excellent. You have added 25% to 50%. And how would you find 10%? Very good, by dividing the 50% by the number 5, or ..... yes, that's right, by dividing whole 100% by the number 10. (It is advisable to use

the term *number* 5, *number* 10 in order not to confuse the children by mixing percentage quantities and pure numbers.)

Splendid, now what do we have to do to get 20%? So let's see if I have understood correctly: we take 10% and multiply it by the number 2.

OK, now it's your turn to give some examples.

Let's try again. What is 50% of 160? Correct, 80. And what is 10% of 160? Now what's 25% of 160? 40. Now, let's try to calculate the percentage of another number, let's say 300. What is 50%? 150. And what about 25%? 75. And sill with the number 300, what is 10%? 30. And 200% of 300? 600, right. What about 150% of 300? 450. Excellent! Do you know what mathematicians call the number next to the % symbol? They call it the percentage rate. So going back to one of our examples: 50% of 160 equals 80. Now, for mathematicians160 is the total, 80 the percentage and 50 the percentage rate. Now it's your turn to make some examples.

4. **Working Out Percentages: Let's Have Some Fun with Numbers.** By now you have become experts with percentages and we are now ready to embark on big scale inverse reasoning. Do you remember in the game when the company grants 300sq cm. of 600sq cm., what percentage rate are they offering? Good 50%. And if they offer 60sq cm of 600sq cm? The rate will be 10%. And if they offered 1,200 of the 600sq cm? Well, the rate would be 200%.

5. **Recap.** Now let's summarise what we have learnt so far… Thanks for your cooperation.

TIME
Briefing 20 mins
Running time 3 hours
Debriefing 30 mins

Evaluation

The methodology includes, aside from the standard final verification, intermediate and comprehension tests (structured and semi-structured) whose aim is to test learning in progress throughout the learning process of the simulation.

Test

The test is illustrated in Figures 11-15.

Table 1. Documents (Phase I)

Firm A
Dear kids,
We are sorry to communicate we cannot help you building your sports centre, because we are busy doing building work outside town. Anyway, we are sure you will manage this difficult task on your own and, to help you along, we have asked the architects and engineers who designed your centre to tell us the quantity of material you will need. So, we ask you to go to the building site of our firm and to collect the following material:
- The...% of the ...strip (...cm^2)
- The...% of the brown strip (...cm^2)

To help you out in this task you have at your disposal the *percentage machine* that will quickly help you to calculate the quantity of each cardboard strip you can collect.
We wish you good work and we are available should you require further assistance!

The .... Firm

Table 2. Documents (Phase I) (continued)

Firm B
Dear kids,
We are happy to hear you are busy realizing the sports centre in our town and we wish to help you. So, we would like to donate some material that we are sure will be useful. Therefore, go to our firm's building site and you will find the following materials:
•a green cardboard strip (...cm^2)
- a grey strip (...cm^2)
•.............
From this material we can give you:
- The...% of the strip
- The ...%of the ...strip

Unfortunately, you will not find us at the building site to help you calculate the materials to withdraw. Never mind, do not worry because we have left you the *percentage machine*.
Good luck!
The ... firm

Table 3. Documents (Phase I) (continued)

Firm C
Dearest kids,
What a good initiative! We are wondering how we can be of service. At our building site there are some materials we could give you. Unfortunately not all of them, because as you well know we need them for our work, but in the following percentages:
•.............
•...............
If you are interested run to our building site, calculate the surfaces using the *percentage machine* and take the quantity you have calculated.
Keep up the good work!
The ... firm

Table 4. Communication from the 3 firms (Phase I)

Dearest kids,
We are sorry to bother you again, but we need to know the surface measurements of the materials you have taken from our sites. If it can help we can lend you the *percentage machine* again. We hope to see your sport centre built soon!
The firm.....

Table 5. Communication new firms (Phase II)

Dearest kids,
We hear your sports centre is not totally complete with all the necessary equipment. We can give you part of the material we have in stock that you can see for yourselves if you call at our sites. So, we ask you to check which of these materials can be useful for you and take only what you need. Like the other companies, we have the *percentage machine* which you can borrow, but this time we want you to express the quantity of material in percentages.
We hope we will soon be able to visit your sports centre.
The firm.....

Figure 11. First group

1. Colour 50% of the strip

Write down the reason why you stopped where you did.

2. Color in the 25 % of the strip. Explain how you did it.

3. Color in the 200% of the strip and then explain how you did it.

4. Color in the 75% of the strip and then explain how you did it.

5. Color in the 150 % of the strip and then explain how you did it.

Figure 12. Second group

1. The drawing has been cut and represents the 50 % of a strip. Finish the drawing of the strip thinking about its 100 %.

2. The drawing has been cut and represents the 25% of a strip. Finish the drawing of the strip thinking about its 100%.

3. The drawing represents the 100% of a strip. Finish the drawing of the strip thinking about 200%.

4. The drawing has been cut and represents the 75% of a strip. Finish the drawing of the strip thinking about 100%.

5. The drawing represents the 100 % of a strip. Finish the drawing of the strip thinking about 150%.

Figure 13. Third group

Observe the two following strips and complete the following sentences.
1. The first is approximately the_____ of the second one. After giving the answer explain the reason for it.

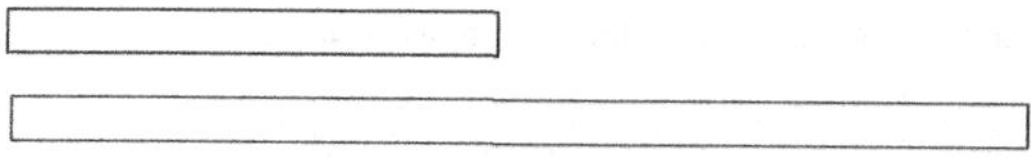

2. The first is _____ of the second one. After giving the answer explain the reason for it.

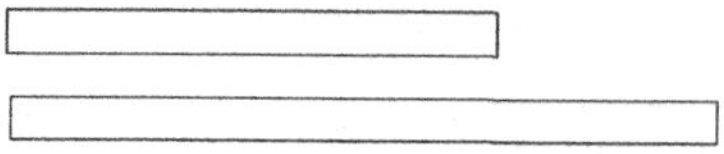

3. The first is the _____ of the second. After giving the answer explain the reason for it.

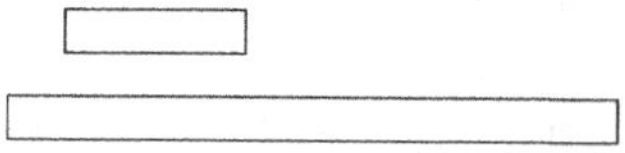

4. The first is the _____ of the second. After giving the answer explain the reason for it.

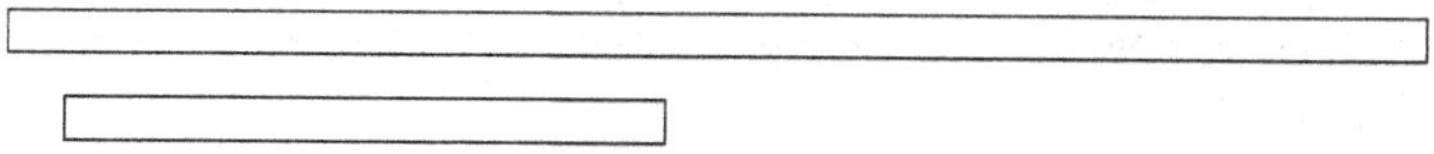

Figure 14. Fourth, fifth, and sixth group

Fourth group			
		Question	**Answer**
		To find the percentage of a quantity	
	1	How much is 50% of 8?	
	2	How much is 25 % of 20?	
	3	How much is 50 % of 90?	
	4	How much is 10% of 120?	
	5	How much is 25% of ?	
	6	How much is 200% of 80?	
	7	How much is 150 % of 80?	
	8	How much is 250 % of 20?	
Fifth group		You are required to find the quantity knowing the percentage and the value of the percentage given.	
	9	20 is 50% of which number?	
	10	13 is 25% of which number?	
	11	21 is 75% of which number?	
	12	15 is 10% of which number?	
	13	30 is 10% of which number?	
	14	20 is 25% of which number?	
	15	180 is 150% of which number?	
	16	44 is 200% of which number?	
Sixth group		You are required to find the percentage value knowing the percentage and the total quantity	
	17	If the cardboard strip found at the company measures 200 cm^2 and you, with the percentage machine, take out 100cm^2 to build the swimming pool, how much is the percentage value?	
	18	If the cardboard strip found at the firm's building site measures 200 cm2 and with the percentage machine you take out 50 cm^2 to build the tennis court, how much is it in percentage value?	
	19	How much is the percentage value of 150 if we refer of a total of 200?	
	20	How much is the percentage value of 50 if we refer to a total of 500?	
	21	How much is the percentage value of 80 from a total of 160?	
	22	How much is the percentage value of 210 if we refer to a total of 280?	

Figure 15. Seventh group

Examples
A swimming pool for kids is filled in for the 25% of its capacity. How many liters of water have been used if the maximum capacity of the swimming pool is 8,000 liters?
Luigi is a great sports person and is training for the marathon in his village, but because of a cramp in his right leg he has to stop after he covered 21 km, that corresponds to the 50% of the total track. How long is the marathon?
One afternoon Mr. Bianchi takes his two children to the cinema. The oldest pays the full price of 12 euro for his ticket, the same as his dad, while the youngest pays the 75% of the price. How much is the cost of the youngest son's ticket?
In front of the entrance of a primary school there is a factory wall 3 meters high and 50m long. It is a grey wall and very ugly. The children from the school have permission to decorate with graffiti 75% of the wall. How big will the graffiti be?
One evening Mr. Bianchi takes his two children to theatre. The oldest pays the whole ticket, like his dad, while the youngest has a 25% reduction and pays 15 euro. How much is a normal ticket?

REFERENCES

Domenici, G., & Frabboni, F. (2007). *Indicazioni per il curricolo. Scuola dell'infanzia, primaria e secondaria di primo grado*. Trento: Erickson.

Fregola, C. (1990). Vol. Aritimetica 4 . In Laeng, M. (Ed.), *Percorsi Didattici. Teramo: Lisciani e Giunti.*

Fregola, C. (1990). Vol. Geometria 4^ e 5^ Elementare Aritimetic . In Laeng, M. (Ed.), *Percorsi Didattici. Teramo: Lisciani e Giunti.*

Fregola, C. & Piu A. (n.d.). *I giochi di simulazione per l'apprendimento della matematica: un progetto pilota,* accettato dalla rivista *Psicologia e Scuola.*

Moss, J., & Case, R. (1999). Developing children's understanding of the rational numbers: A new model for an experimental curriculum. *Journal for Research in Mathematics Education, 30*(2), 122–147. doi:10.2307/749607

ENDNOTE

[1]　It is an approach that contemplates to half a quantity given each time and to rebuild it back doubling it (Moss, Joan & Case, Robbie, 1999). Developing children's understanding of the rational numbers: A new model for an experimental curriculum. *Journal for Research in Mathematics Education,* 30(2), 122-147.uu

Chapter 10
The Conduct of a Simulation Game

Roberta Masci
University of Calabria, Italy

ABSTRACT

The chapter describes the phases of the simulation games presenting the role and functions of the game leader in each phase. The chapter also provides helpful advice on the different ways of conducting the simulation games and discusses the main difficulties that can arise in each phase and how to overcome them.

INTRODUCTION

Simulation games are educational contexts of social interaction, insofar as they satisfy a series of conditions which determine different exchanges and relationships between the pupils and the teacher who share an experience in which a deliberate process of construction of knowledge and abilities takes place.

Both while the simulation game is being carried out and in the final discussion, all participants are involved in an experiential dialogue which offers support for sharing the meaning of what has been learnt. The participants' involvement in the

DOI: 10.4018/978-1-60566-930-4.ch010

game, the sharing of their experience and the acquisition process require careful planning by the teacher. In fact, in the absence of adequate direction much of the game's educational potential risks being lost.

The successful managing of simulation games requires appropriate and detailed preparation, based on knowledge of the games, which can only be gained through hands-on experience.

With the aim of providing a guide which may help to build a successful experience, it is useful to highlight the individual phases of the simulation and the role of the leader in each. What follows is an ensemble of suggestions for those who intend to take part in the project and direct their pupils in simulation games.

The direction of a simulation game often presents some difficulties that may be overcome by experimenting and systematically reflecting upon the objectives of the experience. In any case, it is advisable to start with the more structured games as they possess a pre-established structure, and although this implies less flexibility, they require less ad hoc decision making on the part of the leader during the game itself.

The present chapter will, after a careful description of the phases of the simulation game itself, outline the functions and the role of the director in each of the phases the game and provide some useful guidance for the reader.

THE PHASES OF A SIMULATION GAME

Although there are many ways to organize and direct simulation games, their procedural architecture is made up of four fundamental and indispensable phases: opening, briefing, running and debriefing.

Phase 1. Opening. This initial phase is necessary for creating the relations, conditions and procedures of the game. During the opening phase, the desired aims are specified to the pupils, and the type of activity in which they will take part is carefully described, explained and questions answered.

In this way, attention is focused on the rationale of the game and on the aims and roles assumed in the interaction. This phase is intended to stimulate pupils' motivation also, where possible, by encouraging them to describe previous experiences of participation in games or similar activities.

These first pieces of information allow the participants to become familiar with the simulation game, and the leader to clarify the rules. In other words, this is a phase in which a real educational contract takes place between the leader and the participants, which should give rise to positive expectations of this undertaking. The clarification of the rules and representation of the roles should allow each of the participants to become fully involved in the action, the process, and relations within the group.

Phase 2. Briefing. In effect, this is the preparatory phase of the simulation game, during which the scenery, i.e. the simulated context, within which the pupils will operate, is clarified, inviting the pupils to work hard for the resolution of the problem situation at the core of the game.

In this phase the aims of the simulation are stated clearly and precisely, the context in which it takes place and its characteristics are described in detail, the groups are formed and the roles are allotted to each participant and instructions provided.

The informative phase can also include some test games to allow the pupils to understand fully the simulation procedure, giving them a slow-motion run-through or rehearsal of the activities that will take place in the course of the simulation. In this circumstance, the teacher will explain the unfolding of events, phase after phase, and will try and answer all the questions that may arise on the rules, times and so on. The trial run is not always necessary but, if it does not take place, the teachers need to be ready to deal with any confusion that may arise later on in the first session.

Further information can be provided in the course of the activity when necessary or when the participants themselves ask for greater clarification once they have acquired a certain degree of confidence and familiarity with the activity. In the less structured simulation games, those which necessitate a direct and more immediate involvement, the presentation will have less space, as the participants will be asked to start playing according to the instructions provided, assign the roles themselves and, generally speaking, rely on their spontaneity and desire to participate in the proposed activities. In other cases, on the other hand, careful and meticulous explanation of the instructions may be required prior to involvement (*total briefing*). This type of simulation game can include various types of activity, such as preliminary preparation sessions, technical explanations, briefing sessions, introduction to the themes to be dealt with in video, film and oral presentations, role plays and so on. The phase of the actual game, consequently, will represent an element within the general learning process. This type of simulation game can have certain limitations, however, as it presupposes less freedom for the players.

Phase 3. The unfolding. This is the phase when the actual game is played out, in which an essential clue to the operations to be carried out, step by step, is found in the documents by each of the participants, who are fully involved in the problem situation, taking on the roles, making decisions and utilizing the materials in cooperation with fellow pupils under the guidance of the teacher.

Some highly complex games can be divided into different phases, which may sometimes be separated by intermediate phases for comments and evaluation. Furthermore, if required by the game, some time may be dedicated to researching the documentation in order to carry out a deeper analysis of the problem: sources, testimonies, reports.

Phase 4. The final discussion (debriefing). This is the concluding synthesis. After the unfolding of the game, discussion is useful to place the simulation in perspective, and allow the acquired experience to be digested and consciously taken on board. The time set aside for discussion represents a central element, as it enables the participants to discuss the results and the actions undertaken during the game, comparing different opinions and analyzing the group's behaviour and the obtained results.

The actors are now allowed to detach themselves from their roles in order to reflect upon the concepts and the cognitive processes activated during the development of the game. Naturally, in this phase the tools which were used in the course of the simulation activity, the products achieved and the materials used are all useful prompts to encourage recollection of the considerations which emerged in the context of the game; this re-examination will allow the process of acquisition to start.

Debriefing can be organized in different ways, from an informal discussion to a structured one and other forms of reports or written comments on the experience.

As regards the beginning of the discussion, some authors maintain that there should only be a short break before the final discussion; others suggest there may be some advantages in postponing the final discussion for longer in order to offer the participants time for "mature reflection" outside the tense atmosphere which such activities undoubtedly create.

Debriefing is thus the beginning of the comprehension and consciousness of what happened during the game and it is the phase in which the experiential activity is transformed into learning. However the game is played, it is important to facilitate the communication and confrontation to allow for the emergence of certain factors, in particular:

- Recalling of the experience and impressions of each of the participants to be shared with other players;
- The contents and the processes that took place;

- Analogies with real world situations;
- The codes and symbols which may have been used.

THE ROLE OF THE LEADER

In order to manage a group of children in an effective and functional manner, the leader's role should be essentially that of mediator of the learning process. In fact, the task of the leader is to help the pupils take an active part in the learning process. This implies that the leader assumes the direction of the game, sustaining and monitoring the pupils' learning process and maintaining an ongoing dialogue which guides participation towards learning objectives, both in terms of the final product and, most of all, the individual stages as the game evolves.

All this implies a revision of the repertoire of relational skills that can be employed by the teacher to run the game, maintaining the monitoring of the three dimensions of the conduct of the group: the content, the communicative relationships at individual and group level, and the teaching process.

We shall now see the tasks of the leader in each of the above mentioned phases of the game.

Before starting the game the leader must sound out the knowledge and abilities of the pupils in order to make preliminary decisions on the suitability of the game with respect to the teaching aims and to guarantee the full and profitable participation of all concerned. In this phase the organizational aspects are defined regarding the definition of spaces, the predisposition of materials and the composition of the groups.

Figure 1. Shows the procedural architecture of the game

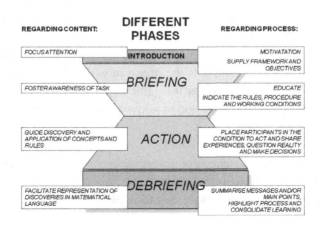

As the simulation game requires the participation of a restricted number of people, 6 or 7, it is useful to establish the criteria for the selection of the pupils who will take part. Certain factors should be considered: in general, heterogeneous groups with diverse backgrounds, capabilities and interests have a number of advantages as they expose the pupils to different perspectives and methods of resolution of the problems and stimulate a higher degree of cognitive development and learning (Johnson W. D. et al, 1996). Thus, it is preferable to form heterogeneous groups, except in the case in which specific abilities must be taught or specific teaching objectives must be met, when it is appropriate to form homogenous groups. In fact, the former there is a tendency to greater reflection and elaboration, more exchange of explanations and more detailed discussion overall, all of which lead to a greater development of reasoning faculties and accuracy of the long term mnemonic retention.

For the groups to be heterogeneous one may utilize: a randomized procedure or, as for our research, a questionnaire to detect different profiles on which to form the group. For the randomized procedure the roles can be drawn from a hat for example, whereas for the other procedure, a questionnaire can be proposed on multiple mental skills, which will provide information on the profile of the pupils which will be distributed in the group in a way to avoid the presence of "similar" profiles based on the repertoire of skills detected through a questionnaire.

Furthermore, it is necessary to organize the spaces and materials along certain lines, which can improve the quality of the learning atmosphere and the relations between students: for instance, making sure that the pupils are close enough together to share the materials and maintain eye contact with all the members of the group, when exchanging ideas and materials.

In the opening phase, the leader must motivate players and encourage participation in the game. It is important in this phase to establish a positive rapport with the participants, maintaining eye contact with them and structuring positive interdependence between them, at the same time as insisting on individual responsibility. In other words, it is necessary to enable pupils to feel responsible for the development of their own learning and that of the group, drawing the pupils together around the common objectives of the game and providing concrete reasons for co-operation.

It is advisable to use a simple, clear and appropriate language avoiding uncertainties and prolixity which may put participants off at an early stage.

In the briefing phase, it is important to illustrate the background, the problem situation and to assign the roles which may be assigned by the group itself or by the leader; often it will be useful to distribute roles in a random manner.

The leader, at this point, explains the characteristics of the task assigned in a clear and well defined way, the procedures to be followed to undertake the task and to regulate the working group. In other terms the leader specifies what is required of the students, providing guidance on when the task is considered successfully completed, and invites them to include all members with a view to the reaching of the common objective. Further, the leader explains the dynamics of the events which may arise in each phase.

In order to verify whether the pupils have fully understood what is required to complete the task and follow the instructions, the leader might need to ask the pupils some specific questions and, at the same time, provide reassurance by telling the students that there will be someone on hand during the game to deal with any problems. Further, the leader can provide a simple demonstration of the game, showing and simulating the necessary actions in the game in slow motion for each of the phases of development.

The leader also has the task of animating the game, facilitating its development and taking care of the group dynamics.

The functions to improve the running of the game are the following:

- Verify that the pupils have understood the task and the assigned material and go through the information and the instructions provided during the briefing whenever necessary;
- Monitor the pupils' behaviour both at individual and group level, by checking progress, group interaction;
- Intervene to improve the work of the group and the task, providing clarifications, illustrations and further instructions;
- Encourage respect for time limits;
- Make sure that all participants are involved in the game and taking on the assigned roles;
- Help children in difficulty by providing assistance, but do not substitute them;
- Facilitate the solution of conflicts between participants on difficulties arising from different interpretations of the phases or of specific activities.

In the case where difficulties are detected in the learning process, in the participation and relations among participants, which may hinder the smooth running of the game, the leader should try to determine the causes and try to overcome them by providing appropriate direction and guidance. In the face of unexpected developments, the leader can intervene by assuming one of the roles in the game and directly join in the simulation to get it back on track.

In the debriefing phase, the leader's task is to use the information generated during the experience to facilitate the learning of the players in the final discussion (Lederman L.C., 1992).

The role of the leader is thus to set the scene, by taking into account suggestions for the preparation of the game session to which are added the observations made during the game itself which can better orientate the conduct of the debriefing. The leader must allow adequate time, draw analogies with relevant areas or situations to use at the right moment, prepare a set of questions to facilitate the evolution of the discussion, and provide a frame in which to work within the given time limits.

Before starting the debriefing, the leader must be able to help the group to come out of the experience and prepare to examine it together. In doing this, the teacher-leader invites the pupils to put the materials of the game to one side, helping them to come out of the role of the player. It is best not to take a break at this moment as the group, which has just emerged from the simulation, feels the need to talk about their experience. Subsequently, the teacher starts to form the circle where the pupils find a place, making sure that the circle is closed without empty spaces. This seemingly cosmetic detail has an important symbolic value as it encourages the pupils to feel united and be in a good listening position.

When all the children present are in a circle, the leader explains what is about to happen and asks for their active cooperation. To do this the teacher can start by saying, for example, that the debriefing is a time to think together what has happened and what it means for the group, that each player holds an important piece of a big puzzle and that, to understand what this represents, it is necessary to gather and examine all the pieces together. The leader, at this point, can reprise, in a sort of action replay, the steps of the game and ask the participants to talk about the steps they took at the different stages and in particular any problems they encountered.

The debriefing is a delicate phase to manage that requires the ability to listen to and empathise with the participants:

The leader is advised to follow certain guidelines:

- The teacher should avoid telling the players what they have (or should have) learnt and be confident that whatever they may have learnt in that moment will be of value to them;
- Be supportive of all those who contribute to the discussion of the simulation game. This will encourage those who voice their impressions to go deeper. When it is deemed appropriate, it may be useful to reinforce the participants' self-esteem, by offering psychological encouragement;
- Reformulate the same question as often as necessary;
- Respect and use the silences as spaces to think and internalise and make sure it is understood that it is necessary to learn to wait for one another (taking turns);
- Help those, who have a tendency to talk for too long to become more sensitive to the needs of others and those who tend to hesitate before expressing themselves to become more confident. To stimulate those who do not speak, the leader can utilize the group, saying for example: "Who would like to help me get some comments from the children we have not heard from yet?";

- Encourage with an appropriate question or prompt those who are thought to have a particular experience to report;
- Intervene when it is noted that the participants are not used to expressing opinions, asking for greater effort; jokingly pointing out, and guaranteeing, for example, that each consideration or evaluation will not be judged by anyone.

At the end of the game, the data and information which have been collected at the beginning and during the game and the examined results obtained by the pupils, are brought together in order to examine closely the effectiveness of the game and its management. To establish how many pupils have achieved the fixed objectives and what has been learnt it is indispensable, in this phase, to examine all the data collected in the initial stages, analyse the project and the process and connect all this information together to verify not only the success of the overall outcome, but also how this has been achieved.

REFERENCES

Fregola, C. (2003). *Riunioni efficaci a scuola. Ridefinire i luoghi della comunicazione scolastica*. Trento: Erickson.

Johnson, D. W., Johnson, R. T., & Holubec, E. J. (2006). *Apprendimento cooperativo in classe. Migliorare il clima emotivo e il rendimento*. Trento: Erikson.

Lederman, L. C. (1992). Debriefing: Toward a systematic assessment of theory and practice. *Simulation & Gaming, 23*(2), 145–160. doi:10.1177/1046878192232003

Peters, V. A. M., & Vissers Geert, A. N. (2004). A simple classification model for debriefing simulation games . *Simulation & Gaming, 35*(1), 70–84. doi:10.1177/1046878103253719

Piu, A. (2001). *Processi formativi e simulazione*. Roma: Monolite.

Steinwachs, B. (1992). How to facilitate a Debriefing. *Simulation & Gaming, 23*(2), 186–195. doi:10.1177/1046878192232006

Section 4
Experimental Research Project

Chapter 11
A Review of Previous Studies

Angela Piu
University of L'Aquila, Italy

ABSTRACT

The chapter presents a critical analysis of the literature on simulation games identifying the research direction along which the studies conducted up until now have been following and the issues that have emerged during the research. On the basis of these considerations, a choice can be made of the most suitable simulation games to employ in a specific learning context.

INTRODUCTION

Research into simulation games in the educational field has produced contrasting results and there are still many contentious issues left to be resolved. From its introduction back in the 1960s the use of simulation games, in particular in primary and secondary education, has enjoyed a steady development especially in the field of computer simulation.

Over the last forty years, therefore, a tradition has been built up that has enabled simulation to be considered today, in many countries, to be founded on an established methodology and seen by many as a valid teaching strategy.

DOI: 10.4018/978-1-60566-930-4.ch011

The value of simulation is confirmed and supported by the fact that in the countries where it is often used, there is a rich and wide-ranging literature on the subject and many simulation games in divers kinds of disciplinary fields are available on the market. However, despite this long tradition, the actual achievement of the research into the use of simulation games in education is quite modest, especially when we think of their widespread use, and there are no commonly agreed guidelines to base simulation games on; indeed, what there is has to be considered fragmentary and by no means scientifically disinterested given the fact that the purpose of many available games is to make a profit rather than purely educational in which the aims, concepts and structures are stated explicitly.

In fact, the results achieved so far are not univocal because of the different characteristics of the studies conducted, the eclectic nature of the research that involves different sectors or fields and the lack of an ontology that is able to provide a sound conceptual footing for the scientific discourse which is indispensable for any reliable assessment of the educational effectiveness of simulation games.

Many studies devoted to evaluating simulation games, moreover, are basically of an anecdotal nature: they describe the games in a detailed manner, often emphasising the characteristics and the experience of using the games with students, rather than on their effectiveness within an overall project in which the educational aims and objectives to be met are rendered explicit.

This chapter aims to present the typologies of research on simulation games and the significant results on which there is widespread agreement. The analysis intends to focus attention on the problems that have arisen from the literature and, from this, to put forward various suggestions on the development of further work and underline the ambits and directions for future research.

CERTAIN RESULTS

The results on the effectiveness of simulation games, notwithstanding the 50 years of fruitful experience (Wolfe & Crookhall, 1998), have not always been supported by the research, and even where there has been research, one has to exercise considerable caution when reading the results. As various authors point out, for example Randel, Pierfy, Bredemeier and others, numerous studies have not been adequately structured, there is no shared taxonomy of simulation games and the final results frequently lack thorough documentation.

Three categories of research into simulation games have been identified in the literature:

- descriptive studies of the effects of a particular game on the participants;
- explanatory studies that place the results achieved by various players in relation to other variables;
- comparative studies that compare the effectiveness of simulation games with other teaching methods (Fletcher, 1969 in Keach & Pierfy, 1972).

To the first group belong those studies that describe what the participants have learnt from the experience through subjective observations supplied by the designer of the game and the teachers involved. Though many studies examine a single group of subjects, some also assess students' perceptions of the game by asking them what they have learnt; other studies provide the learning results.

Research projects of this kind can be considered pre-experimental: they do not allow for a valid contrast and comparison with other experimental situations, since the individuals are distributed between the groups in a random manner and the research plan is open to numerous possible sources of error as regards the internal and external validity of the experimentation. In other words these research methods do not allow researchers to verify the existence of a causal relation between the independent variable and the dependent variable, i.e., to be in a position to assert that it was actually the game that was responsible for the observed changes in the final results, or whether there were extraneous factors. Hence, they are unable to generalise from the results, i.e. to extend the results to other subjects and contexts. Moreover, in the research plan there is no provision for comparing the results of the group that took part in the project- the players of the simulation game- with the result of another group who have not played the game. Nevertheless, these studies are still of considerable interest in that they provide a useful basis for future research. "Although considered by most scholars as minor research, descriptive studies can make important contributions toward the development of simulation game research. Descriptive research studies are often simply case studies of the experiences of persons who have field tested, observed, or participated in a simulation game exercise. This kind of research contributes significantly as rich sources of testable hypotheses and potential explanatory variables. Secondly, descriptive studies may identify user problems that help avoid certain common errors in use, choice, or timing of simulation games. Thirdly, they may prove useful in identifying or devising new evaluation methods. Finally, since many descriptive studies are written by researchers in specific academic fields, they may identify common discipline problems, help to clarify requisite skills and devise educational outcomes, and raise questions about sequencing of activities within courses" (Edwards, 1975).

To the second group belong those studies that put the results obtained in relation with other variables that can influence the results. Bredemeier and Greenblat (1981) present a thoughtful discussion of a number of important variables: personality, cognitive learning style, gender of the players, group variable, academic ability, game ability, and administrative variable. Researchers should be aware of these and other variables.

Some studies, for example, have shown how the attitude of the leader towards the group, as well as his or her background knowledge can have an influence on performance. Significant differences have been found in the attitudes of groups that have participated in the same game with different leaders. Other procedural variables such as the introduction, variations in how the game is played and the final debriefing influence in various ways the experience of the players and their results.

The internal structure of the games can also lead to variations in the experience and the results; this is equally the case with personal variables. For example, when the content of the game does not sufficiently reflect reality it can happen that the players enjoy themselves but do not learn as much as expected from playing the game. Character differences also seem to have an influence on how the game is experienced as well as on the results. The same is true for the attitude of players prior to the game, their relationships with each other, whether they know already each other, gender differences and so on (Bredemeier & Greenblat, 1981).

In other cases it has been found that lack of empathy, a preference for symbolic methods based on reading and writing and for working independently, all have a negative effect on the results of the simulation game, while other studies have shown that the use of simulation can produce significant results with disadvantaged students with linguistic difficulties.

These studies, some of which are referred to above, constitute a necessary step towards assessing simulation games insofar as they provide useful information about the conditions in which the game can be played most effectively. All these considerations, however, still leave open one question that will be addressed later on, that could provide a justification for all the claims (tackled in the third group) for the efficiency of educational simulation games (Keach & Pierfy, 1972).

This group contains elements both of descriptive and exploratory studies, but essentially focuses attention on assessing the value of simulation games compared to other educational methods. It is difficult to generalise on the results obtained from these research works both because each study is characterised by different elements and because of the errors made by researchers that can weaken the quality of their research methods. Despite claims that the differences in research projects can undermine attempts to compare the results, Cherryholmes (1966 in Pierfy, 1977) goes on to form generalisations on the effectiveness of educational simulation games because "convergent findings based on a variety of measures and experiments increase the validity of inferences based upon the findings".

Many other authors following his example have produced interesting round-ups of the literature on comparative studies.

The first of such studies was the work of Pierfy (1997) who examined 22 research studies comparing simulation games for social science with conventional methods of teaching. The author came to the conclusion that simulation games are not much more effective than other methods. The comparison was carried out taking into consideration: the learning results, memorisation, changes in attitude and interest. The works seem to imply that there is a positive link between retaining information and both a change of attitude and an increase in interest. With reference to the results of learning, feedback in the form of a test administered immediately after the experiment, appeared to show no significant differences. Out of the 22 research efforts studied 15 did not find any significant differences, 3 found in favour of simulation games and 3 in favour of conventional teaching methods. As regards retention of what was learnt, measured in the same way, after a certain length of time, 8 found significant differences while 3 found no differences. The other 11 studies expressed reserve for the post test administered after some time. As regards changes in attitude, changes in attitude only 11 of the studies deemed it a worthwhile subject of attention and 8 of these revealed that simulation games had a considerable impact on attitudes in a positive sense. Finally as regards interest, 7 of the 8 studies found greater interest for simulation games rather than conventional teaching.

The aforementioned round-up of Bredemeier and Greenblat (1981) adds to that of Pierfy (whose revision was mentioned by the authors together with the data) the results of other works that, while adding further information gathered from later studies, come to the same overall conclusions. Concerning the learning results, for example, there are no significant differences whereas, as regards retention or memorisation and changes of attitude and motivation, the results of simulation games are better. For the first, the authors specify that the better results gained by simulation games in as regards a change of attitude very much depend on the conditions in which the game is played, while as for the better score on motivation the authors add the findings of later studies which confirm Pierfy's assessment.

His summary widens the debate by introducing other results, that are critically discussed by the author. Some relate to the category "learning about the self" and others "learning atmosphere". As regards the former a number of studies are mentioned that reveal that the "participants in a simulation game report a variety of outcomes, including release of tension, receipt of valuable affective feedback from others or from the experience of the game, increased self-awareness, and greater sense of personal power or self-confidence" (Bredemeier & Greenblatt, 1981, p. 324). In certain cases research has shown that subjects who are sensitive to the disapproval of others and have difficulty in playing roles have negative results. As regards the second category, however, the author suggests that the change in atmosphere in the class and in the social relations that various researchers attribute to participation in simulation games could be closely correlated to the variable relating to teaching style and personality, a variable that needs to be taken into account.

After this comes the work of Randel et al. (1992) covering a period of 28 years, from 1963 to 1991. This work features 68 studies excluding others that are merely descriptive and do not present any research data. One aspect of Randel compared to other works is that the analysis includes games and simulation games, the latter being considered a subcategory of the former. Hence, the results of the 68 studies concern the comparison of both games, many of which are computer games, and simulation games and conventional teaching methods in various disciplines, such as social science, maths, art, physics, biology and logic (while business games were put aside to be studied at a later date). The results reported by Randel are as follows: 56% find no differences whatsoever; 32% is in favour of simulation games and games in general; 7% is in favour of simulation games and games in general but the results were considered unreliable and thus excluded; 5% in favour of conventional teaching. As regards mathematics, 7 out of 8 studies showed that the use of simulation games and games led to better results. Overall, simulation games and games produced a better result than conventional teaching as concerns retention of what was learnt. In 12 of the 14 studies students reported greater interest in simulation games and games than in conventional teaching.

All these comparative studies contain weaknesses that the above-mentioned authors underline, while adding various useful suggestions for the conduct of future comparative research.

One of the main problems inherent in scientific research has been encountered by the designers of simulation games themselves when they unconsciously try to influence the data as a result of enthusiasm or the desire for a particular outcome. Although there are studies that have avoided this, the problem remains with others so that when the same studies are conducted by third parties the results change. Another problem concerns the reliability of the instruments used to measure the dependent variable. As Pierfy points out many studies give no indication of the origin of the tests, while for others the reliability coefficient is low both when the instruments are used to assess cognitive aspects and when they are used to assess affective ones.

When attention turns to the formation of the groups, the authors show that the assigning of places in the experimental group and the control group is carried out on the basis of a pre-test. The danger of this is that the pre-test could interfere with the independent variable. In order to overcome this problem many researchers have utilised whole classes and split the pupils into the experimental and control group on a random basis. This method of group formation, however, runs the risk, especially with small samples of excluding a further variable, i.e., the two groups have a different leader. As regards the mode of teaching for the control group, moreover, it often occurs that the researchers do not supply detailed information on the administration of the game. In particular, there are differences in the debriefing, which, in some games is considered an integral part of the game while in others it is not. This difference makes it even more difficult to make comparisons between studies. Furthermore, a considerable number of researchers have completely ignored the Hawthorne effect, that is to say, the fact that the control group receives the same teaching as normal, while the experimental group have different expectations because of the novelty of the simulation.

Another problem concerns the employment of the same test to verify the dependent variable; this could increase the chances of invalidating the research through the learning effect of the pre-test, in the sense that the final results could be attributed not so much to the game itself but rather to the expectations raised by the questions in the pre-test. The likelihood of this occurring is greater when the time lapse between the pre-test and the final test is short.

From this summary of the previous research efforts, the need for a rigorous classification of the games and their design, especially as regards their theoretical basis and their teaching aims, emerges clearly. Moreover, more attention should be paid to the scientific grounding and methodology of the research: in other words, a reflection on method and instruments and how to tie these to the overall aims of the study (Lucisano, 2006; Dewey, 1951). Because of all the problems that characterise educational research work such as the use of different, sometimes conflicting, methods, it is essential to apply a unified scientific approach in order that, as Dewey taught us, the ideas of the different scientific schools of thought can be compared with each other and, above all, compared with the results of their work (Lucisano, 2006). This process can only be achieved if the scientific community renders not just the outcome of their experiments available but also the data and the evidence on which their results are based (Visalberghi, 1978).

RECENT RESEARCH

The works mentioned in the previous section are only some of the most important round-ups of the research literature on simulation games illustrating not just the results achieved so far but the problems thrown up by researchers from the 1970s up till the 1990s. After the 1990s, even if computer simulation had already been discussed in Randel et al., the attention of many researchers turned towards simulation games on the computer, an area covered by a growing body of literature, while there has been a fall in interest in business games that are not included in analyses of simulation games with a few notable exceptions.

As regards computer simulation, interest has been focused mainly on the perceptions of students to simulation games; these studies are often preceded by vague descriptions of the games themselves and on comparisons between educational simulation games on the computer and other forms of teaching.

On a wave of enthusiasm for the new medium initial research focused attention on the comparison between computer simulation and traditional forms of learning. Yet, the results of these studies are conflicting and in some cases no particular advantages were found in the use of computer simulation in an educational context vis-à-vis traditional methods of teaching the curriculum (Rivers & Vockell, 1987). Other studies, on the other hand, produced more encouraging results on knowledge acquisition of the arguments dealt with, i.e. the pupils who studied through the means of computer simulation appeared to have a better grasp as regards the transfer and application of knowledge (Grimes & Willey, 1990). When computer simulation was compared to activity in the laboratory, the former scored better in terms of speeding up learning time (Shute & Glaser R., 1990; Lewis, Stern J., Linn, 1993). However, even if computer simulation appeared more efficient from the point of view of learning time, this was not the case when it came to overall understanding and the construction of knowledge.

Now it seems that the attention of researchers in this ambit has turned towards the use of computer simulation not as an alternative way of teaching the curriculum but rather in terms of didactic support and the results of these studies have been positive.

Today the results of these studies are basically orientated in four directions (Piu A., 2007):

a.   the first relating to the potential of computer simulation in helping learners familiarise themselves with new concepts and/or examine their basic concepts through using the computer as a means of exploration. In particular, certain studies have shown that computer simulation can represent valuable support to face-to-face lessons as regards the acquisition of concepts insofar as the initial exposure to such concepts helps the student not only to a better understanding, but also in their ability to transfer and apply what has been learnt (Brant G., Hooper E. & B. Sugrue, 1991; Sarantos P., Macri-Botsari E., Paraskeva F., 2005-2006). In the ambit of the PRIN project 2003-2005 carried out by the University of Calabria Research Team on Simulation and Training, it was found that simulation was effective in the construction of knowledge in training courses in simulation: to be more precise, in courses where the experience of simulation was accompanied by guide and support on the use of computer simulation (Piu C., 2006). Finally, another study has shown that, by linking computer simulation with direct experience in the real world on which the simulation is based, we can help students connect what they learn from the simulation with concepts discussed in class, while the direct experience is of greater help to students whose ability to contextualise learning is weak. As regards the other variables, however, there have been no significant findings.

b. The second direction relates to advantages in understanding and in the use of symbols, linked to the ability to transfer from one representation to another and in abstraction; various studies have shown that computer simulation is effective in helping students who have difficulty in understanding and using symbols as it provides an important stepping stone between the real phenomenon considered and the abstracted form of the model in the process of understanding. Positive results have been recorded, in fact, in the ability to transfer from one representation to another, i.e., from a description in terms of objects and events to their respective symbolic representation (Teodoro, 1998).

c. The third direction concerns better understanding not only through the use of a descriptive model but also an explanatory one. Various studies have found greater learning benefits from computer simulation than from laboratory work, in the sense that processes of visualisation have provided an explicit bridge between the every day understanding that the students have of certain phenomena (in this case, an electric circuit) and the principles and models that underlie such phenomena. By setting up a virtual environment it was possible to visualise the underlying phenomenon and understand the reasons for the behaviour of the different components, thanks also to the possibility of being able to manipulate them. This proved to be more useful than working with real circuits in the lab (Finkelstein, Adams, Keller, Kohl, Perkins, Podolefsky, Reid, LeMaster, 2005). The advantages are essentially to do with the presentation of a model, in which patterns can be observed due to the simplification of the information, the greater extension in time and space and the visualisation of what cannot be seen directly. All these factors can allow the student to observe the model of reality in a complete fashion so that, rather than being merely descriptive, the learning process is rendered explicit (Winn, Stahr, Sarason, Fruland, Oppenheimer, Lee, 2006);

d. The final direction, which is the same for computer simulation and other means of simulation, has to do with the question of motivation in the teaching process that generates simulation; simulation is something that students find intriguing and this creates interest and the desire to participate (Stipek, 1996). Some research studies have shown that the active resolution of problems and comprehension tasks and the personal assessment of students, which are all part of the simulation process, inevitably encourages students to go beyond the information given and to express a critical evaluation; in other words, to choose freely and guide their own conduct on the basis of the choices made (Piu A., 2006).

RESEARCH INTEREST IN SIMULATION GAMES

The conclusions drawn from much of the research into simulation games underline the need for unified and rigorous research methods in this field. However, the initial results can be considered an encouragement to proceed in the direction taken in order to find further confirmation of the results so far. Memorisation, changes in attitude and an increase in motivation are all aspects worthy of investigation, especially when we consider the close connection between affective- motivational aspects and cognition that has recently found further confirmation by psychological and educational research and the need for life-long learning required by present day society.

The time is right to take stock of the line taken by various researchers in the field who have abandoned the study of simulation games as an alternative to traditional teaching methods to concentrate on their support role within the curriculum (de Jong, Van Joolingen, Brant, Hooper, Sugrue, Piu c. et al.) and, therefore, also from the point of view of a quantitative as well as qualitative research approach to focus on the process that develops during the simulation game with the results obtained.

If future research follows this direction, a great deal of further work will be needed on various issues as they arise.

The problems that require investigation seem to concern not just the best way to integrate simulation within an overall educational project, but also the need to reflect on the design and evaluation criteria for the courses in which simulation is employed and the selection of the right support instruments.

There is also a need to reflect on the role of simulation in teaching in the initial or intermediate phase of learning and the support instruments to use. With reference to this De Jong et al. identify three characteristics on which to base a classification of support instruments that could be useful for these ends (De Jong, Van Joolingen, 1998). The first concerns "direction", i.e. the question of when and whether to offer advice. The second characteristic refers to the typology of support tools, that could either be restrictive in the sense that they could restrict the field of action of the student to such an extent that he/she is no longer able to deal with the complex situation posed by the simulation, or supportive, in the sense that they guide the students along the right lines. The final characteristic is the opportunity to utilise these support tools, in the sense that the choices made in the design phase depend on the learning characteristics of the students and their background knowledge.

One area of major interest will be the effectiveness of simulation as a support in learning processes that enable participants to develop, and subsequently apply their knowledge outside the protected confines of the teaching environment in the real world; in particular, the aim is for simulation to help students to a deeper understanding of various concepts so that their newly acquired knowledge becomes integrated into their cognitive map in place of previous vague ideas and intuitions. In this context the study of the scaffolding and modalities of representation in the construction of concepts assumes a certain importance. Another relevant aspect, moreover, will be the study of the change not only in terms of epistemological beliefs of the students and their expectations with regards to the processes of learning and acquisition of concepts, but also in terms of teachers' expectations of the abilities of their students.

In conclusion, it should be remembered that there are other relevant issues concerning the relationship between virtual and real environments in the construction of knowledge. The virtual world, in effect, as various researches have shown, provides students with the opportunity to take part in different systems that make up our environment.

REFERENCES

Brant, G., Hooper, E., & Sugrue, B. (1991). Which comes first the simulation or the lecture? *Journal of Educational Computing Research, 7*(4), 469.

Bredemeier, M. E., & Greenblat, C. S. (1981). The Educational Effectiveness of Simulation Games: A Synthesis of Findings. *Simulation & Gaming, 12*, 307. doi:10.1177/104687818101200304

De Jong, T., & Van Joolingen, W. (1998). Scientific discovery learning with computer simulations of conceptual domains. *Review of Educational Research, 68*, 179–201.

Dewey, J. (1951). *Le fonti di una scienza dell'educazione*. Firenze: La Nuova Italia.

Edwards, S. D. (1975). *The use of Descriptive Studies in Simulation Game Research*. Paper presented at The Annual Meeting of the National Council for the Social Studies. Atlanta, Georgia: November 26-29.

Finkelstein, N.D., Adams, W.K., Keller, C.J., Kohl, P.B., Perkins, K.K., Podolefsky, N.S., Reid, S., & LeMaster, R. (2005). When learning about the real world is better done virtually: A study of substituting computer simulations for laboratory equipment. *PhysRev Special Topics-Physics education research, 1*.

Grimes, P. W., & Willey, T. E. (1990). The effectiveness of microcomputer simulations in the principles of economics course. *Computers & Education, 14*, 81–86. doi:10.1016/0360-1315(90)90025-3

Keach, E. T., & Pierfy, D. A. (1972). *The effects of a Simulation Game on Learning of Geographic Information at the Fifth Grade Level. Final Report.* Athens: University of Georgia. (ED068889). Lewis, E.L., Stern, J.L., Linn, M.C. (1993). The effect of computer simulations on introductory thermodynamics understanding. *Educational Technology, 33,* 45–48.

Lucisano, P., & Salerni, A. (2002). *Metodologia della ricerca in educazione e formazione.* Roma: Carocci.

Pierfy, D. A. (1977). Comparative Simulation Game Research: Stumbling Blocks and Steppingstones. *Simulation & Gaming, 8,* 255. doi:10.1177/003755007782006

Piu, A. (2006). Simulation, Training and Education between Theory and Practice . In Cartelli, A. (Ed.), *Teaching in the Knowledge Society: New Skills and Instruments for Teachers* (pp. 205–219). Hershey, PA: IGI Global.

Piu, A. (2007). La simulazione al computer in ambito educativo. Prospettive di ricerca. In A. Curatola & O. De Pietro O. (Eds.). *Saperi, competenze, nuove tecnologie. Metodi e strumenti nella formazione* (pp. 199-208). Roma: Monolite.

Piu, C. (2006). La sperimentazione . In Piu, C. (Ed.), *Simulazione e competenze. Gli effetti della simulazione nella certificazione delle competenze e nella loro corretta gestione.* Roma: Monolite.

Randel, J. M., Morris, B. A., Wetzel, C. D., & Whitehill, B. V. (1992). The effectiveness of Games for Educational Purposes. A Review of Recent Research. *Simulation & Gaming, 23,* 261. doi:10.1177/1046878192233001

Rivers, R. H., & Vockell, E. (1987). Computer simulations to stimulate scientific problem solving. *Journal of Research in Science Teaching, 24,* 403–415. doi:10.1002/tea.3660240504

Sarantos, P., Makri-Botsari, E., & Paraskeva, F. (2005-2006). A computer simulation: before or after instruction? *International Journal of learning, 12*(8).

Shute, V. J., & Glaser, R. (1990). A large-scale evaluation of an intelligent discovery world: Smithtown. *Interactive Learning Environments, 1,* 51–77. doi:10.1080/1049482900010104

Stipek, D. J. (1996). *La motivazione nell'apprendimento scolastico.* Torino: SEI.

Teodoro, V. D. (1998). *From formulae to conceptual experiments: interactive modeling in the physical sciences and mathematics.* Invited paper presented at the International CoLos Conference New Network based Media Education, Maribor, Slovenia.

Visalberghi, A. (1978). *Pedagogia e scienze dell'educazione*. Milano: Mondadori.

Winn, W., Stahr, F., Sarason, C., Fruland, R., Oppenheimer, P., & Lee, Y. L. (2006). Learning Oceanography from a Computer Simulation Compared with Direct Experience at Sea. *Journal of Research in Science Teaching, 43*(1), 25–42. doi:10.1002/tea.20097

Wolfe, J., & Crookall, D. (1998). Developing a Scientific Knowledge of Simulation/Gaming. *Simulation & Gaming, 29*(7).

Chapter 12
Research Outline

Angela Piu
University of L'Aquila, Italy

ABSTRACT

This chapter describes how the research was developed: the hypotheses and the decisions taken in the planning stage are explained and the documentation on the carrying out of the project provided along with the research protocols.

INTRODUCTION

Interest in the role of simulation games in the learning/teaching process represents a research area which the promoters of the *Simulandia* project presented herein first began to reflect on at the beginning of the new millennium.

The aim of the early research efforts conducted in those years was to consider the theoretical basis of simulation games in education, from the perspective of recent findings into the learning and teaching process, and the ongoing research on knowledge acquisition and the different ways of learning that have emerged with the growth of the *knowledge society.*

DOI: 10.4018/978-1-60566-930-4.ch012

In other words, with reference to the educational needs of contemporary society, we put together recent research on learning and its emotive-motivational aspects with the characteristics of simulation games in a learning environment in order to identify their potential uses in guided educational contexts.

The operation of systematizing the theoretical and practical work (an investigation carried out in the Province of Cosenza on a sample of secondary school students who took part in the IG students programme)[1] allowed us to assess how the simulation game was perceived, experienced and appreciated by the student as a useful strategy for knowledge acquisition, thanks to the fact that it offers the chance for active participation in the learning process and group work in a context which was unusual if compared to normal teaching methods; these aspects, indeed, favour the growth of motivation, by facilitating self-awareness and helping the students to acquire knowledge skills (Piu A., 2002).

Subsequently, a practical research project carried out into the teaching experiences of primary and junior secondary school teachers at the Istituto Comprensivo "Don Milani" in Crotone, Calabria provided researchers with the opportunity to reflect on the employment of new learner-centred teaching strategies and different kinds of interaction both between teacher and learner and between learner and subject. The reflection triggered learning processes within the research group itself: the subjects were involved in a simulation game that provided the opportunity to experiment in a supportive environment where they could test themselves in the logics of communication and their own relationships with organisationally complex environments and, at the same time, experience both outdoor and indoor adult courses for designers and teachers of training courses[2] (Fregola, 2004; Piu A., 2006).

The considerations made by the research group at the end of the training course have enabled us to analyse a number of characteristics of simulation games from the inside and draw up various options on how the game could be used in schools. The theoretical background has been steadily widened and a decision taken to re-interpret simulation games from the perspective of the ecology of human development (Bronfenbrenner, 1986), in which games are configured as an expansion of the phenomenological world of the subject and appear to be functional part of the process of learning/teaching that goes to determine the learning conditions (Gagné R., 1973).

After the initial work of bringing together the theory with the results obtained, the members of the research group, on a wave of enthusiasm, felt the need to further their investigations and field work to be in a position to carry out data recognition.

in order to examine the advantages and pedagogical value of simulation as an intervention strategy. The work presented in this book illustrates the direction taken by the group as regards in which ambits simulation games were assumed to be most relevant and fruitful. This is the result mainly of classroom observations of geometry and arithmetic lessons and of the spatio-temporal dimensions of the learning process, that can be shown to ensure development in the areas of learning and motivation in the process of acquiring mathematical concepts in relation to the level of involvement and level of significance of the results. Having said that, there are undoubtedly problem areas to be explored.

In light of the evolution of the studies and comparisons, two more research actions have been started which, although not strictly relating to simulation games per se but rather to simulation activities, have nevertheless made a contribution and improved the project's expertise in the ambit of simulation with particular reference to education:

a. research-action, in the technological ambit, which has allowed us to reflect on the possible effects of the simulation in the certification and construction of the competences and in their correct management in the university teaching (Piu C., 2006). Here simulation activities have allowed for the interaction of the theoretical acquisition from previous works with ambits related to the more complex and articulated learning process. The results were significant and provided evidence within a broader project, representing added value for the educational work developed in e-learning.

b. research-action, in the ambit of mathematics teaching, through the construction of a shared route between the concrete and the abstract in a semi-structured learning environment close to the simulation field (Fregola, 2006). The research has highlighted the possibility of studying certain processes of abstraction related to learning which lead the student to the discovery of a concept in virtual loci through immersion. (Maragliano, 1998, 1998: Levy, 1997).

Conscious of the complexities of the research matters raised in recent years and thanks to the competence acquired by the group in the planning of simulation activities, the members of the group decided to focus attention on research into simulation games applied to the learning process in a specific subject area: logic-maths.

RESEARCH FRAMEWORK

The underlying of assumption of this research effort is that simulation games can provide a dynamic venue for learning and, in particular, for math teaching. Our research aim is to immerse the students in a complex mesh of virtual and everyday reality at the centre of the didactic process and stimulate their motivation as well as their sense of self-efficacy. The issues behind our work are the *mathematization* of reality, learning processes and motivation required to sustain the acquisition of mathematical language and its possible applications in primary and lower secondary school.

Within this context the research concerns the design, realization and experimentation of simulation games applied to math teaching with three basic goals in mind:

- experiment with certain aspects of the evolution of educational science that have provided learning and teaching models that can guide the teaching practice in order to act as a catalyst for motivation that can sustain, over time, the acquisition of math knowledge;
- investigate certain structures and dynamics of simulation games applied to the learning and construction of mathematical language through abstraction and formalization;
- promote meta-cognitive control mechanisms that develop inside the simulation game and guide the growth of self-efficacy.

The aim of the research program is to encourage a reflection on the environments that can lead to a motivating and effective system of math teaching and create a framework for the research into the role of simulation games in terms of:

- Systemizing previous research;
- Identifying the criteria that guide the design of simulation games;
- Identifying the dynamics of administering the games with reference to contents and ways of interaction.

OBJECTIVES

The research aims to spark a reflection on the building of learning environments to construct a motivating and effective repertoire for math teaching with specific reference to simulation games.

Through simulation, we aim to provide learning immersion situations combining virtual environments with more traditional aspects of math teaching. The assumption is that every child is capable of abstract thought that can be elaborated and drawn towards the construction of a conscious system of planning, action and monitoring of his or her learning process.

Within this context we propose a social learning experience based on sharing to promote learning processes, social participation and emotional maturity through the structure of the game that requires cooperation, respect for the rules and a shared objective.

Simulation games create a dynamic context within which all players have to tackle problems, question reality, take decisions, abide by the rules and pursue common objectives. They differ from other teaching practices in that they provide a molar activity that develops through group work, has a clear goal, continues in time and can lead to a broadening of horizons, by encouraging learners to find connections with other situations.

The process of *mathematization* of reality that leads to the discovery of concepts, rules and structures as well as covering complex concepts of arithmetic and geometry, can encourage learners to find patterns in reality and develop a gradual understanding of reality itself.

The teaching approach is based on the pattern of transcoding that, from a didactic point of view, is intended to organize the language, the setting and the learning environment, defining the teaching content on various levels of abstraction in order to facilitate the construction of a language that is meaningful and enjoyable and can act as a bridge towards the attainment of mathematical language.

As can be seen from a study of the literature, which is still fragmentary and incomplete, simulation games for math learning deal almost exclusively with economic themes, such as handling money, or probabilities; they often require the use of the computer and, overall, it is clear that many aspects have been insufficiently explored up till now:

- process of abstraction, encoding, decoding, transcoding and the learning transfers involved in acquiring mathematics;
- the construction of representations in code that gradually becomes more formal through the use of mathematical language;
- the interaction between cognitive, affective and social aspects that play a fundamental role in math learning;
- the development of relational and meta-cognitive areas.

PHASES

The program is structured in 3 phases:

1. Theoretical and methodological analysis. The aim of this phase is to: analyze the literature on simulation games for math learning in order to define criteria for the classification of previous research on simulation games; define the epistemological environment for math learning, using educational psychology to identify the methodological aspects that orientate the decision making process in the design phase.

2. The design of simulation games. After identifying the criteria from the relevant literature and theories of educational psychology, we will concentrate in this phase on studying the repertoire of relational competences to be stimulated by the teacher in directing the game, at the same time as monitoring the three areas of conduct of the learners: the contents, individual and group relationships, and the didactic process. Since the simulation games, as well as the instruments for verifying and monitoring, are designed for transcoding patterns, this phase also includes a try-out to test the game and carry out an item analysis in order to check the feedback procedures. Our aim is to involve math teachers, the real experts in the field, in the design process.

Experiment. The hypothesis at the base of the *Simulandia* project, is that- with respect to traditional methods- simulation games and the exercises used in them can influence not only the specific learning of mathematical concepts, different learning functions and variables that facilitate acquisition, but also develop and consolidate skills that characterise mathematical thought and the construction of language. We intend to ascertain whether, by using simulation games as learning environments, one can contribute to developing strategies that improve learner self-efficacy and autonomy. Action in simulation contexts helps focus attention on the process of *mathematization* by bringing together aspects from the complexities of daily life with problem solving activities that require the use of learning strategies, which, in turn, develop and take shape through the activity.

The overall paradigm guiding the methodological integration can be traced back to that of self- efficacy (Olmetti Peja, 2007). In particular, the target that will be used in the project relates to a teaching method aimed at introducing primary school children to the study of isometrics and the study of percentages.

The following research hypotheses have been formulated: In a primary school class the use of simulation games (on the introduction to isometrics or the introduction to percentages) with respect to the traditional lesson:

H(1)= facilitates the learning of skills and the ability to think mathematically
H(2)= facilitates the memorising of skills learnt and the ability to think mathematically
H(3)= improves the motivation in maths learning
H(4)= improves scholastic and social self-efficacy

The simulation games are designed with a specific aim to replace those currently on sale or found in the literature that are unsuitable and inadequate. One for geometry and one for arithmetic. Alongside these games are the verification tests and observation instruments. In this phase of the research we intend to involve maths teachers who have a certain expertise in the syllabus planning of their subject.

The design of the games entails, moreover, a necessary try-out phase to asses the working of the game and carry out a detailed analysis of the tests in order to confirm the suitability of the research instruments.

From the methodological point of view the project aims to adopt both an experimental and a qualitative approach.

The experimental approach can be divided into two groups:

a.   the experimental group who will play the simulation game;
b.   the control group who will participate in a face to face lesson.

For the formation of groups a questionnaire was administered on multiple intelligences (Mc Kenzie, W., 2005), from the results of which the children were divided into groups in such a way as to avoid similar profiles with respect to intelligence repertoires revealed by the questionnaire. To do this cluster analysis was used. Later the groups were given pre-tests and post-tests to assess the learning results of the mathematical contents of the experiment as well as questionnaires on self-efficacy and on the motivation to learn mathematics.

The objective is to test the hypothesis of a change between pre-test and post-test as a result of the intervention, and to look for correlations between the results of the maths learning and cognitive, meta-cognitive and affective variables that the other instruments employed will allow us to observe. The two groups share the same syllabus and the same teacher. It was not possible to carry out the experiment in perfect laboratory conditions with rigorous control and isolation of the variables as this is difficult to achieve in field work experiments with children. Yet the aim was to carry out the work in a scientific manner following valid protocols and research procedures.

As regards the qualitative approach, we shall assess though the feedback from the questionnaires the materials used and/or produced by the two groups in the classes to tackle the problem situations and the discussion on the hypotheses of possible solutions put forward by the pupils. Moreover the behaviour of the pupils during the activities will be observed and assessed through the relevant descriptive learning lists. The open questions contained in the tests will be carried out through a coding based on an ordering, defined by a group of experts, of the correctness of the definitions given in natural language. On account of the somewhat vague nature of natural language, the coding will be carried out through the definition of a group of fuzzy sets[3].

To sum up, the procedure for experimentation and analysis is as follows:

Step 1.
- administration of the McKenzie test to the pupils of each class on the basis of which the groups taking part in the experiment will be selected
- formation of two groups through cluster analysis
- random selection of students in non homogenous manner to two groups of the same class determined by cluster analysis
- Face-to-face lesson group
- Simulation game group

Step 2.

Administration of following tests to each pupil:

- cognitive performance
- motivation in learning maths
- perceived scholastic and social self-efficacy
- Data analysis for each of the two macro-groups
- Paragon analysis of two groups

Step 3.
- Experimental teaching phase for two macro-groups

Step 4.
Administration of post-test to all pupils regarding:

- cognitive performance
- motivation in learning maths
- perceived scholastic and social self-efficacy
- Administration of learning verification after 30 days
- Data analysis for two macro groups
- Paragon analysis of the two learning groups
- Paragon analysis between before and after Step 3

Step 5.
- Analysis of the most sensitive variables in the learning phase
- Interpretation and communication of data

The realisation of the experimentation is preceded by the presentation and sharing of the group aims with the school director and teaching staff of the classes selected to participate in the project and by the selection and training of the project coordinator.

In order to make the research process explicit to all the actors involved, ensure that the objectives are clearly understood and shared, and guarantee uniformity in the conduct both of the lesson and the simulation game, two documents on the experimentation have been drawn up (see section 5).

The research project concludes with the final report in which the data obtained in the trials and the completed questionnaires received from both the experimental and control is analysed, and the information is considered in relation to the theoretical hypotheses of the research.

In addition to this, we shall include all the elements employed in the research from the assumptions made in the choice of procedures to the instruments and how these have been utilised in order to communicate the work undertaken to the scientific community, who will assess its merits and validity.

EXPERIMENTATION DOCUMENTS

For those who would like to try the experiment themselves, this section will include the documentation drawn up for the schools participating in the project with all the relevant information. This however, only concerns one of the two games used, but the procedure of the first game can be easily applied to the second. The games we refer to with their respective verification tests are, on the other hand, presented in chapter 9.

For the direction of the research it was necessary to establish a guide for the games not just to describe and explain the rules and procedures, but also to define the stages:

rather than create inflexibility they enable the teacher to impose a structure and control of the contributions that develop creatively in the group communication, providing direction for the contents to be abstracted and formalized in mathematical language.

The Director

Dear...

The chair of Experimental Education in the department of the "Science of Primary Education" at the University of L'Aquila in association with the University of Rome Three and the University of Calabria have begun a field work research project, whose aim is to test a number of teaching strategies for learning mathematics and to assess the results of primary school pupils.

The aim is to identify the teaching methodologies than could integrate the usual techniques with an approach that includes emotional and relational aspects, often unconscious, in strategies for teaching mathematics. The objective is to act on the motivational process and overcome certain obstacles to learning mathematics.

Thanks to the collaboration with the teacher..., who has agreed to coordinate the necessary activities, we would like to invite your school to be part of the group of schools involved in this research.

We thank you for your attention and look forward to your participation in the project. In the meantime we remain at your disposal for any clarification on the matter.

Kind regards

L'Aquila

Angela Piu

Associate professor

Department of Experimental Education

University of L'Aquila

Dear colleague,

We are happy you have accepted to take part in this experiment conducted by the Universities of Aquila, Rome 3 and the University of Calabria. The experiment proposes to test a number of didactic strategies for learning mathematics and to assess results of primary school pupils.

The subject chosen for the research is isometrics.

In order to made our research more rigorous we have attached to this letter two documents containing information and instructions on how to carry out the work, the materials to use and documentation we would ask you to return after the work has been completed.

We would further like to point out that we have chosen a coordinator for your school, who will be on hand to clarify any doubts that might arise during the course of the experiment.

We thank you for your kind cooperation and offer our best regards.

L'Aquila, ...

Angela Piu

Associate professor

Department of Experimental Education

University of L'Aquila

DOCUMENT ON EXPERIMENT: SIMULATION GAME

This document:

1. Presents the activities to be done;
2. Gives information on how the simulation game is played and its timing
3. Gives instructions on the documentation to be handed out at the end of the experiment.

INTRODUCTIONARY NOTE

The activity we ask you to carry out with your pupils aims to introduce the study of isometrics through a specially made simulation game (attachment 1A) to be carried out with the following instructions.

The specific aims to pursue are the following:

1. Identify direct and indirect congruent shapes.
2. Define the concept of isometry
3. Identify the characteristics of isometrics in relation to shape, direction and movement.
4. Identify direct and inverse congruent shapes using translation, rotation and symmetry or a combination of translation and rotation.

5.   Invent and use an economic "code" shared by the group to communicate isometric characteristics.

    In order to pursue these aims you are invited to involve the pupils in a simulation game, set in a small town called Cardland. The activity consists in involving the students in the solution of a problem situation presented in this scenario, making sure the students are able to work actively and freely during the game, but still following the rules and acting out the roles given. This will allow them to "enter" the spirit of the game and to make decisions and adopt coherent behaviors within the context of the task.

    As regards the teacher, you have the task of directing the simulation game. At the beginning it will be your job to explain the scenario to the students, the instructions and the different phases of the games, trying to motivate and interest them; during the game it will be your task to help and monitor the running of the game, stepping in when problems arise, while at the end it will be your task to promote and conduct the final discussion that is of fundamental importance as it is the moment when the concepts, the rules and the geometrical operations that emerged during the simulation are analyzed and placed in relation to each other.

HOW TO CONDUCT THE SIMULATION GAME

The game is divided into four main stages: opening, briefing, running of the game and debriefing.

    In the following table suggestions are presented for every phase on how to conduct the game. We advise you to read these suggestions along with attachment 1A for specific information on the simulation game.

Opening

- Raise interest, curiosity, attention (refer to the participants' experiences)
- Establish a positive rapport with the participants (maintain visual contact, explain the rules).
- Explain the characteristics of the simulation game.

Briefing (Presentation of the Game)

- Clarify the scenario and the problematic situation of the game.
- Explain in a clear and precise way the aims of the simulation.

- Give instructions on how to do the activity, avoid uncertainty and long-winded explanations that could put the participants off even before the game has started.
- Illustrate the phases and the rules
- Assign roles.
- Use a language that is simple, clear and appropriate.

Running of the Game

- Help pupils play the game.
- Monitor the different phases.
- Step in if problems occur.

Debriefing (Final Discussion)

Conduct the discussion according to the guidelines in the project document to involve all the participants, to listen to them and analyze and systemize the contents and the mathematical processes.

Instructions on the Documentation and Timing

The phases of the experiment involve:

1. Filling in tables: where confidential information on the students is requested (privacy laws) and on the duration of the different phases of the game, the task must be completed by the teacher;
2. Giving out worksheets and a final test, to be filled in by the students.

In the following table information is given on the timing of the various tasks.
Preliminary phase. This phase must involve all the class. At the end the documentation must be given to the coordinator indicated to the school by the research group.

1. Fill in the table (attachment 2)
2. Hand out the test (attachment 3)
3. Hand in the documents to the coordinator and await instructions on the names of the pupils who will play the simulation game.

The following phases will involve only the students selected by the coordinator:

- Give the coordinator all the completed documentation
- Give the completed documentation to the coordinator

DOCUMENT ON EXPERIMENT: LESSON

The following document:

1. Presents the activity to be done
2. Gives indications and suggestions on how to run the lesson and the timing.
3. Gives instructions on the documentation to be handed in at the end of the experiment.

INTRODUCTORY NOTE

The aim of the activity we ask you to run with your pupils is to introduce them to the study of isometrics using the "face to face" lesson (attachment 1B) to be carried out with the following instructions

The specific aims to be pursued are the following:

1. Identify direct and inverse congruent figures.
2. Define the concept of isometry
3. Define the characteristics of isometrics in relation to shape, direction and movement.
4. Identify direct and inverse congruent figures using translation, rotation, and symmetry or a combination of translation and rotation.
5. Invent and use an economic "code" shared by the group to communicate the characteristics of isometrics.

Table 1.

Before starting the game.	1. Hand out the test (attachments 4 and 5) 2. Hand out the verification test (attachment 6)
During the game:	1. Fill in the table (attachment 7)
At the end of the game:	1. Hand out the verification test again (attachment 6) 2. Hand out the test (attachment 4 and 5)

Table 2.

30 days from the day the game ended	1. Hand out the verification test (attachment 6)

In order to achieve these aims you are invited to involve the pupils in a face to face lesson, full of examples that will make the presentation more concrete, and to involve them in exercises. This will allow them to use the concepts introduced in the explanation.

So, the teacher has the task of directing the lesson. At the beginning it will be your role to illustrate to the pupils a frame of reference for the lesson, making sure to motivate and capture their interest; during the lesson you will have to present, develop, and interconnect the key concepts using examples and organizing the exercises so as to help the students remember such concepts, while at the end of the lesson you will have the fundamental task of summarizing the contents of the lesson.

HOW TO CONDUCT THE LESSON

The lesson is divided into three main stages: opening, body, conclusion.

In the following table suggestions on how to conduct the lesson are reported for each stage. It is advisable to read these suggestions along with attachment 1B which provides specific information on the conduct of the lesson.

Opening

- Raise interest, curiosity, attention (refer to the participants' experiences)
- Provide a frame of reference for the lesson (explain the scope of the lesson, announce the structure of the explanations, explain possible connections with concepts dealt with previously)
- Establish a positive rapport with the participants (maintain eye contact, explain the stages of the work)

Body

- Develop the lesson around key concepts (mark the importance of key concepts with concepts that demonstrate their validity and importance, organize the content in relation to students' needs)
- Inductive sequence (presentation of a problem, analysis of the various aspects of the problem with reasoned generalizations based on a reference theory)
- Use examples, which make the presentation more concrete and help the transmission of complex concepts
- Repeat key concepts to help their memorization, reformulating the same concepts using different terminology
- Use a language that is simple, clear and appropriate

- Check comprehension of the content by asking questions
- Give feedback on the questions
- Organize exercises

Conclusion

Recapitulate the contents of the lesson.

INSTRUCTIONS ON THE DOCUMENTATION AND ON THE TIMING

The experimental phase presents:

1. The filling in of various tables: where confidential information on the students is requested and information on the times of the different phases, this is to be carried out by the teacher;
2. The handing out of work sheets and the verification test to be given to the students.

In the following table information is given on the timing for the filling in of the tables and the handing out of the work sheets and the verification test.

Phase 1. This phase must include all the class. At the end the documentation is to be handed to the coordinator indicated to the school by the research group.

The preliminary phase is common to the two activities, so the necessary documentation will be collected at the same time.
1. Fill in the table (attachment 2)
2. Hand out the test (attachment 3)
3. Hand out these documents to the coordinator and await directions on the names of the students chosen for the next phase.
The following phases involve only the students chosen by the coordinator
Before starting the lesson:
1. Hand out the work sheets (attachment 4 and 5)
2. Hand out the verification test (attachment 6)
During the lesson:
1. Fill in the table (attachment 7B)

At the end of the lesson:
2.   Hand out the verification test once again (attachment 6)
3.   Hand out the tests again (attachment 4 and 5)
Hand all the completed documentation to the coordinator
30 days after the end of the lesson:
1.   Give out the verification test
Hand all the completed documentation to the coordinator

ATTACHMENT 1B: LESSON INTRODUCTION TO ISOMETRY

Requirements

Define in your own language the meaning of:

- Equality
- Distance
- Movement
- To be able to cut out shapes.

Specific Aims

- To identify direct and inverse congruent shapes.
- To define the concept of isometry.•
- To identify isometric characteristics in relation to the shape, direction and movement.
- To identify direct and inverse congruent shapes using translation, rotation, symmetry or by combining translation and rotation.
- To invent and use an economic "code" shared by the group to communicate isometric characteristics.

Lesson

Refer to the classic functions of a classroom lesson.

Materials

- transparencies;
- drawing pins;

- markers for transparencies;
- blank sheets of paper;

MAIN CONCEPTS AND SUGGESTIONS

1. **Congruency**. During the game you have superimposed many footprints and shapes. Were they all the same or congruent as mathematicians say? When can we say two pictures are congruent? (If two footprints, shapes or pictures overlapped precisely! That is if we are able to match two pictures in every point). That's good enough for the moment!

2. **Direct and inverse congruency.** What movement have you used to superimpose the shapes? Did you use the same movement to superimpose the right outline with the right one and the left one with the right one? Did you notice any differences when you made the superimposition? (For example, to superimpose the outline of the right foot you have to drag the transparency or you have to rotate it. While to superimpose the footprint of the left foot with the footprint of the right foot you have to turn the picture on the transparency over. Therefore, in the first case you have superimposed the two footprints of the right foot by a movement in the plane, while in the second case you have superimposed the right footprint with the left one with a movement in space). Well done! So in the first case we talk about direct congruency, in the second case about inverse congruency. Now let's try to make a geometrical picture! Which one do you suggest? What happens in this case?

3. **Direction of the path covered and surface affected.** Which other differences did you notice about the surface after making the movement? And what about the distance of the path covered? (The direction of the path and the surface do not change in the case of a direct congruency but they vary, instead, in the case of inverse congruency).

4. **The symbols of the code.** Mathematicians, when they speak among themselves, often use symbols in order to be precise and to make their discussions quicker. What symbols would you use to refer to all these changes? How would you choose these symbols? Let's compare and discuss them together! Mathematicians call the "dragging" translation, for rotation they use the same word and they refer to turning something over as symmetry.

5. **Isometric definition.** Up to now we have analyzed what varies and what does not after you have done the movements with the footprints. So, what doesn't change? (The figures remain the same after the movement: the dragging, the rotation and the turning over. In particular, the distance, "metry" (metros) from the word isometry, between the points of the pictures remains the "same"

Table 3.

	Translation	**Rotation**	**Axial symmetry (with an external axis)**
The direction of the path covered on the border	Remains unchanged	Remains unchanged	Changes
The surface of the shape	Remains unchanged	Remains unchanged	Changes
The movement	Occurs on the plain	Occurs on the plain	Occurs in the space
The shape	Is not distorted	Is not distorted	Is not distorted
In the figure	The distances between its points remain constant	The distances between its points remain constant	The distances between its points remain constant

(i.e., iso). For this reason mathematicians have decided to call the movements that leave unchanged the distances between the points of a geometric figure "isometries")

6. **Summary.** Now let's sum up what has been said so far! And...thank you for your participation!

Duration

2 hours.

Evaluation

The methodology helps us take into consideration, not just the planned verification along the usual lines but also intermediate and final learning strategies, with the scope of achieving results by using structured and semi-structured verification tests in the simulation process.

ATTACHMENT 2

School.......................................
Class...
Teacher......................................

Table 4.

Pupil	Sex (M/F)	Age	Mark in math of the previous year	Disability Certification (yes/no)
1.				
2.				
3.				
4.				
5.				
6.				
7.				
8.				
9.				
10.				
11.				
12.				
13.				
14.				
15.				
16.				
17.				
18.				
19.				
20.				

ATTACHMENT 7A: SIMULATION GAME

School...
Class..
Teacher...

Table 5.

Phases (report the phases indicated in the second paragraph of the document)	Time (report the duration of every phase)
Phase:opening	
Phase: briefing	
Phase: carrying out of the task	
Phase: debriefing	

Report the list of the names of the participants (or numbers or codes for everyone)

Table 6.

1.
2.
3.
4.
5.
6.
7.
8.

ATTACHMENT 7B: LESSON

School...
Class...
Teacher...

Table 7.

Phases (report the phases indicated in the second paragraph of the document)	Time (report the duration of every phase)
Phase: opening	
Phase: body	
Phase: conclusion	

Report the list of the names of the participants (or numbers or codes for everyone)

Table 8.

1.
2.
3.
4.
5.
6.
7.
8.

REFERENCES

Ausubel, D. P. (1995). *Educazione e processi cognitivi*. Milano: Franco Angeli.

Bronfenbrenner, U. (1986). *Ecologia dello sviluppo umano*. Bologna: Il Mulino.

Bruner, J. (1997). *La cultura dell'educazione*. Milano: Feltrinelli.

Cengarle, M. (1989). L'uso delle tecniche di simulazione nella formazione dei negoziatori . In Cecchini, A., & Indovina, F. (Eds.), *Simulazione. Milano: Franco Angeli. Cornoldi, C. (1995). Metacognizione e Apprendimento*. Bologna: Il Mulino.

Curatola, A., & De Pietro, O. (Eds.). (2006). *Saperi, competenze, nuove tecnologie. Metodi e strumenti nella formazione*. Roma: Monolite.

de Kerckhove, D. (1991). *Brainframes, Mente, Tecnologia, Mercato. Come le tecnologie della comunicazione trasformano la mente umana*. Bologna: Baskerville.

Delors, J. (1998). *Nell'Educazione un Tesoro*. Roma: Armando.

Dorn, D. S. (1989). Simulation Game: One more tool on the pedagogical shelf. *Teaching Sociology*, 17.

Fischbein, E. (1998). *Conoscenza intuitiva e conoscenza logica nell'attività matematica*. Bologna: Pitagora.

Fischbein, E., & Vergnaud, G. (1992). *Matematica a scuola: teorie ed esperienze*. Bologna: Pitagora.

Fregola, C. (2004). I livelli d'astrazione nell'apprendimento matematico attraverso i materiali montessoriani. In Centro di Studi Montessoriani. *Annuario 2003 – Attualità di Maria Montessori*. Milano: Franco Angeli.

Fregola, C. (2007). La bussola, il sussidiario, la virtualizzazione nell'educazione matematica . In Curatola, A., & De Pietro, O. (Eds.), *Saperi, competenze, nuove tecnologie. Metodi e strumenti nella formazione*. Roma: Monolite.

Gagnè, R. M. (1973). *Le condizioni dell'apprendimento*. Roma: Armando.

Lèvy, P. (1997). *Il virtuale*. Milano: Raffaello Cortina.

Lucisano, P., & Salerni, A. (2002). *Metodologia della ricerca in educazione e formazione*. Roma: Carocci.

Maragliano, R. (1996). *Esseri Multimediali*. Firenze: La Nuova Italia.

Maragliano, R. (1998). *Nuovo manuale di didattica multimediale*. Bari: Laterza.

Mc Kenzie, W. (2005). *Intelligenze multiple e tecnologie per la didattica*. Trento: Erickson.

Montuschi, F. (1987). *Vita affettiva e percorsi dell'intelligenza*. Brescia: La Scuola.

Montuschi, F. (1993). *Competenza affettiva e apprendimento*. Brescia: La Scuola.

Olmetti Peja, D. (1998). *Teorie e tecniche dell'osservazione in classe*. Firenze: Giunti.

Olmetti Peja, D. (2007). Diventare studenti strategici. In D.Olmetti Peja & C. Fregola C. (Eds.), *Superare un esame. Come trasformare ansia, emotività e studio in risorse strategiche*. Napoli: EdiSES.

Piu, A. (2002). *Processi formativi e simulazione. Fondamenti teorici e dimensioni operative*. Roma: Monolite.

Piu, A. (2006). Simulation, Training, and Education between Theory and Practice . In Cartelli, A. (Ed.), *Teaching in the Knowledge Society: New Skills and Instruments for Teachers* (pp. 205–219). Hershey, PA: IGI Global.

Piu, C. (2006). *Simulazione e competenze. Gli effetti della simulazione nella certificazione delle competenze e nella loro corretta gestione*. Roma: Monolite.

Pontecorvo, C. (Ed.). (1993). *La condivisione della conoscenza*. Firenze: La Nuova Italia.

Vergnaud, G. (1994). *Le rôle de l'enseignement à la lumière des concepts de schème et de champ conceptuel*. In M. Artigue, R. Grass, C. Laborde & P. Tavignot (Eds.), *Vingt ans de didactique des mathématiques en France* (pp. 177-191). Grenoble: La Pensée sauvage.

ENDNOTES

[1]   The IG Students programme involved senior secondary students from across Italy in a project to create and run enterprises through simulation. This initiative was part of a larger one conducted throughout Europe called Young Enterprise Europe which, in Italy, was led by the non profit organisation IG Students, that gave its name to the proposed programme based entirely on business simulations in Italy

[2]   In particular the training programmes was centred on the internal staff of the Region of Umbria and it soon became an environment in which adults were involved in simulations requiring full personal and professional commitment, stimulating the cognitive, socio-affective, emotional relational and psycho-motor spheres. Through this initiative it was possible to witness adults who were able to rediscover aspects of learning in a context sheltered from the power games dynamics of many organisations, a context in which they could feel at ease both with themselves and others.

[3]   The quality of what is fuzzy affirms that everything is measurable. The quality of what is fuzzy has a formally scientific name, i.e., polyvalence. The opposite of fuzzy is bivalent or having two values, two ways to respond to every question: true or false, 1 or 0. The quality fuzzy means polyvalence, i.e., two or three options, maybe an infinite spectrum of options, rather than only two extreme alternatives, or to put it another way instead of binary, infinite shades of grey between white and black. It means everything that judges or lawyers during a debate seek to exclude when they say, " Answer yes or no." (Kosko B., 1997). The use of fuzzy logic is still being debated in the epistemology of science. We have chosen to connect our decision to make use of it with a strategy of educational evaluation in a learning environment that, in turn, is the object of our research and thus of evaluation. The possibilities of fuzzy logic have led us to apply it in our research as an experimental element to be placed in relation to validation of efficiency of the transcoding pattern, with a methodology based, in any event, on qualitative and quantitative aspects.

Chapter 13
Research Results

Angela Piu
University of L'Aquila

Cesare Fregola
Roma Tre University

Claudia Abundo
Roma Tre University

Salvatore Fregola
IanusLab Catanzaro

ABSTRACT

In this chapter, we present the research process followed in the work from the try out phase for each game, the testing of materials and methods, the definition of research protocols, thus the experimental procedure, the description data analysis and the interpretation of the results. Finally, we present the primary results of our work in the primary school classroom, where we proposed the Cartolandia experiment.

THE TRY-OUT PHASE

Cartolandia

The try-out phase of the Cartolandia simulation game was carried out with Class 3 of the St. Foruli primary school (Scoppito), which is part of the Comenio comprehensive institute in Aquila with the collaboration of teachers Mauro Ciotti and Michele Di Lisio, who were both engaged in the construction of the materials for the game.

DOI: 10.4018/978-1-60566-930-4.ch013

In particular, Mauro Ciotti and Michele Di Lisio constructed the map, chose the image for Cartolandia, designed and constructed the "carto-carpet" and selected the images for the shapes. It was decided to construct the carto-carpet in a size that would not take up too much room (2x3 metres) in order to allow the children to move round it and work more easily in collaboration with each other. Shapes were chosen in which the feet would correspond to the footprints in order to make the investigation more real and logical. In this phase both teachers introduced various useful modifications to improve the performance of the game and began to whet the pupils' appetite before the start of the game proper.

The actual workability of the simulation game, one of the main objectives of the pilot project was tested on Class 3, in which Mauro Ciotti conducted the game with three groups of pupils from his own class at different times in February 2008. In rotation, the children divided into groups of five took part in the game, while their classmates were involved in other activities outside the classroom with other teachers. Meanwhile, Michele Di Lisio, who was already familiar to the pupils having carried out his teacher training practice in that class, was able to participate in the role of observer, without being seen as an outsider by the children.

For the three groups, the presentation of the scenario and the explanation of the problem situation lasted thirty minutes on average, while an average sixty five minutes was calculated for the simulation game itself, excluding the debriefing phase, which took thirty minutes.

From the work of observation it emerges that there were no interruptions during the activity of any of the three groups. The pupils manipulated the materials, utilised the transparencies accurately, kept to the rules, followed the recommended procedure (albeit with some variations but nevertheless within the determined limits of the task analysis) and achieved the object of the game by finding out and providing the name of the culprit.

Every child was actively involved. With reference to this, the indicators used in the observation work, are mainly based on the frequency of dialogues, interactions, exchanges and actions using the transparencies on which the shapes and footprints were traced. Only one child in the second group did not participate in the group work. It was also recorded that one child in the third group introduced only inverse and direct congruence; moreover, another pupil in the first group and a pupil in the third group intuited rotation before the teacher's explanation.

All the children were given a test the results of which were used to carry out an item analysis, following this a number of modifications were made.

In relation to the learning objective of the simulation game, through the considerations that emerged during its realisation a grill of descriptors was drawn up to be used to conduct the observation and evaluation both during and at the end of the game. Furthermore a decision was reached to add another learning objective that despite being one of the authors' intentions had not been adequately expressed. This objective is as follows: "Identify direct and inverse congruent figures by using translation, rotation and symmetry or a combination of translation and rotation". Following the redefinition of the objectives, the rules for the *carto-lab* were also improved and are now formulated in this way:

1. You can let the footprint or shape on the transparency slide sideways, up or down, without removing the sheet from the surface.
2. You can rotate the figure by sticking a pin at the corner of the transparency.
3. You can turn over the transparency keeping the edge of the sheet at the same distance from the respective figure (footprint or shape).
4. You can let the footprint or shape on the transparency slide sideways, up or down, and then also rotate it by putting a pin at the corner of the transparency.

At the end a decision was taken to indicate the maximum number of players. After the try-out phase, Eledia Mangia coordinated the task of preparing all the materials to be employed during the game itself.

The City in Percentages

The try-out phase of the "city in percentages" simulation game was carried out with Class 1 at the L. Milani Scuola Media, part of the Istituto Comprensivo Montessori, in Giuliano Milanese (MI) and managed by Anna Santoro, a teacher. In particular Anna Santoro together with teaching assistant Girolamo Pagano constructed a percentage machine on the basis of indications supplied by the designers of the game. A4 was the choice of size in order to keep the length of the material to be inserted uniform, while the width of the different sheets to be inserted could be variable.

The game's workability was tested by three groups of pupils of the aforementioned class at different times in December 2008. In rotation the children divided into groups of seven participated in the game, while their classmates were involved in other activities outside the classroom with different teachers.

For the three groups the presentation of the scenario and explanation of the problem situation lasted an average thirty minutes, while the simulation game itself lasted an average three hours for each group, excluding the debriefing phase that took thirty minutes.

The results of the observation show that there were no interruptions to the game for any of the groups. Pupils manipulated the materials, kept to the rules following the recommended procedure and achieved the objective of the game, presenting the chart with the plan of the sporting facilities both in the initial specifications of the firms and the ones later suggested by the children themselves to improve the centre. On the charts, therefore, we can find, besides the common features, also bowling greens and other swimming pools. All the children were involved in the activities and displayed active participation, as can be seen from the observation through the frequency of dialogues and interaction recorded, and the use of the machine to calculate the percentages, especially by the children given the role of machine operatives.

Following the try-out phase Anna Santoro supplied a number of useful indications for the final definition of the project. In particular, she suggested the need for a clearer explanation in the first phase of the game in order to supply the children with advice on how to define a sketch of the plan to draw on the chart that would make it easier to complete the task. The suggestion taken on board is the following: starting with a sketch, prepare the chart on which to add, one at a time, the strips of card obtained from the percentage machine for the realisation of the plan.

Ms Santoro also suggested that the roles should be alternated at the teacher's discretion so that each participant can have a chance to utilise the percentage machine.

EXPERIMENTAL PROCEDURE

The aim of the research is to find out whether there is better learning and better retention of what has been learnt, better motivation and greater self-efficacy in the simulation game compared with traditional method of face-to-face teaching.

The statistical analysis of the data on the experimental work carried out has been developed in stages through the study of research results.

Group Selection

Two groups were defined for each class, an experimental and a control group. The former took part in a learning game, while the second had a face-to-face lesson.

For the subdivision of the classes a Gardner test was given to each pupil with 90 questions on multiple intelligences (verbal, visual, logical, musical, kinaesthetic, naturalistic, existential, interpersonal, intrapersonal).

The responses were then studied through cluster analysis, which is a data reduction technique that groups cases or variables on the basis of similarity measures. From the results obtained with this method three groups were determined, two experimental and one control with the same external structure but with a different internal one.

The two experimental groups can be analysed as a single group, since the three groups have a similar structure with respect to the observed characteristics, i.e., the variables identified through the Gardner test.

The Tests

Later the pupils were given:

- the social self-efficacy test, on self evaluation of learning and organising the study of the different school subjects, with respect to a numerical scale of ability;
- the scholastic self-efficacy test on learning and organising the various school subjects with respect to a numerical scale of ability;
- the motivation test for learning geometry; his test, including both positive and negative judgements on the subject evaluated on the same scale, is then recoded on a new scale in order to draw all the responses simultaneously;
- a verification of the learning of isometrics.

All the tests were analysed first at a descriptive level in order to have an overview on the pupils' self-evaluation and the information on certain preliminary learning conditions.

The descriptive analysis of the data was carried out separately on each of the two macro-groups for all the tests.

After playing the game the tests previously administered to the pupils were given out again and the learning test once again after 30 days.

The data supplied provides information on the variations of the pupils regarding

- social self-efficacy
- academic self-efficacy
- motivation
- learning
- learning retention after a predefined period of time.

A statistical analysis of the data was carried out, therefore, separately for each of the two learning groups on the results of the second series of tests and a comparative analysis of the two learning groups.

The Formulation of the Data Analysis

The comparative analysis between the test results before and after the experiment with the two teaching methods will be carried out with different techniques depending on whether it concerns single classes or a study of the whole school, or the total of all the schools involved in the research for methodological reasons.

In particular, for the comparative analysis of a single class a variance analysis will be used (ANOVA) with repeated measurements in order to determine whether there are significant differences between the scores obtained on the learning tests both before and after the experiment for each type of lesson.

In the multi-variance approach to data analysis the designs that contain both fixed and random factors are mixed designs. Among these we can find, therefore, designs in which one or more factors are compared by repeating the measurements of the same subjects.

ANOVA with repeated measurements can thus be substituted by a suitable linear mixed model. The comparative analysis of the total of the information from the different classes will, in this way, be carried out with a linear mixed model in which the classes are coded and inserted in the model as contingent effects.

The statistical analysis of the learning tests, as aforementioned, concern the quantitative analysis that will not take account of the open questions contained in the tests. The analysis of the responses supplied by the students has been carried out through a coding based on an ordering, defined by a group of experts, of the correctness of the definitions given in natural language. On account of the somewhat vague nature of natural language, the coding was executed through the definition of a group of fuzzy sets. The statistical analysis, elaborated with analytical techniques on the fuzzy data of the distances between such sets, can allow the researcher to make an evaluation of which of the pupils' responses are closer to reality.

DATA ANALYSIS

The main objective of the quantitative and qualitative analysis of the data is to define a research protocol that can be considered in the ongoing exploration stage. The preliminary phase has been completed, however, and the project overall confirmed through the use of established methodological research criteria.

Around 300 children are involved in the current phase of the work. The simulation game employed is called Cartolandia. Since the project has covered different schools across the whole of the country, not all the data have been collected and the conclusion regarding the class project should be completed by the end of April 2010.

The data elaborated so far refers only to one primary school class of third year and one fifth year, where the work has already been concluded: one in Genzano (Rome) and one in San Giuliano Milano (Milanese). In these schools 40 children were involve overall 20 of these for the experimental group and 20 for the control group. The two groups were analysed separately, then together.

The aim of the conducted study is to analyse the dependence between the data in order to identify the existence of a model that can relate the two phases. The

ANOVA model for repeated measurements, in fact, contains a parameter that takes into account the specific characteristics of each subject in the two different phase in which the relevant data is recorded, i.e., of the individual variable. This parameter has been eliminated from the analysis, on account of the difference in the responses of the same subject in the various experimental conditions. The model assumes, therefore, that the individual variability is the same for all levels of treatment.

The repeated measurement variance analyses estimate the importance of the effect of the lessons, in order to refute the hypothesis that the differences are not significant.

The data analysis on the motivation to study the subject based on a test containing polarity questions was conducted after a preliminary recoding phase carried out by assigning the minus sign to concordances with affirmative responses with negative polarity.

The statistical analysis was then performed to verify the collective responses of the students of the two schools, regarding learning, and the retention of learning and the starting points indicated by the previous year's marks of the two classes together. In this case the model utilised was a mixed effects model, in other words a type of factor modelling containing both fixed factors- in our case the hypotheses to be verified- and contingent effects- in our case constituted by the pupils' own class. This type of method also can be utilised in a way to compare two experimental conditions on the same subjects. The analysis elaborated through an ANOVA model in the first part of the study, therefore, can be substituted whenever more classes are analysed with a mixed effects model. With this type of model we can also check whether the hypotheses to be tested are statistically significant.

From the study it emerges, the subjective nature of the participants and the small amount of data on which to work notwithstanding, that the statistical evidence is significant with respect to the reduced quantity of students involved; this opens up interesting prospects, different at the level of the two schools, which in any case allow us to confirm the statistical analytical choices made.

In the next section, we shall examine more closely those cases in which the comparative analyses led to significant statistical evidence of an improvement in the passage from a face-to-face lesson and a lesson structured around a simulation game.

The Children at the Montessori School in Milan

Before and After Teaching Analysis of Social Self-Efficacy

In the Montessori school the children provide evidence, through the results reported in the tests, of an increase in so-called social self-efficacy in the case of simulation game with respect to the classical face-to-face lesson. In particular, the average differences between post and pre learning, in the scale of reference, are 1.73 in the classical lesson, and 2.8 in the simulation lesson, respectively.

Figure 1 represents the models in black for the face-to-face lesson and red for the simulation lesson. As the figure illustrates, both have increased but the model of the simulation game shows how children take advantage from the social point of view of an interactive teaching method based on play.

Before and After Teaching Analysis of Academic Self-Efficacy

Also from the point of view of scholastic self-efficacy before and after the experience there is sufficient evidence to refute the idea that there is no difference between face-to-face teaching and simulation. As can be seen in Figure 2, which is similar to the previous one, the teaching model leads to positive perceptions from the students also in the case of academic self-efficacy. The results show that, on average, the difference between pre and post experience is 0.45 for face-to-face teaching, while for teaching with the Cartolandia simulation game it rises to 1.5.

De Amicis School in Genzano

Statistical Analysis of Social Self-Efficacy Before and After the Teaching Experience

As in the case of the school in Milan the children's results in the case of teaching in a simulation context are clearly better than those attained with face-to-face teaching.

Figure 1.

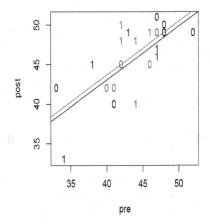

Figure 2.

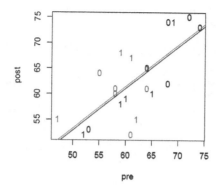

The results on the average differences indicate a variation from a 0.5 improvement in face-to-face teaching to one of 1.25 for simulation.

Statistical Analysis of Motivation for the Subject (Geometry) Before and After Teaching Experience

In the school in Genzano the relevant data on motivation to learn geometry show a greater improvement in motivation after the lesson based on simulation game that was the case with the traditional teaching method.

The graph in Figure 4 makes it clear that pupil motivation improves in both cases, but for simulation it is much more marked. The average differences between before and after the teaching experience with regards to motivation are 1.14 for the face-to-face lesson and 4.25 for the Cartolandia simulation lesson, respectively.

Comparative Analysis of the Marks at the Beginning (based on Previous Year's Reports) and Learning Retention

Figure 5 for the Genzano school shows that there are clear differences between the starting marks in the subject in question and learning retention in the two experimental situations. In particular, in the face-to-face lesson there is an improvement of 7.42 points on the reference scale, whereas with the Cartolandia simulation it rises to 8.5.

The analysis of the data on the two classes elaborated on the basis of the research hypotheses has substantially confirmed the hypotheses and the analytical protocols.

In the albeit limited number of cases on the constructs taken in consideration (self-efficacy, motivation, learning retention) the improvement is statistically sig-

Figure 3.

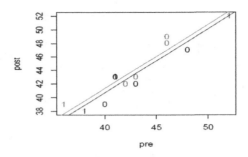

Figure 4.

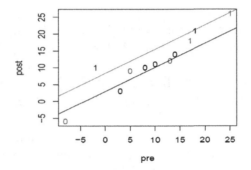

Figure 5.

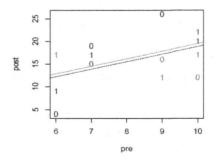

nificant over the two experimental control groups. The simulation game was shown, therefore, to be a better environment compared to the classical teaching model.

Although we must wait to extend the analysis to the groups where work is still in progress, we can nevertheless draw some inferences with regards to the effects school can have by varying their learning environments to take into account the evolution of ways children actually interact in today's world, especially when it comes to increasing their motivation to learn mathematics.

This experimental work is being placed in a wider analytical perspective involving the perceptions, and emotions that direct the learner to study and improve, and in the intervention on meta-cognitive processes that can influence self-efficacy and learner autonomy as part as a life-long process.

EVALUATION PROCESS USING FUZZY LOGIC

The transcoding process, described in Section 1, Chapter 2, has led the authors to reflect on the criteria for evaluating the learning achieved in the sense that the more traditional evaluation instruments such as objective tests have been shown to be only partly effective. The concepts/objectives matrix that has provided an implicit backdrop for the design of the verification tests can be placed in relation to the nature of concepts and the aims that guide the learning objectives.

In particular, with reference to Bloom's taxonomy we have examined the level of consciousness, understanding and application.

With regards to levels of consciousness we focused on the mastery of a definition or representation of a concept with the codes of a possible mathematical language, always in line with the appropriate level of the primary school. In this case the objective tests proved effective.

With regards to application, the nature if the simulation game itself allowed the observation of the discoveries and their application in the curse of the game. In this case too the objective tests proved effective.

With regard to level of understanding, the difficulty in codifying the tests in a closed form, led us to formulate the request for definitions and explanations through open questions.

We therefore decided to start an evaluation process using fuzzy logic that enables the researcher to codify a taxonomy of meanings.

The functional characteristics of fuzzy logic can be connected to three distinct phases in the construction of a model to be applied in the representation of the phenomenon to be measured:

The first phase refers to the construction of the domino, i.e., the fuzzy set or the sets that define the variables that are the object of the evaluation.

These second phase refers to the search for the functions that determine the classification criteria for the variables.

The third phase deals with the construction of the condominium, i.e., the fuzzy measure of the phenomenon (Talarico 2002).

The aim of this phase is of the elaboration of the research data is to contribute to the construction of the model that will be defined when all the data on the 300 pupils still involved in the experimental phase are available.

DATA ANALYSIS OF UNDERSTANDING WITH FUZZY LOGIC

For the analysis of the comprehension tests (Figures 6-16), a decision was made to design and realise a model based on fuzzy logic.

Figure 6. The classification of the tests, the sets and the representation of the model. In fuchsia the definitions that come closest to the formal one (with the necessary nuances), in blue those that have some interesting elements, and yellow those that differ the most.

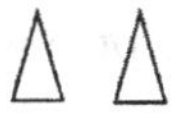

ISOMETRY		
Learning retention		
Group game:		
	☆	the same distance
	☆	Same distance
	★	
	★	
	★	
	☆	Same distance
	★	Same distance, that does not change shape
Group lesson:		
	★	
	☆	Same angle
	☆	It takes place in space and is the same distance
	☆	Same distance
	☆	Two figures are equal
	☆	Movement of the figures in space
	☆	The two forms are equal

Figure 7. Classification of tests (continued)

Proof		
Group game:		
	☆	the same metre
	★	The same distance that is the distance between the points does not change
	★	Same distance from the same point and so the same
	★	
	★	Equal distance between two points of a figure even if it moves
	★	
Group lesson:		
	☆	Same distance
	☆	"Iso" means the same, metre means distance
	★	Movement that conserves the distance between the points of the figures.
	☆	It means the distance between the points never changes
	☆	Same distance
	★	It is a movement that does not change the distance between the points

In this phase of the research, given the limited size of the sample, the objective is to experiment and test the model as regards its structure and functioning in particular. For this reason an algorithm was selected that provides a bi-dimensional representation of the data. Nevertheless, the fuzzy procedure applied makes the process of linguistic transformation clear, thanks to the various nuances of the three fuzzy sets characterising each of the colour responses

- yellow: far from the formal definition
- blue: near the formal definition
- fuchsia: "inside" the formal definition.

Each of the three colours can have infinite grades of intensity.

On the basis of these characteristics, we can read the graphs directly, make a comparison between the results of the group that have taken part in the simulation game and the group that followed a traditional lesson.

Figure 8. Translation

TRANSLATION	
Learning retention **Group game:**	
★	movement, like the car before it was behind then in front
★	
★	
★	
★	
★	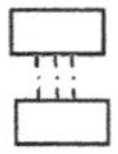
★	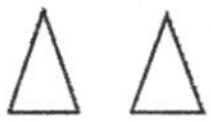

Figure 9. Translation (continued)

Group lesson:	
★	
★	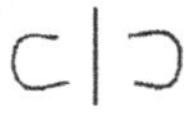
★	When a hand moves from up to down 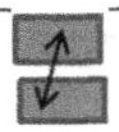
★	The figure moves
★	The movement of figures on a plane
★	A thing moves right-left, up and down
★	The shape moves

Figure 10. Translation (continued)

Proof		
Group game:		
	☆	When we move an object forwards, for example a foot
	★	▲ - - ▲
	☆	When a body slides on a plane
	★	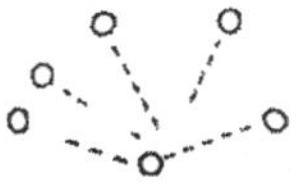 (figure of circles)
	★	Straight movement on the plane of the figures
	★	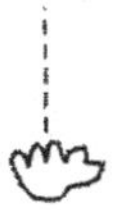 (hand figure)
Group lesson:		
	★	If you have two figures and one moves and they are congruent
	☆	The two faces look in the same direction
	★	This way:  (figure of two squares with arrows)
	☆	When something moves either to one side or up and down
	★	When a thing moves and stays the same
	☆	When a thing moves
	☆	When a figure moves

Figure 11. Rotation

ROTATION		
Learning retention		
Group game:		
	☆	When an object rotates
	★	
	★	
	★	
	★	
	★	
	★	
Group lesson:		
	★	
	★	

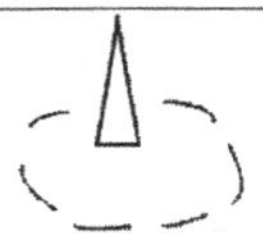

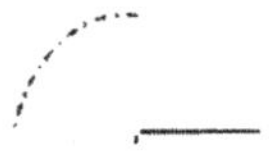

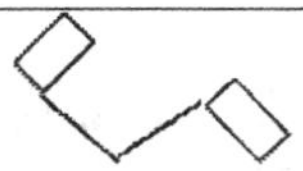

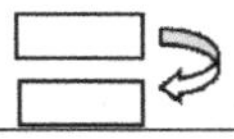

Figure 12. Rotation (continued)

	★	This way: 
	☆	A figure rotates on itself
	☆	The figure rotates
	★	When a figure rotates on a surface
	☆	The two shapes rotate in different directions -
Proof		
Group game:		
	★	When you rotate an object, on the desk or on the ground
	★	
	☆	When a body slides on a surface
	★	It rotates 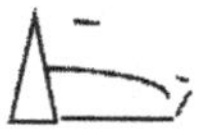
	★	
	★	Rotation on the surface of a figure
	☆	
Group lesson:		
	★	If you have two figures and you rotate them they don't change
	☆	This means that the object turns
	★	This way:

Figure 13. Rotation (continued)

This way: 
Means that the object moves
when a thing moves above a surface
When a figure turns round on itself
Two neighbouring figures, one moves and turns

Figure 14. Symmetry

SYMMETRY	
Learning retention	
Group game:	
★	
★	
★	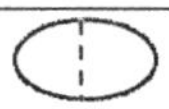
☆	The figure is overturned
★	
★	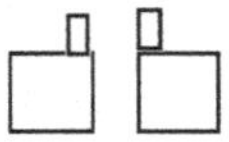
★	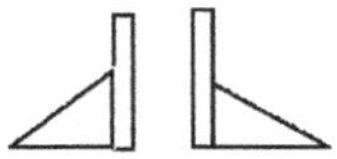
Group lesson:	
★	

Figure 15. Symmetry (continued)

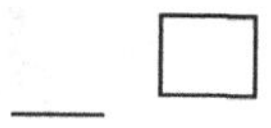

	☆	⬜
	☆	From one point to another
	☆	An object turns around
	☆	Same value
	☆	When a figure moves in space
	☆	Same measure
Proof		
Group game:		
	☆	Means overturning
	★	When a figure is moved in space
	★	When a body is overturned in space
	★	Like a mirror 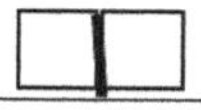
	★	△△
	★	⌃ ⌃
	★	
Group lesson:		
	★	If you turn a figure it doesn't change
	☆	It opens and there is the symmetrical axis

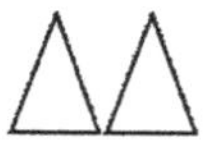

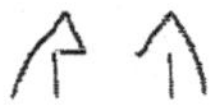

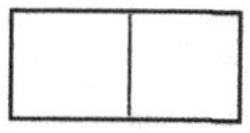

Figure 16. Symmetry (continued)

	★	This type: 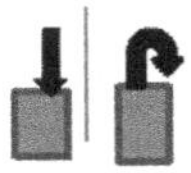
	★	Means that an object divided in two in space
	☆	When you separate one thing from another
	★	When a figure overturns but doesn't change
	★	Two equal figures overturned and divided by a symmetrical axis

Data Interpretation and Comparison

For the concept of **isometrics** (see Figure 17) we can observe that:

- with regards to **retention** there are no substantial differences between the simulation game group and the traditional lesson group, other the presence of a lager blue area with the simulation group and larger yellow one for the

Figure 17. Isometrics

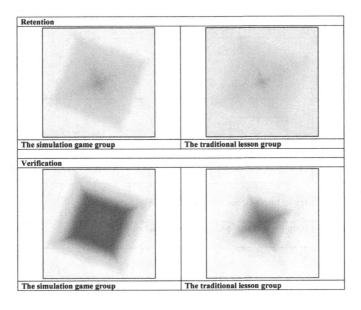

traditional lesson group. The implication of this is that the difference between the two representations is minimal.

- with regards to **verification** the fuchsia areas have the same size, while there is a notable absence of any representation of the traditional lesson group in the blue areas.

For the concept of **translation** (see Figure 18) we can observe that:

- with regards to **retention,** the simulation group expressed themselves in an optimum way with a predominant number of responses close to the formal definition. It is worth noting the absence of yellow areas. As regards the traditional lesson group the graph is close to the complementary; in this case the yellow substitutes the fuchsia area entirely.
- with regards to **verification**, the simulation group presents a marked depth in the fuchsia area which implies that the, albeit limited, number of responses that almost coincide with the formal definition are formally correct. One can observe on the graph a significant blue area that reveals significant intermediate responses in line with the transcoding pattern. As regards the traditional lesson group, on the other hand, we can note a substantial yellow area with highly significant depth.

Figure 18. Translation

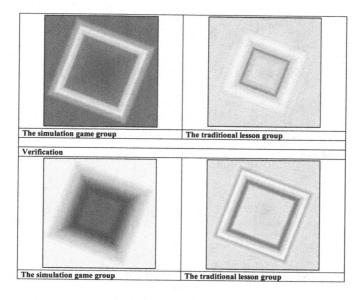

For the concept of **rotation** (see Figure 19) we can observe that:

- with regards to **rotation** the simulation group is shown to have intuited the concept of rotation (the fuchsia area is predominant); there is, however, despite the expression of the formal definition given, a certain lack of precision. In the traditional lesson group the overall level of comprehension of the concept of rotation was weak, apart from a few cases.
- with regards to **verification,** in the simulation group blue is widespread; this means that what was presented during the retention phase was not sufficiently consolidated (the fuchsia area is found at the edges of the graph and not at the centre). During retention the concept of rotation was understood but it was difficult to express it in a formal way. As regards the traditional lesson group, during the verification the yellow area was predominant and very deep: the concept, therefore, had not been understood and there was no response close to the formal definition.

For the concept of **symmetry** (see Figure 20) we can observe that:

- with regards to **retention** the simulation group understood the concept, apart from a limited number of cases, while the traditional lesson group was complementary with a high number of response far from the formal definition.

Figure 19. Rotation

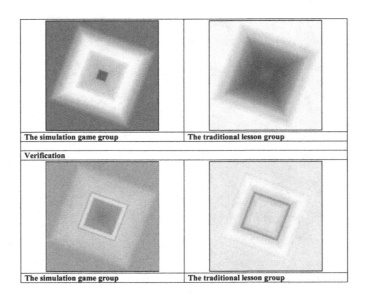

Figure 20. Symmetry

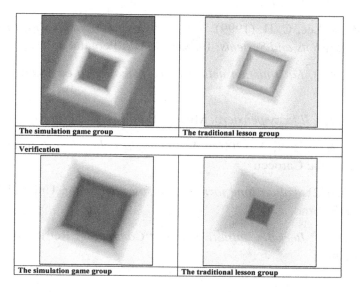

- with regards to **verification**, both groups present similar representations but the fuchsia area is more consistent in the simulation group that revealed a higher number of responses close to the formal definition.

Finally, as regards the transcoding pattern C, we can state that the simulation group presents a wider variety of definitions compared with the traditional lesson group. This implies that the definitions close to the formal one show a level of confidence and understanding of mathematical language in the formal rigour but also in the ability to articulate and this makes it clear that a good understanding of the concept has been achieved. We recall the terms used by the children in their own language that can, in a nuanced way, lead to a full understanding of mathematical linguistic codes (limited here to concepts to do with isometrics).

Finally, from the graphs we can identify the areas of intervention to redirect the learning process, thanks to the effectiveness of the analogical code that the colour representation provides.

REFERENCES

Biswas, R. (1995). *An application of fuzzy sets in students' evaluation. Fuzzy Sets and Systems. Kaaragpur: Department of Mathematics.* Indian Institute of Technology.

Celi, F., & Fontana, D. (2003). *Fare ricerca sperimentale a scuola. Una guida per insegnanti e giovani ricercatori.* Trento: Erickson.

Chen, S.-M., & Lee, C.-H. (1999). *New methods for students's evaluation using fuzzy sets. Fuzzy Sets and Systems.* Tarrytown, NY: Pergamon Press.

Cottini, L. (1999). *La statistica nella ricerca psicologica ed educativa.* Firenze: Giunti Editore.

Kosko, B. (1997). *Il fuzzy pensiero.* Milano: Baldini e Castoldi.

Lucisano, P., & Salerni, A. (2002). *Metodologia della ricerca in educazione e formazione.* Roma: Carocci.

Talarico, F. (2002). *Valutazione formativa e soft computing.* Unpublished thesis. Università di Salerno.

Zadeh, L. (1994). *Berkeley Initiative in Soft Computing.* Retrieved from http://cs.berkeley.edu

Bibliography

Eledia Mangia
Roma Tre University, Italy

	Published monograph
Year	1987
Clearing House	
Author	A. Cecchini et Al.
Title	**I giochi di simulazione nella scuola**
City / Editor	Bologna: Zanichelli
Pages	241
Descriptors	Educational games, experimentation, problem solving, simulation, primary school, lower and higher secondary school
Abstract	The text contains important theoretical reflections on simulation games, followed by practical advice for their design and realisation. Six examples of simulation games, that can be applied in a primary or secondary school environment, are illustrated. For each game the following features are presented: detailed explanation of the game's procedure, materials employed, hints on how to conduct the game with reference to the educational objectives. In these games the pupils naturally take on roles in problem solving situations entailed in the application of the rules and the development of the game. In this way, the children become active participants and attain greater awareness of their own learning process.
*	Immediately useful work for educational purposes

	Published monograph
Anno	1989
Clearing House	
Author	Bruno D'Amore
Title	**Progetto MA.S.E. Un'ipotesi di curriculum matematico nella scuola elementare secondo i nuovi programmi.**
City / Editor	Milano: Franco Angeli
Pages	324
Descriptors	mathematics, didactics, teaching material, learning units, primary school.
Abstract	The project presents ideas for the yearly mathematics curriculum for primary schools on the basis of ministerial programmes for the year 1985. The work is a teaching guide containing theoretical reflections followed by practical advice for teachers. The proposed activities are divided into 136 teaching units to be covered over a five year period. Each teaching unit presents the objectives, certain methodological indications and interdisciplinary exercises and activities. Indications are also provided on checks and final tests and evaluation criteria. In the appendix, beside the text of the ministerial programmes for 1985, the author describes his own experiences on useful activities for teaching mathematics to young children.
*	A useful reference work, though some examples and educational proposals require updating.
	Published monograph
Year	1989
Clearing House	
Author	Zoltan Paul Dienes
Title	**Six stages in the process of learning mathematics**
City / Editor	Firenze: Organizzazioni Speciali
Pages	62
Descriptors	mathematics, education, teaching material, learning, process of abstraction
Abstract	Z.P. Dienes is famous for the realisation of the structured teaching materials he brought to the attention of teachers at the end of the 1970s. His studies had, in fact, a theoretical basis in the evolution that, in those years characterised development psychology, in particular the work of Jean Piaget. The text became a classic with an approach to the teaching of mathematics that can be defined as concrete-constructivist. The abstraction of concepts does nor derive from the exploration of *phrases* from mathematical language, but from the experiences which the child is able to have, depending on their own individual rhythm, in the stages that lead to the construction of concepts. This implies knowledge of learning mechanisms and the action of mathematical thought and, more in general, that of logical abstraction. After the presentation of the six phases, their characteristics and functions, the book proposes three alternatives: one referring to logic, one to the isometrics of an equilateral triangle and one to the realisation of order. One can observe the value of the deliberate and competent use of Logical Blocks, the material proposed by Dienes, who more than anyone else found effective applications for the teaching of mathematics for children from an early age onwards.
*	Document of direct use in practical teaching and the planning of teaching courses.

	Published monograph
Year	2007
Clearing House	
Author	Richard D. Duke
Title	**Gaming.** *Language for the Future*
City / Editor	Bari: La Meridiana
Pages	215
N.standard	
Descriptors	Means of communication, learning environment, problem solving, simulation, cognitive processes, teaching material
Abstract	In this volume the author deals with and reflects on the educational uses of ludic activities, that he refers to as *gaming* or *gaming simulation*. The basic thesis is that *gaming* is a new form of communication: *Language for the Future*. After analysing different alternative means of communication, the author identifies clearly the characteristics and the inherent procedures of a played out simulation, in particular the techniques, design and practice of the gaming simulation. The text is accompanied by images, two appendices and a glossary.
*	Theoretical and practical work of reference for anyone interested in simulation games and their design
	Published monograph
Year	1988- 1991
Clearing House	
Author	Edited by Mauro Laeng
Title	**Disciplinary themes** according to the ministerial programmes for 1985
City / Editor	Teramo: Lisciani & Giunti
Pages	4.057
Descriptors	Disciplinary themes, teaching proposals, updating, teaching material, illustrations, primary schools
Abstract	Prof. Mauro Laeng, an educational expert, who chaired the commission responsible for the ministerial programmes for the year 1985, coordinated the work, which consists of nine volumes divided into theoretical and practical parts. It is structured around teaching modules and classes in primary school; these, in turn, are organised into subject matters, conceptual frameworks and teaching objectives. Each volume presents epistemological aspects of the subject in question, accompanied by disciplinary and interdisciplinary teaching material, entry tests, final tests and progress and final evaluations. Structured yet also flexible and easily applicable, this project is a stimulating and still relevant instrument through the application of the innovations introduced in teaching programmes in schools. This choice, moreover, gives the interested teacher the possibility to design teaching practices suitable for their own classes. The work can be considered one of the first to integrate the evolution of educational psychology, post Piaget, into a possible system for the teaching of mathematics.

*	A very useful work for teaching purposes even if the some of the solutions proposed are somewhat dated, being from a different social and technological context (before the Euro, for example, or the introduction of Windows etc.).
	Published monograph
Year	2006
Clearing House	
Author	Mckenzie Walter
Title	**Multiple intelligences and technologies for teaching. Strategies and materials to diversify teaching provision.**
City/ Editor	Gardolo di Trento: Edizioni Centro Studi Erickson
Pages	230
Descriptors	Technology, didactics, multiple intelligences, teaching, didactic proposals, strategies.
Abstract	Based on Howard Gardner's theory of multiple intelligences, this volume provides an informative guide on how to apply the multiple intelligences theory to teaching through the use of digital technologies. An understanding of Gardner's theory can help the teacher develop a balanced and effective approach, that respects the different potential learning needs of the pupils, and amplify the range of possible intervention. In the light of socio-cultural and technological changes, the author offers the reader the chance to reflect on the identity of the contemporary teacher, the learning-teaching process, the role of information technology as a teaching resource and the position of the pupil and different subjects with regard to the process of education. In proposing these reflections, Mckenzie aims to encourage the formation of a new kind of teacher: "the techno-constructivist teacher", who can bring out various intelligences through the use of technological instruments. The term "technological" is used in the same sense as "technical discourse", and thus concerns the decisions interpreted, understood and taken thanks to the technology. The text contains numerous examples, teaching units and schemata of projects that integrate technology as a teaching aid in the educational process. Finally, the book is provided with PEP modules (Pre-software, Experience Post-software), POMVT (Procedure, Objective, Materials, Evaluation, Technology) e OPP (Objective, Procedure, Product) with the aim of providing an analysis of the lessons and available resources. The appendix contains a questionnaire on the pupils' multiple intelligences, a questionnaire for assessing multiple intelligences for the teachers and national standards for educational technology (National Educational Technology Standard/ NETS).
*	A directly useful work as regards design, methodology and teaching.
	Published monograph
Year	1983
Clearing House	
Author	Michele Pellerey
Title	**Mathematics teaching with a human face**
City / Editor	Torino: Società Editrice Internazionale
Pages	157

Descriptors	Mathematics teaching, learning, affettive dimension, "mathematicisation", ministerial programmes, objectives, lower secondary and primary school.
Abstract	This volume integrates, collects and develops studies and reflections on the teaching of mathematics in Italian schools, in particular *Scuola Media* (lower secondary). In the first part of the volume the author traces an outline of the different components in the changing perspective of the school system: historical, theoretical, social, political, psychological and educational aspects that have interacted and conditioned in recent years (and continue to do so) educational developments in schools and, in particular, in the *Scuola Media*. In the second part the author develops an analysis of the contents of the mathematical syllabus from 1963 to 1979, focusing on a number of essential points: the affective dimension, the urgent need for a project, the process of mathematical learning, and certain aspects of evaluation. The school, as a locus of humanisation, can rediscover an active and human approach where every concept is developed through progressive awareness in a process in which the pupil is protagonist.
*	A work of direct practical use as regards methodology.
	Published monograph
Year	2002
Clearing House	
Author	Angela Piu
Title	**Processi formativi** **e simulazione** *Fondamenti teorici e dimensioni operative*
City / Editor	Rome: Monolite
Pages	176
N.standard	
Descriptors	Didactics, learning strategies, problem solving, simulation, cognitive processes, teaching material, research.
Abstract	The volume presents the theoretical basics and the operative procedures of simulation games, focusing attention on their inherent learning/teaching processes. With regards to the simulation the author pays particular attention to the most suitable strategies for enriching the educational content and facilitating the learning process with respect to the changing needs of the scholastic and social context. The Appendix contains the results of the *IG Students field investigation*, carried out in the province of Cosenza, the aim of which was to verify whether: 1) students experienced simulation as a useful learning strategy; 2) students appreciated the way the simulation was organised in terms of active participation and group work; 3) the simulation favoured learning motivation by furthering self-awareness of their knowledge and actions.
*	A work of direct practical use. Recommended reading for anyone working in the field of education.

	Published monograph
Year	2006
Clearing House	
Author	Carmelo Piu
Title	**Simulazione e competenze.** *Gli effetti della simulazione nella certificazione delle competenze e nella loro corretta gestione.*
City / Editor	Rome: Monolite
Pages	187
Descriptors	Training, simulation, competence, research
Abstract	This volume has collected various work in the field of research activity into *Simulation and Training*, developed by the Local Research Unit of the University of Calabria (PRIN 2003-2005), with the aim of assessing the possible effects of simulation on the certification and construction of competences and how to teach them correctly. The theme of simulation is dealt with both from the perspective of privileged didactic strategy and from the point of view of knowledge acquisition. With reference to the latter there is a need to put into action strategies based on a personalised approach able to express quality teaching in order to develop higher cognitive processes and specific forms of intelligence.
*	A work of direct practical use. Recommended reading for anyone working in the educational field both on site and on line.
	Published monograph
Year	1991
Clearing House	
Authors	Lauren B. Resnick, Wendy W. Ford
Title	**The psychology of mathematics and scholastic learning**
City / Editor	Torino: Società Editrice Internazionale
Pages	251
Descriptors	Psychology of mathematics, scholastic learning, problem solving mathematics
Abstract	This volume covers the history of the psychology of mathematics with the aim of clarifying and understanding the nature of the processes and methods of organisation and expression of the mind when learning mathematics. The authors examine the contributions of different psychological schools: from Thorndike's work on association, to Gestalt psychology, to the contributions of Piaget, up to the contributions of the behaviourists and American cognitive psychologists. Each chapter deals with a different theory and examines the relative psychological research considering the implications of the concepts, rules and integrated procedures. The definition of mathematics in the sense of problem solving is implicit in every chapter.
*	A work of epistemological value rather than on the application of learning theories to mathematics teaching. However, the methodological insights can be transferred to the teaching of mathematics.

	Published monograph
Year	1967
Clearing House	
Author	Various authors
Titolo	**Nuffield project for mathematics**
City / Editor	Bologna: Zanichelli
Pages	249
Descriptors	Mathematics, didactics, educational activities, classroom innovation, teaching material, primary and lower secondary schools, illustrations.
Abstract	The aim of the project is to increase awareness of the issues surrounding the teaching of mathematics to children from the ages of five to thirteen. It is composed of monographic guides covering the main themes of basic mathematics. Each section focuses on *how to learn* more than on *what to teach*, from the idea the children should be allowed freedom to discover and manipulate reality in order to acquire knowledge and awareness. The motto of the project is, "if I can do it, I can understand it" Each part supplies theoretical and practical indications for the teaching and learning of mathematical concepts; moreover, suggestions, practical examples and arguments are provided that can support the intuitive development of the learner of mathematics. In the appendix can be found the work of pupils in English schools who have participated in the Nuffield Project, an initiative which deserves a place in the history of maths education.
*	A reference work containing educational advice on innovations that have become standard practice.
	Published monograph
Year	1985
Clearing House	
Author	Various authors
Title	**RICME Project. Guide for mathematics teaching in primary and lower secondary schools.**
City / Editor	Roma: Armando
Pages	341
Descriptors	Mathematics, geometry, teaching, conceptual representation, primary school.
Abstract	The RICME project is a research into teaching delegated by the *Consiglio Nazionale delle Ricerche* to a committee of *the Società Mathesis*, with the aim of identifying and experimenting a form of teaching in primary schools in the years in which the ministerial programmes for 1985 were introduced. Made up of small volumes, the guide offers theoretical and practical advice regarding maths teaching and the learning of concepts and mathematical procedures in primary schools. One important aspect that should be underlined is the work does not propose a rigid chronological sequence of the different arguments. This leaves interested teachers the possibility to design and adapt to their own classroom context. The arguments refer to: geometrical space, relations and functions, sets and logic, combinations, probability, the concept of natural numbers, the introduction of arithmetical operations. The guide puts forward practical ideas and activities to introduce in schools to cover motor and manipulation aspects of learning. Project is accompanied by worksheets divided for use with different
*	Practical and useful document for teaching purposes

About the Contributors

Angela Piu is an associate professor of Experimental Pedagogy at the University of L'Aquila, Italy and she is currently coordinator and teacher of Master "Progettare e valutare nella formazione" at the University of Calabria and teacher of Master "Didactics of Mathematics" at the University of RomaTre. She received her PhD in Pedagogy in 2000 at University of Calabria, where she has been a part-time university teacher of assessment in the degree course at the Faculty of Primary. She also has been a specialist teacher working in a lower secondary (junior high) school providing support for children with special needs. She has carried out studies and research on simulation in training and on theme such as distance learning and education technology. She is continuing her research into these areas, in particular in the use of simulation games in the teaching of mathematics and into training and university laboratories for distance learning. She is author of various books, articles and papers which have been widely read both on a national and international level.

Cesare Fregola is professor in mathematics didactic and learning difficulties. (L'Aquila University); teacher of mathematics and educational psychology on the Masters Course in Math Teaching: Art, Science and Reality at the Roma Tre University and teacher on the 2nd level Masters Course in "teaching planning and evaluation" at the University of Calabria. Transactional analyst in the educational ambit, Cesare has participated and led research into various themes such as the emotional, cognitive and socio-relational aspect of learning processes as well as into other area in the educational field. He is author of monographs, articles and papers of national repute and co-author of an internationally recognized paper on themes concerning distance learning.

* * *

Daniela Olmetti Peja is an associate professor of Experimental Pedagogy (SSD M-PED/04) at Università Roma Tre, Faculty of Science of Education since 1st March 2007 which belongs to the Department of Education. She is scientific coordinator of the training activities at the Laurea Degree Corse of Science of Primary Education, Coordinator of Master in Didactics of Mathematics between Arts, Sciences and Reality and Member of the Commission entrusted of the control of the student's acquired curriculum. She wrote and edited several books and many articles.

Carmelo Piu is a professor of Experimental Pedagogy and scientific director of the Master in "Progettare e valutare nella formazione" at the University of Calabria. Since the academic year 1981/1982 he has participated at many researches and directed some experimentation on the integrated formative system, teachers training and evaluation of training. For several years he has dealt with new technologies applied to education. His current research is focused on the area of e-learning, media education and simulation gaming. He has been serving as a referee reviewer for some educational journal, conference proceedings and books. He wrote and edited several books and many articles.

Anna Santoro took a degree in Biological Science at Milan University and she has been teaching Maths and Science in a Junior High School since 1976. She is also qualified as a Science teacher in the Senior Secondary School. She used to be member of the Committee assessment of teachers, headmaster's aide and new Mathematics teachers' tutor. She worked with Padua University on the topic of "bullying", and with Milan Bicocca University on European Social Funds ("School and Family time"). She also cooperated with local institutions on projects to prevent school dropout and organized and supervised workshops for students in difficulty. At present she is in charge of mathematics games (Bocconi University) for her school where she usually makes her students use the "Cabri" Geometry computer program and she belongs to a research team on Mathematics didactics with Professor Piu and Professor Fregola; she plans simulation games and she runs university laboratories to train teachers on duty.

Claudia Abundo is a statistician and a high school teacher. She graduated with a BA in Statistics in 2004 and received a PhD in Methodological Statistics in 2009 from Sapienza University of Rome. In 2006 was research collaborator at the University of Bristol, UK. Now she has a temporary position at Roma Tre University and at a high school in Rome. Her main research interests are fuzzy entropy and fuzzy statistical regression methods, also with bayesian aspects.

Salvatore Fregola is a computer analyst. He works in the field of information science and has been founder of Ethos Multimedia, a software house operating in Italy since 1996. His research interests concern the construction of fuzzy models for the Risk Management, Development of Human Resources and Decision Support System in the field of formative assessment. He consults for public and private companies. Since 2010 is the scientific director of Ianus Lab, an association of research working in academia and in collaboration with various scientific organizations.

Eledia Mangia was born in Genzano (Rome) on the 1th of November, 1983. In 2005, she gratuated with a degree in Scienze dell'Educazione e Formazione at "La Sapienza" University of Rome and in 2007 she took the after degree in Scienze della Formazione Primaria at "Roma Tre" University of Rome. Since 2007 she has been teaching in Primary School and since 2008 she has been collaborating with the Faculty of Scienze della Formazione Primaria at "Roma Tre" at University of Rome.

Roberta Masci was born in L'Aquila (Italy). She is a PhD student in Psychology of Programming and Artificial Intelligence at the University of Calabria. In 2004 she got a degree in Sciences of the Education at the University of L'Aquila. In 2005 she attended a post-graduate course in Comunicare nella scuola, tra relazione educativa e aspetti cognitivi at the University of Florence. In 2005 she was a speaker at IV International Conference La qualità dell'integrazione scolastica, Centro Studi Erickson – Trento, in Rimini (Italy). She wrote some articles on integration of the deaf child in a regular school. She is currently involved in a research project on the use of simulation for deaf and blind children.   •

Index

L

laboratories 16
language 26, 28, 29, 36, 48, 49, 52, 53, 54,
    83, 84, 85, 86, 88, 89, 92, 93, 97,
    99, 100, 102, 106, 109, 184, 185,
    186, 187, 189, 193, 195, 197
learning 206, 208, 209, 210, 211, 212,
    213, 214, 215, 227,
learning atmosphere 172
learning devices 16
learning environments 3, 4, 5, 7, 13, 16,
    51, 67, 69, 83, 84, 85, 88, 90, 91,
    104, 106, 183, 184, 185, 186, 204,
learning math 58
learning mathematics 47, 53, 58, 62
learning mechanisms 5
learning models 15, 21, 22
learning of skills 186
learning processes 66, 67, 68, 69, 70, 71,
    77, 114, 116, 117, 182, 184
learning retention 209, 213
learning strategy 34, 35
libraries 16
light and shadows 124
linear 3
linguistic code 88
linguistic intelligence 75
locus of control 60
logical 206, 208
logical capacity 66
logical-mathematical intelligence 75
logical structures 17, 22
logical thought 90
longitudinal studies 65
ludic activity 52

M

macro 53
main learning stages 113
Massachusetts Institute of Technology
    (MIT) 37
mathematical code 86, 109
mathematical concepts 2, 4, 5, 6, 53, 54,
    117, 125, 132, 133, 183, 186

mathematical interpretation 53
mathematical knowledge 17, 18, 19, 54,
    87, 88
mathematical language 1, 3, 6, 7, 8, 13,
    14, 54, 84, 85, 86, 88, 99, 100, 102,
    106, 117, 121, 125, 132, 184, 185,
    189
mathematical learning 84, 89
mathematical meta-theory 6
mathematical relationships 87
mathematical structures 51, 112
mathematical territory 88
mathematical theory 88
mathematical thought 132
mathematicization of reality 83
mathematics 15, 16, 17, 18, 19, 20, 21, 24,
    57, 58, 59, 60, 61, 62, 63, 64, 112,
    113, 116, 124, 130
mathematization 183, 185, 186
mathematophobia 58
math teaching 1, 2, 3, 183, 184
Mauro Ciotti 205, 206
mechanisms 50, 52
memorising of skills 186
meta-cognitive 4
meta-cognitive aspects 87
meta-cognitive awareness 51
meta-cognitive control mechanisms 184
meta-language 84
methodological analysis 185
methodological aspects 185
methodological frame 113
methodological innovation 53
methodological investigation 113
methodological value 2
methodology 168, 174
Michele Di Lisio 205, 206
micro 53
models of reality 33
Modern Mathematics 7
Monopoly 38
motivation 208, 209, 211, 213, 215
motivational effectiveness 2
motor skills 69
multimedia systems 16
museums 16